M000238951

# Conducting Multinational Research

# Conducting Multinational Research

*Applying Organizational Psychology in the Workplace*

*Edited by*
**Ann Marie Ryan, Frederick T. L. Leong, and Frederick L. Oswald**

American Psychological Association • Washington, DC

Copyright © 2012 by the American Psychological Association. All rights reserved. Except as permitted under the United States Copyright Act of 1976, no part of this publication may be reproduced or distributed in any form or by any means, including, but not limited to, the process of scanning and digitization, or stored in a database or retrieval system, without the prior written permission of the publisher.

Published by
American Psychological Association
750 First Street, NE
Washington, DC 20002
www.apa.org

To order
APA Order Department
P.O. Box 92984
Washington, DC 20090-2984
Tel: (800) 374-2721; Direct: (202) 336-5510
Fax: (202) 336-5502; TDD/TTY: (202) 336-6123
Online: www.apa.org/pubs/books
E-mail: order@apa.org

In the U.K., Europe, Africa, and the Middle East, copies may be ordered from
American Psychological Association
3 Henrietta Street
Covent Garden, London
WC2E 8LU England

Typeset in Goudy by Circle Graphics, Inc., Columbia, MD

Printer: United Book Press, Baltimore, MD
Cover Designer: Mercury Publishing Services, Rockville, MD

The opinions and statements published are the responsibility of the authors, and such opinions and statements do not necessarily represent the policies of the American Psychological Association.

Library of Congress Cataloging-in-Publication Data

Conducting multinational research : applying organizational psychology in the workplace / edited by Ann Marie Ryan . . . [et al.].
    p. cm.
  Includes index.
  ISBN-13: 978-1-4338-1141-8
  ISBN-10: 1-4338-1141-3
  1.  International business enterprises—Research. 2.  International business enterprises—Cross-cultural studies. 3.  Psychology, Industrial. 4.  Organizational behavior.  I. Ryan, Ann Marie.
  HD2755.5.C6377 2012
  338.8'8072—dc23

2012004009

British Library Cataloguing-in-Publication Data
A CIP record is available from the British Library.

Printed in the United States of America
First Edition

DOI: 10.1037/13743-000

# CONTENTS

# CONTRIBUTORS

**Anne-Grit Albrecht, PhD,** Department of Psychology, University of Mannheim, Mannheim, Germany

**Soon Ang, PhD,** Division of Strategy, Management, and Organization, Nanyang Technological University, Singapore

**Dave Bartram, PhD,** SHL Group, Surrey, England

**Jürgen Deller, PhD,** Institute for Strategic HR Management Research and Development, Leuphana University of Lüneburg, Lüneburg, Germany

**Stephan Dilchert, PhD,** Zicklin School of Business, Baruch College, The City University of New York, Lüneburg, NY

**Emily E. Duehr, PhD,** SHL Group, Surrey, England

**Michele J. Gelfand, PhD,** Department of Psychology, University of Maryland, College Park

**Cristina B. Gibson, PhD,** School of Business, University of Western Australia, Crawley, Australia

**Frederick T. L. Leong, PhD,** Department of Psychology, Michigan State University, East Lansing

**Brent J. Lyons, MA,** Department of Psychology, Michigan State University, East Lansing

**Dana McDaniel, PhD,** Department of Psychology, California State University, Long Beach

**Kok-Yee Ng, PhD,** Nanyang Business School, Nanyang Technological University, Singapore

**Deniz S. Ones, PhD,** Department of Psychology, University of Minnesota, Minneapolis

**Frederick L. Oswald, PhD,** Department of Psychology, Rice University, Houston, TX

**Frieder M. Paulus, PhD,** Department of Psychology, Leuphana University of Lüneburg, Lüneburg, Germany

**Ann Marie Ryan, PhD,** Department of Psychology, Michigan State University, East Lansing

**Juan I. Sanchez, PhD,** Department of Management and International Business, Florida International University, Miami

**Paul E. Spector, PhD,** Department of Psychology, University of South Florida, Tampa

**Betina Szkudlarek, PhD,** University of Sydney, Sydney, Australia

**Linn Van Dyne, PhD,** Department of Management, Michigan State University, East Lansing

# FOREWORD

The movement for multiculturalism in psychology has generated a dual focus on domestic and international multiculturalism. Although the former type of research is more common than the latter, researchers are becoming increasingly aware of the need for studies that span multiple nations. This trend in psychology is particularly important for organizational psychology. Contemporary organizations are both domestically and globally diverse, and researchers face new challenges in conducting organizational studies that are generalizable and relevant to today's workforce.

Multinational psychology research requires not only an understanding of the set of psychological variables that might vary in their type, level, and relationships with one another but also a major logistical effort when translating measures across several languages, administering those measures across countries and organizational settings, and determining whether the measures operate in a similar statistical manner across cultures in terms of their factor structure, reliability, and predictive validity. This book addresses these and other challenges by describing best practices and lessons learned. Specifically, the chapter authors describe their research projects and address questions such as the following:

- What issues did you struggle with in conceptualizing the cross-cultural research questions being investigated?
- What operational challenges did you encounter in designing and executing the study?
- What analytic challenges occurred?
- What lessons can you pass on to others seeking to undertake large-scale, multinational studies?
- What common criticisms are faced in this type of work? Which criticisms have some legitimacy, which are specious, and how were both types addressed?
- What major potential confounds (i.e., cultural features bound by other group-level characteristics, such as socioeconomic status, race, country, religion) did you consider in conducting the research, and how were they handled?
- What conceptual and methodological trends are important to consider in future efforts of this kind?

The impetus for this book was a symposium held at Michigan State University (MSU). The symposium, "Conducting Multinational Research: Applying Organizational Psychology in the Workplace," brought together researchers who have successfully conducted large-scale, multinational research projects in organizational psychology. The symposium series is administered by the MSU Consortium for Multicultural Psychology Research, whose mission is to generate and apply psychological science that increases understanding of multicultural issues in both domestic and international contexts.

This book is the inaugural volume of the Multicultural Psychology Series launched by the American Psychological Association (APA) in collaboration with MSU. By emphasizing multicultural theories and research in psychology, the new series will expand on the traditional Eurocentric focus of mainstream psychology and will help develop a multicultural mind-set in the field of psychology. It is my hope that this series will be a guidepost for the field in advancing multicultural perspectives in theory, research, and practice.

Frederick T. L. Leong, PhD

# Conducting Multinational Research

# INTRODUCTION

ANN MARIE RYAN, FREDERICK T. L. LEONG,
AND FREDERICK L. OSWALD

The globalization of business markets has created enormous opportunities for organizational psychologists (Ang & Inkpen, 2008). The increased connectivity across borders means that applications of psychology to the workplace require a greater understanding of cultures, both in their own right and when they interact and evolve. Organizations today source, place, and develop their talent around the globe (Ryan & Tippins, 2009). On a regular basis, individuals interact virtually with coworkers who may work in geographically dispersed locations and have different cultural backgrounds. Supervisors must be capable of leading culturally diverse teams (Ernst & Chrobot-Mason, 2011). Because of this, organizational psychology researchers and practitioners are challenged to bring their expertise to workplace issues that span continents, time zones, and cultures, and to do so in a way that promotes the well-being of workers wherever they may hail from or reside.

The organizational psychology practitioner who works for or with multinational organizations continually addresses the question of cultural influences: What is globally applicable? How will I know which practices are meaningful and acceptable in each location and with each cultural group with which I work? How will I know whether a given research finding has limited or broad cross-cultural generalizability? Despite the widespread internationalization of business, the answers to these questions are not readily apparent, as the field of organizational psychology has for a long time possessed only limited research on cross-cultural issues related to workers and the workplace. However, that limitation is rapidly disappearing as careful examinations of the cross-cultural applicability of research and practices are being undertaken (e.g., Gelfand et al., 2011; House et al., 2004), largely of necessity as organizations demand these answers for their global workforces.

Table 1 provides some illustrative examples of questions that managers and organizational psychologists in corporate and consulting settings are raising with regard to the role of culture in some of the topic areas that have been long standing foci for the field of organizational psychology. What is surprising is that although each of these topics is associated with much research activity, only a tiny portion of that activity is focused on these cultural research questions. Although some of these questions have been the target of large-scale multinational research projects (i.e., questions on leadership), others have garnered at most two-country comparisons or just passing mention as a concern. Gelfand, Raver, and Holcombe Ehrhart (2002) noted that many organizational psychology theories have only been tested in Western contexts. Clearly, organizational psychologists can do much to expand current theoretical perspectives and research streams to incorporate multicultural views. The aim of this volume is to provide some illustrations as to how that can and should be done.

There are many examples of how culture influences topics of interest to organizational psychologists: Team effectiveness is influenced by the cultural heterogeneity of the team (Shapiro, VonGlinow, & Cheng, 2005); what is considered an effective leader varies by culture (House, Hanges, Javidan, Dorfman, & Gupta, 2004); and what is considered rewarding and motivating varies by culture (Brown & Reich, 1997). There have also been some large-scale research efforts to establish the ways in which cultures vary that might underlie these differences: Schwartz's (e.g., Schwartz & Boehnke, 2004) work on value differences, Bond et al.'s (2004) work on social axioms, House et al.'s (2004) framework of cultural differences in values and practices, and Gelfand and colleagues' (Gelfand, Nishii, & Raver, 2006; Gelfand et al., 2011) work on social norm sanctioning and the construct of tightness/looseness.

Still, the process of conducting multinational research in organizational settings is viewed as a particularly daunting one. Faculty warn graduate students and junior colleagues away from pursuing multinational research—as it is "too messy," "too difficult to conduct," "takes too long," and "won't yield enough publications quickly so it will negatively impact your career" (O'Meara, 2011). Researchers often express an interest in conducting such

# TABLE 1
## Questions Related to Organizational Psychology Practice in Multinational Organizations

| Topic | Illustrative questions |
|---|---|
| Selecting employees | Is the same assessment tool (or interview questions) usable and relevant globally for the same job? |
| Training and developing employees | Should my approach to training and development be tailored to different cultures, or should it instead be standardized and similar across cultures? |
| Motivating employees | Are employees in different cultures equally motivated by the same types of incentives? Are psychological and financial incentives viewed in the same manner? |
| Leading employees | Around the world, do supervisors, team leaders, and subordinates view the same leadership behaviors as effective? |
| Effective multinational teams | What are the best practices in forming and leading a team composed of individuals with diverse cultural backgrounds? What are cross-cultural differences in team-level cohesion, coordination and communication? |
| Work–life balance | Is the meaning of work, family, and work–life balance the same across cultures? Does workplace flexibility provide the same value to employees globally? |
| Employee attitudes | Are the attitudes of job satisfaction, employee commitment, and employee engagement similar or different across cultures? Are the relationships with outcomes (performance, counterproductive behaviors) similar globally? |
| Turnover | Do influences on turnover intentions differ across cultures? |
| Recruitment | Are the factors that lead to attraction to organizations relatively similar or different in different countries? Does the management of social capital vary in culturally relevant ways that affect differences in recruiting? |
| Managing performance | Are there cultural influences on how performance feedback is sought, provided, accepted, and related to change? |
| Occupational health concerns | Are employee reactions to physical, social, and psychological stress affected by cultural background? |
| Justice | Are there cultural differences in what individuals see as fair treatment in the workplace? How do national differences in employment law affect organizational culture and practice as they pertain to employee fairness? |

research, only to back away when it is perceived as too difficult to successfully pull off.

We must acknowledge that these concerns have real merit. Many of these well-known multicultural research efforts (e.g., the GLOBE study of House et al., 2004; the collaborative work discussed by Sanchez and Spector in Chapter 5 in this volume; the International Generalizability of Expatriate Success Factors (iGOES) project described in Chapter 4 in this volume) are the products of many, many years of effort. Further, although individuals have found funding sources for their efforts, multinational efforts may often require multiple, country-specific funding sources in conjunction to pull such large-scale projects off. Organizational sponsorship of projects may arise from practice concerns and can be a key source of funding, participants, and other resources needed for such an effort. However, the researcher must work to balance the needs and goals of the organization (a practical solution for a practical problem, answered quickly for the least expenditure of time and money) and the desires and goals of the research enterprise (understanding of a phenomena through high-quality designs, with considerable control and attention to measurement quality). Finally, Ryan and Gelfand (2012) noted that most organizational psychology training programs provide an insufficient focus on training students in the requisite skills in research methodology, statistical analysis, and cross-cultural competence to carry out multinational research effectively.

Despite these concerns, it is possible to conduct high-quality, multinational organizational psychology research. This volume showcases such research as a means of demonstrating that it can be done and done well. The volume brings together researchers with a wide variety of substantive interests to provide illustrations and reflections of multinational organizational research. Some of the authors provide a detailed description of their methodology and findings; others focus more on broad strategic and practical issues encountered in conducting such research. Some of the researchers document large-scale collaborative efforts involving large research teams, multiple funding sources, and years of work; others describe organization-specific efforts with specific practical aims. Together, these chapters provide insights for the individual seeking to conduct or apply cross-cultural research in organizational settings.

This book is organized so that the first few chapters provide some more in-depth illustrations of cross-cultural research efforts and lessons learned. The book then funnels out to the more broadly focused chapters that offer general reflections on conducting multinational research.

In Chapter 1, Gibson, Szkudlarek, and McDaniel draw on examples from their own investigations to illustrate how remaining open to the inductive process can lead to stronger contributions. They describe a large, multinational, multifirm, multimethod research project that resulted in theoretical advancements regarding team effectiveness.

Chapter 2 provides an in-depth review of the collaborative efforts of Ng, Van Dyne, and Ang to develop the theoretical basis and empirical measurement of the construct of cultural intelligence, and their expansion of those efforts to document the nomological network of correlates, antecedents, and outcomes of cultural intelligence.

Bartram devotes Chapter 3 to illustrating the very practical issues related to using research measures across cultures. He provides examples of how to evaluate construct invariance across culture, nation, and language; when it is reasonable to aggregate samples of people to create norm groups; and how to interpret test scores in cross-cultural contexts.

Chapter 4, by Ones, Dilchert, Deller, Albrecht, Duehr, and Paulus, describes how one can use meta-analytic techniques to determine whether relationships found in one cultural context generalize to others. They illustrate this process with a large, global sample of expatriates.

Sanchez and Spector contribute specific insights into how cross-national research projects might be organized and executed in Chapter 5. They discuss recruiting researchers, setting up roles and boundaries, and leading a cross-national research team. They also provide insightful illustrations of measurement issues as well as sampling bias challenges that are common to cross-cultural efforts.

In Chapter 6, Lyons, Leong, and Ryan discuss the ethical dilemmas that may arise in conducting multinational research. They review ethical codes and guidelines relevant to cross-cultural researchers, and provide some scenarios of difficult situations researchers may face.

The final chapter, by Gelfand, provides some personal reflections from an individual whose career focus has been cross-cultural organizational psychology. She provides insights on the challenges faced at each stage of the process, from theorizing to data collection to presentation, and offers directions for addressing those challenges.

This book is intended for individuals in a wide range of career stages and a wide range of settings. There is value here for the student who wonders what it takes to conduct multinational research. There is value here for the early or midcareer researcher who is making decisions about conducting cross-cultural studies in a given area of substantive interest and needs guidance on how to determine the appropriate scope for the research and how to do it well. There is value here for the practitioner faced with implementing a practice on a global scale and wondering about how to approach the task and what should be considered. And there is value here for the merely curious, who may not be eager to wade into cross-cultural research or practice themselves, but who have the desire to know, How did they manage that?

# REFERENCES

Ang, S., & Inkpen, A. C. (2008). Cultural intelligence and offshore outsourcing success: A framework of firm-level intercultural capability. *Decision Sciences, 39*, 337–358. doi:10.1111/j.1540-5915.2008.00195.x

Bond, M. H., Leung, K., Au, A., Tong, K.-K., De Carrasquel, S. R., Murakami, F., . . . Lewis, J. R. (2004). Culture-level dimensions of social axioms and their correlates across 41 cultures. *Journal of Cross-Cultural Psychology, 35*, 548–570. doi:10.1177/0022022104268388

Brown, C., & Reich, M. (1997). Micro–macro linkages in high-performance employment systems. *Organization Studies, 18*, 765–781. doi:10.1177/017084069701800503

Ernst, C., & Chrobot-Mason, D. (2011). Flat world, hard boundaries: How to lead across them. *MIT Sloan Management Review, 52*, 81–88.

Gelfand, M. J., Nishii, L. H., & Raver, J. L. (2006). On the nature and importance of cultural tightness–looseness. *Journal of Applied Psychology, 91*, 1225–1244. doi:10.1037/0021-9010.91.6.1225

Gelfand, M. J., Raver, J. L., & Holcombe Ehrhart, K. (2002). Methodological issues in cross-cultural organizational research. In S. Rogelberg (Ed.), *Handbook of industrial and organizational psychology research methods* (pp. 216–246). New York, NY: Blackwell.

Gelfand, M. J., Raver, J. L., Nishii, L., Leslie, L. M., Lun, J., Lim, B. C. . . . Yama-guchi, S. (2011, May 27). Differences between tight and loose cultures: A 33-nation study. *Science, 332*, 1100–1104. doi:10.1126/science.1197754

House, R. J., Hanges, P. J., Javidan, M., Dorfman, P. W., & Gupta, V. (Eds.). (2004). *Culture, leadership, and organizations: The GLOBE Study of 62 Societies.* Thousand Oaks, CA: Sage.

O'Meara, K. (2011). Inside the Panopticon: Studying academic reward systems. In J. C. Smart & M. B. Paulsen (Eds.). *Higher education: Handbook of theory and research* (Vol. 26, pp. 161–220). New York, NY: Springer.

Ryan, A. M. , & Gelfand, M. (2012). Internationalizing the I-O psychology curriculum. In F. T. L. Leong, W. Pickren, M. M. Leach, & A. J. Marsella (Eds.), *Internationalizing the psychology curriculum in the United States* (pp. 245–262). New York, NY: Springer.

Ryan, A. M., & Tippins, N. (2009). *Designing and implementing global staffing systems.* New York, NY: Wiley-Blackwell. doi:10.1002/9781444310924

Schwartz, S. H., & Boehnke, L. (2004). Evaluating the structure of human values with confirmatory factor analysis. *Journal of Research in Personality, 38*, 230–255. doi:10.1016/S0092-6566(03)00069-2

Shapiro, D. L., Von Glinow, M., & Cheng, J. L. C. (2005). *Managing multinational teams: Global perspectives.* Oxford, England: Elsevier.

# 1

## TALES FROM THE (MULTINATIONAL) FIELD: TOWARD DEVELOPING RESEARCH CONDUCIVE TO PROXIMAL THEORY BUILDING

CRISTINA B. GIBSON, BETINA SZKUDLAREK, AND DANA McDANIEL

Sampling champagne in Paris. Swimming in the Indian Ocean. Salsa dancing in Puerto Rico. And mud slides. And getting lost. And (never-ending) jet lag. And yes—cockroaches the size of cats (we swear!). Ah, the joys of multinational field research! Even if it is not always glamorous, it is always and forever enlightening. We three coauthors are addicted—and no, we do not plan on ever recovering. Over the past decade, we have become particularly enamored with an approach to multinational organizational research— the *proximal* approach, which is characterized by openness to the unexpected, acceptance of uncertainty, and appreciation of multiplicity. This approach can be contrasted with more *distal* approaches, which emphasize end states, linearity, and ordered structure (Cooper, 1992; Cooper & Law, 1995). In this chapter, we endeavor to explain why we so much appreciate the proximal approach and to provide practical suggestions for carrying out research in a manner incorporating its insights.

To do so, we tell the story of a comprehensive multimethod, multinational, multiyear research project. This project was not explicitly (initially) guided by a proximal approach. Rather, most of the work has unfolded within a traditional distal mode, involving deductive, quantitative hypothesis test-

9

ing. By most standards, the project has been highly generative—seven major academic articles have reported findings in top scientific journals (Gibson, 2001; Gibson, Cooper, & Conger, 2009; Gibson & Vermeulen, 2003; Gibson & Zellmer-Bruhn, 2001; Gibson, Zellmer-Bruhn, & Schwab, 2003; Zellmer-Bruhn, 2003; Zellmer-Bruhn & Gibson, 2006). Two practitioner articles (Gibson & Zellmer-Bruhn, 2002; Kirkman, Gibson, & Shapiro, 2001), two book chapters (Gibson, Conger, & Cooper, 2001; Gibson & Kirkman, 1999), a doctoral dissertation (Zellmer-Bruhn, 1999), and one book manuscript (Earley & Gibson, 2002) have also resulted from it. In addition, coauthors have disseminated project findings at conferences in Austria, Italy, Peru, Mexico, Turkey, Canada, Puerto Rico, and five U.S. states.

Perhaps the most important, and certainly the most interesting, findings from the research emerged inductively using the proximal approach. Quite candidly, this came as a big surprise to the researchers. But that is one of the beauties of multinational organizational research: It is full of surprises.

Our plan for the chapter is as follows. We first describe the project as a whole, providing an account of how it unfolded over time and several of the findings that emerged from it using a distal approach. In the second section, we discuss the "Big Surprise"—the meaning of team work analysis—that emerged using a proximal approach. We then explain the key principles of the proximal approach that are illustrated in this analysis, on the basis of those that have been identified by prior research (Szkudlarek & McDaniel, 2010), as important components of the approach. Along the way, we provide practical tips for researchers who might like to try incorporating these principles into their own research. We conclude with a reflection on opportunities and challenges of using a proximal approach for multinational organizational research.


## THE PROJECT

Although intercultural theories of organizational behavior have long suggested that teams should be implemented in a manner that incorporates the cultural backgrounds of their members, as of 1996, a unifying theory explicating this process was nonexistent. Hence, the lead author on this chapter (Cristina B. Gibson) launched the Implementation of Work Teams Project. The project was originally conceived of as a comprehensive multimethod investigation of team effectiveness across cultures. The working definition of a *team* was "a group of individuals who work together interdependently to produce products or deliver services for which they are mutually accountable." Key factors expected to impact team effectiveness included degree of direction provided by external leaders, group efficacy, motivational beliefs, cultural phenomena, and various facets of the organizational context. The National

Science Foundation's (NSF's) Decision Risk and Management Science division awarded Gibson a 3-year grant for the project in 1996 (NSF #9631748).

The research design included interviews, surveys, and deductive statistical analysis using data from six multinational organizations—Merck & Co., Inc.; GE Medical Systems; SmithKline Beecham; Kodak Health Imaging; Pfizer, Inc.; and Johnson & Johnson—across four cultural regions (the United States, France, Puerto Rico, and the Philippines). The primary research assistant and coauthor (Mary Zellmer-Bruhn, who was at that time a PhD student at the University of Wisconsin and is now a tenured professor at the University of Minnesota) commenced collaborating on all phases of the project. Over the course of the data collection, the project also involved 16 additional administrative, translation, and research assistants.

In Phase I, Gibson and Zellmer-Bruhn traveled to facilities in each country owned by each multinational corporation (MNC) and conducted intensive exploratory interviews pertaining to the function of the teams, teamwork knowledge, the management of the teams, and the context in which the teams work. Interviews were conducted in the interviewees' first language, with a native of the region serving as translator, and interviewees were asked to discuss which factors they felt were the most important facilitators and inhibitors of team effectiveness. A total of 111 individuals were interviewed, representing 59 teams across the six organizations and four cultures. All interviews were tape recorded and transcribed by professional linguists and transcriptionists.

Using comprehensive, computer-facilitated text analysis, the authors found numerous important issues for subsequent study, including the leadership of teams, team learning, feedback and reward systems, and sharing of knowledge and practices. Phase I also involved the empirical development of a set of culturally equivalent team assessment survey instruments in three languages (English, Spanish, and French) for multiple constituents (team members, leaders, and customers) measuring team effectiveness, process, context, culture, and practices. Gibson, Zellmer-Bruhn, and Schwab (2003) chronicled the cross-cultural development of these measures and explained why such measures are critical for both research and team diagnosis. These tools, which were used for Phase II quantitative research, have also been adopted by colleagues around the world for conducting team research and continue to be used by the firms involved in the project to monitor team progress.

Phase II of the project involved quantitatively capturing the teaming practices in the MNCs and statistically modeling the predictors of team effectiveness. The survey was administered to more than 3,000 participants (including team members, leaders, and customers) in five of the multinational organizations across the four countries in three languages. A total of 1,041 completed surveys were returned, representing 166 teams. On the basis of survey results, customized team-level feedback reports (also in three different languages) were distributed to all teams to disseminate major findings of the project and facilitate team development among industry participants. Managerial implications and suggestions for action were proposed. These findings have subsequently impacted the ability of the firms to better manage their teams in the global marketplace as they respond to competitive pressures, resulting in substantial performance improvements.

In Phase III of the research, comprehensive multivariate statistical modeling of the survey data was conducted to test a series of complex hypotheses about team processes in a deductive (distal) mode. Three articles demonstrate some of the major contributions made by this study. First, Gibson and Vermeulen (2003) demonstrated that, in contrast to traditional arguments that subgroups in teams create dysfunctional factions, mild subgroups based on demographic and cultural differences *improved* learning behavior in teams. In addition, both very homogeneous and very heterogeneous teams, in terms of demographic and cultural characteristics, were more inclined to engage in learning behavior. Finally, leader encouragement, team empowerment (i.e., allowing teams the discretion to make decisions), and the availability of a knowledge management system in an organization were also significantly and positively related to team learning behavior. In demonstrating that team learning is predicted by factors both internal and external to the team, this research represents a substantial contribution to the innovation and learning literature, as well as theory regarding team effectiveness.

In a second article (Zellmer-Bruhn & Gibson, 2006), again using deductive statistical analysis, the authors integrated and extended literature on international management and team effectiveness by examining how the macrocontext in MNCs influences learning in work teams, and how team learning influences task performance and interpersonal relations. With controls for microcontextual features including team type, training, feedback, and autonomy, the authors found that organizational contexts emphasizing global integration reduced team learning and those emphasizing responsiveness and knowledge management increased team learning. Team learning in turn positively influences both task performance and quality of interpersonal relations. This study supports assertions that team learning depends on the organizational context—but it pushes the idea of context far beyond the team's immediate microcontext to demonstrate that macrocontext matters as well. On a practical level, the authors emphasized that in MNCs certain processes (e.g., procurement) will need to be globally integrated; however, enabling subsidiaries to meet the needs of their local context by adjusting practices and acting somewhat independently will facilitate team learning. Stated another way, the findings indicate that local team-level learning should be encouraged within parameters that consider an MNC's need for global efficiency.

In a third article, Gibson, Cooper, and Conger (2009) explored what happens when a leader and the team he or she leads do not see eye to eye. Most of the literature uses survey measures gathered from leaders and teams. It is treated as error when there is not agreement, and often the data are thrown out. But the authors reasoned that the disagreement was an important phenomenon to better understand. Drawing from the extensive literature on teams, leadership, and cognitive models of social information processing, they developed the concept of *leader–team perceptual distance*, defined as differences between a leader and a team in perceptions of the same social stimulus. They developed hypotheses regarding leader and team perceptions of goal accomplishment, constructive conflict, and decision-making autonomy. They found that greater perceptual differences about goals and conflict are associated with decreased team performance. However, even more interesting is that they then used a unique application of an analytical technique (quadratic polynomial regression with response surface modeling, in which responses are graphically depicted along three axes: performance, leader perception, and team perception) to show that it is not just any deviation from perfect agreement that matters. The effect is strongest when team perceptions are more positive than the leader's (as opposed to the reverse). For example, if the team thinks that goals are being met, but the leader does not, this is highly detrimental—even more detrimental than if the leader thinks goals are being met and the team does not. This pattern illustrates the pervasive effects that perceptions can have on team performance, highlighting the importance of developing awareness of perceptions to increase effectiveness.

The project also resulted in a book (*Multinational Work Teams: A New Perspective*; Earley & Gibson, 2002) that extends and consolidates the evolving literature on multinational teams, integrating the authors' own research with that of others in this domain. Earley and Gibson (2002) developed a comprehensive model that incorporates a dynamic, multilevel view of multinational teams. The model focuses on various features of the team's members, their interactions as a team, and the organizational context in which they operate. The concepts of integration and differentiation and the notion of equilibrium are presented as general forces guiding the specific processes that link various levels of analysis in the overarching model.

Taken as a whole, the project has achieved much of what it intended to achieve: the development of a unifying theoretical framework and set of practical guidelines for implementing teams in a manner that incorporates the cultural backgrounds of the members. In terms of research, the program represents the first large-scale study of teams across cultures and an innovative application of triangulation of methods. Theoretical developments have made contributions to the literature regarding work teams and to the body of theory that has been referred to as "international and intercultural management." Finally, the research has also informed practice, in that it provides guidance regarding the motivational processes that must be managed to successfully implement teams internationally. More specifically, results shed light on the appropriate leadership and human resource practices needed to maximize the quality of the work experience, the effectiveness of the teams, and the competitiveness of MNCs.

## THE BIG SURPRISE

Stepping back from the larger project and examining the variety of contributions it has made, it is quite likely that the most important contribution was one that was completely unintended. Here, we refer to a frame-breaking insight: There are fundamental differences in the meaning of the concept of teamwork across cultures. Further, these differences can be revealed in the metaphors people use to talk about teams, and the metaphors have implications for what is expected from team management (Gibson & Zellmer-Bruhn, 2001). Thus, the most basic assumptions about what workers understand to be a "team" cannot be universally applied across cultures, necessitating a reassessment of theories of group behavior with special attention to cultural differences in the concepts of teamwork they hold.

And it is here where the authors must come clean. This insight arose not because Gibson and Zellmer-Bruhn (2001) read the literature and a priori noticed that a universalistic (and ethnocentric) assumption had been made, and then set out to show evidence to the contrary. Rather, as described above, the researchers embarked in distal mode on a program of interviews to gain insight into a set of hypothesis about team implementation that had been detailed in a comprehensive NSF grant proposal. To be sure, the interviews provided knowledge regarding many of the important features of team implementation that had been identified in the research proposal. But as the interviews unfolded, it became apparent to the researchers that there were unanticipated yet discernable differences in the manner in which participants talked about the very definition and conceptualization of teams.

This discovery started with just a few comments uttered while reviewing initial interview notes (yes, many of these occurred late at night, to the tune of scurrying cockroaches), such as "Isn't it interesting that all three of our interviewees today (in the United States) mentioned something about baseball. We didn't hear that in France." Specifically, one interviewee from the United States said,

> I think it's easy to have individual recognition within the team and still have a clear direction, but the team results are what's important. We have outstanding individuals on the team. And, very similar to a sports

team, somebody needs to hit the home run; somebody needs to stop the ball. You know, somebody needs to catch 'em and drag 'em out. So I think it's a combination, but I think it's very difficult to play together as a team now. You know, we have bench players too. And we need bench players. We need the people that can get up and go fix the equipment every day. (Gibson & Zellmer-Bruhn, 2001, p. 288)

At first, the authors scratched their heads and wondered what in the world baseball had to do with the implementation of pharmaceutical production teams. But as the interviews continued, Gibson and Zellmer-Bruhn began to notice systematic patterns in the use of metaphors by the participants. As they then went back to the literature, they realized that metaphors allow people to understand abstract subject matter in terms of more concrete, familiar terms. In a technical sense, *metaphors* are "mappings across conceptual domains" (Lakoff, 1993, p. 245), and metaphor is evoked whenever a pattern of inferences from one conceptual domain is used in another domain. In this way, metaphors are a key mechanism through which people comprehend abstract concepts and perform abstract reasoning. People's behavior reflects their metaphorical understanding of experience. This link between metaphorical understanding and behavior makes the study of metaphorical language interesting for organizational researchers (Gannon & Associates, 1994).

By systematically analyzing their interviews using an inductive qualitative approach, triangulation of methods, and a team of multinational coders, Gibson and Zellmer-Bruhn (2001) were able to derive five different categories of metaphors for teamwork: military, sports, community, family, and associates. They were also able to show that although the specific content of teamwork conceptualizations varies across cultures, at a general level, most definitions are likely to include what a team does (*activity scope*), who is on the team (*roles*) and why (*nature of membership*), and why the team exists (*objectives*). For example, when some people think of a team, they picture a project team whose activity is limited to the time during which members work on the project, whereas others may picture a team more like a family whose activity is broad and extends across a number of domains in life (McGrath, 1984). Likewise, some concepts of teamwork may include clearly differentiated roles, such as leaders and members, whereas others may be less structured (Cohen & Bailey, 1997).

Consider the following metaphorical statements Gibson and Zellmer-Bruhn (2001) documented in U.S. teams: "Among the sales people on our team, Jack is the star quarterback" and "Our team leader acts more like a coach than a referee." These statements demonstrate the work-team-as-sports-team metaphor, which involves referring to one (*target*) domain of experience (work teams) in terms of a very different (*source*) domain of experience (sports teams). In contrast, the Filipino teams that used family-themed metaphors made statements such as, "It's something in the team, everyone is caring for each other" and "It's very clannish." There are ontological correspondences between entities in the domain of work teams (e.g., the leader, the team members, their roles, their objectives) and entities in the domain of a sports team (e.g., coach, players, players' positions) or family (caring, being a part of a clan, bonding). It is via such mappings that an individual in either nation is likely to project source domain patterns of inference (e.g., expectations about sports teams or families) onto the target domain (e.g., work teams; Lakoff, 1993, p. 245). Furthermore, the metaphor is a source of cognitive priming in that it brings forth semantic, behavioral, and affective responses (Blair & Banaji, 1996) that are characteristic of the source domain.

In a companion article for practitioners, Gibson and Zellmer-Bruhn (2002) documented important implications of these different concepts of teamwork for the success of managerial practices in teams, demonstrating how the metaphors for teamwork illuminate a person's understanding about teamwork and also how the language involved in the metaphor communicates their expectations about teaming practices. It is via such mappings that individuals project expectations they hold about teams onto the work-team domain. Further, Gibson and Zellmer-Bruhn (2002) showed that when an organization adopts practices that are consistent with culturally salient metaphors, teams are more effective.

Demonstrating such underlying differences in the ways people understand teamwork provides at least two major contributions to the literature. First, specifically related to research concerning teams, verifying variance in teamwork conceptualizations provides insight into the differences in preferred practices that have been noted across cultural contexts in other empirical research. Second, and more far reaching, doing so challenges scholars to build specific theories of teamwork that incorporate these differences, and challenges practitioners to adapt teaming practices to become congruent with the prevailing conceptualizations in a cultural setting.

## OUR SURPRISE AS PROXIMAL RESEARCH

The meaning of teamwork analysis within the Implementation of Teams Project was more than just an exciting adventure and a great learning experience. It is also a good illustration of several principles of a proximal approach to research. As Szkudlarek and McDaniel (2010) summarized, the proximal approach acknowledges the dynamic nature of the world and allows the generation of multiple interpretations as understood from within the system rather than imposed by the researcher from the outside. Such an approach may be most appropriate for examining phenomena that are not well understood

(Edmondson & McManus, 2007), in attempts to increase understanding of local perceptions (Miles & Huberman, 1994), to help to gain understandings of dynamics associated with a concept rather than the properties of a concept (Bartunek & Seo, 2002), and for theory generation (Lee, Mitchell, & Sablynski, 1999) rather than testing.

In contrast, the distal mode focuses on stable end products, and the object of study is perceived as a self-contained unit of analysis, with firmly delineated borders (Szkudlarek & McDaniel, 2010). As Cooper and Law (1995) summarized:

> Distal thinking privileges results and outcomes, the "finished" things or objects of thought and action. It privileges the ready-made. So the distal is what is preconceived, what appears already constituted and known, what is simplified, distilled; it's a bit like fast food—packaged for convenience and ease of consumption. The distal stresses boundaries and separation, distinctness and clarity, hierarchy and order. (p. 239)

This can be a concern, as openness to the unexpected, acceptance of uncertainty, and appreciation of multiplicity are particularly crucial in multinational research (Jack, Calas, Nkomo, & Peltonen, 2008). This is because the implicit assumptions people unconsciously use in decoding the world around them, and the alleged universality of many management theories, will be inevitably questioned and contested in novel contexts (Szkudlarek & McDaniel, 2010). This may leave the researcher unable to make sense of witnessed events, or particular events may not even be seen at all as a result of the narrow lens shaped by these assumptions.

Specifically, the meaning of teamwork analysis conducted by Gibson and Zellmer-Bruhn (2001) illustrates five of the 10 principles for conducting multinational research using a proximal lens identified by Szkudlarek and McDaniel (2010): maintaining self-awareness, staying open to doubt, remaining open to discomfort and paradox, using multiplicity and reflexivity in data analysis, and considering the interplay of researcher and researched. Next, we elaborate on each of these principles and how they are manifest in Gibson and Zellmer-Bruhn's (2001) analysis.

**Maintaining Self-Awareness**

Self-awareness is one of the prerequisites for a successful intercultural communication (Bird, Mendenhall, Stevens, & Oddou, 2010). It may also serve as a useful first step in multinational organizational research. Sometimes early in the process of securing interviews, Gibson shared her working definition of a *team* with organizational contacts. Little did she know that in doing so, she may have been changing the very nature of the phenomenon that was most interesting to study—the variation in the meaning of *teamwork*. After only a couple of interviews, it was evident that traditional definitions needed to be suspended (and interviewees needed to be encouraged to express their own conceptualizations), but this became clear only upon self-reflection regarding initial assumptions.

Epistemological reflexivity is important for stimulating researchers toward methodological and paradigmatic intercultural dialogue (Szkudlarek & McDaniel, 2010). One of the first tactical steps may be to reflect on one's own training. A researcher may think to herself or himself: What has been my preferred lens, and how may that lens be shifted or expanded? What are my personal strengths, abilities, or skills with particular methodologies? We encourage reflective acknowledgement of how one's lens is influencing the processes and products of research projects.

## Staying Open to Doubt

Although clarity might be a default preference in management research, we follow Eisenberg (1984) in his claim that ambiguity could be an equally successful strategy. This is aptly illustrated in the meaning of *teamwork analysis*. As Gibson first began conducting interviews on team processes outside the United States, she quickly began to doubt whether the interviewees were on the same page—it did not appear that they were consistently describing "teams" (as traditionally defined in the literature). Could it be that what was considered a team in France was different from what was considered a team in Puerto Rico or the Philippines? This initially led to concern (and yes, distress!)—if participants weren't describing processes in comparable entities, how could implementation be compared across cultures? Such doubts threw the entire research design into jeopardy. Would Gibson have to return the NSF funding?

Scholars such as Locke, Golden-Biddle, and Feldman (2008) have argued that doubt is actually a generative aspect in the research process. The authors argued that doubt is a state of being which is conducive to the process of abduction, or generating ideas for what "may be," as compared with induction (what "actually is") or deduction (what "must be") (Locke et al., 2008, p. 907). Applied to multinational organizational research, this may mean entering field settings with an open mind-set and a willingness to wade through feelings of doubt to let data speak to the researcher (Szkudlarek & McDaniel, 2010). Doubt may mean remaining open to multiple viewpoints and resolving false dichotomies. Gibson and Zellmer-Bruhn remained open to the possibility that the intercultural variation in concepts of teams and teamwork was an interesting phenomenon in its own right. Rather than deductively assuming the concept of *team* was defined in ways denoted by prior theory, they remained open to their feelings of doubt, providing an open forum for the generation of new and fruitful ideas. This led to more systematic analysis of the variation, and further insights into the implications of the patterns the analysis revealed. Hence, by embracing doubt, they were able to view and use it as a source of ideas rather than a source of insecurity (and no, they did not have to return the funding).

### Remaining Open to Discomfort and Paradox

In a related vein, a proximal approach embraces the asking of questions such as "What if the independent variable were the dependent variable?" "What if existing theory did not explain a certain outcome, what could be an alternative theoretical explanation?" early in the research. Asking these questions and remaining open to paradoxical or unexpected thought processes may usefully expand research design options (Szkudlarek & McDaniel, 2010). For example, a distal question ("What is the relationship of A to B?") may become proximal ("What are the processes that explain why A changes the nature of B?"). In the meaning of teamwork analysis, what started out as an exploration of "How does culture moderate the relationship between team implementation and team effectiveness?" became instead an examination of "How does culture change the meaning of the concept of team?"

Like embracing doubt, the process of exploring paradox is often uncomfortable. In a field in which linear thinking is the default, attempting to engage in circular or nonlinear thinking may be challenging. There may be awkwardness in attempting to submerge in unfamiliar conceptual or empirical territory. Yet, the largest theoretical or conceptual advancements may have stemmed from just such type of risk taking, that is, in the leaps from the known to the unknown (Szkudlarek & McDaniel, 2010). Discomfort may be generative and conceptually fruitful.

### Using Multiplicity and Reflexivity in Data Analysis

Because a proximal approach embraces multiplicity of perspectives and interpretations, the data collection process needs to be accompanied with appropriate analytical strategies (Szkudlarek & McDaniel, 2010). The focus areas of the proximal perspective are processes and constant transformation. Research accounts produced in this perspective are indeterminate and are often open to further reinterpretation. One of the important steps taken by Gibson and Zellmer-Bruhn (2001) in their meaning of teamwork analysis was to involve participants from each of the cultural regions in the study in the coding and labeling of the metaphor categories. Specifically, their first step in identifying teamwork metaphors was to develop a list of words that capture how people conceptualize teamwork. If there had been adequate theoretical background, such a list could have been derived from previous research, extant scales, or even a dictionary. But for the teamwork metaphors, Gibson and Zellmer-Bruhn (2001) did not use these methods for two reasons. First, there was little extant research concerning teamwork metaphors. Second, and more important, they reasoned that because their sample was multicultural, and their emergent research question concerned whether such metaphors vary across cultures, developing word lists from U.S.-based theories or dictionaries would have made little sense. These sources may have omitted culturally embedded terms or applied alternative or inappropriate meanings to words other than those intended by non-English speakers.

Therefore, Gibson and Zellmer-Bruhn (2001) used a process that captured cultural nuances in meaning, as well as words that were not readily translated into English. First, they created an alphabetical list of the 6,661 unique words in their interview database. Copies of the list were then given to two raters from each country in the sample. The full list contained many words that were irrelevant (e.g., *the*, *a*) and many intonations (e.g., *um*, *aaah*) because the database was transcribed verbatim from interviews. To remove all irrelevant terms, they asked raters to independently circle any they felt were entirely irrelevant to the questions being asked in the interview. Across all raters, 1,740 words remained and were deemed relevant. Eliminating spelling variants of the same word root (e.g., *family* also occurred as *families*) resulted in a list containing 589 words.

Next, the authors printed the words onto cards and asked five raters from each country involved in the study to sort them into groups they felt represented metaphors for teamwork. The raters had themselves been members of work teams in their native countries, had some work experience together, were similar to each other, and resembled the interviewees in terms of demographic characteristics. They were told to broadly define *teamwork* and were not given a definition of the term. The researchers emphasized that they were to work collectively as a team[1]. The raters worked collaboratively for 8 hours to sort the words. They asked each other about why a given word was placed into a pile and expressed unique ways in which a term could be used in their native culture. Through a process of discussion, negotiation, and elimination, the raters arrived at five piles, each representing a different metaphor. They developed the names for each pile (*family*, *sports*, *community*, *associates*, and

---

[1]The specific instructions given were "Your job is to read a number of words and work together to sort them into piles or groups, each of which represents a different metaphor for teamwork. We do not have prescribed groupings for you, so please create the necessary piles on your own. Please sort the words into piles in such a way that the words that seem similar to each other are in the same pile, words that seem dissimilar are in different piles. In case of doubt, you should create more piles rather than fewer. You can redistribute the words and develop a new pile whenever necessary. When you have arrived at your final set of piles, please develop a name for each pile that captures the content."

*military*). These five metaphor piles contained an average of 100 unique words each and included both English and non-English words (i.e., words that were not translatable to English). The raters defined the metaphors broadly and placed words in them that they felt elaborated the metaphor from their native language point of view.

By taking these (time-consuming) steps, Gibson and Zellmer-Bruhn (2001) were able to ensure that their own biases, assumptions, and training did not dominate the analysis. They incorporated a multiplicity of views from the regions in which the research was conducted into the analysis. Linking the multiplicity and fluidity embraced by proximal research with the complexity of studied phenomena adequately aligns the scholarly perspective with the dynamic nature of global business (Szkudlarek & McDaniel, 2010). This is especially crucial in an ever-changing, intercultural context, where individuals are constantly confronted with unfamiliar circumstances, which often cannot be decoded with home-culture values and behavioral conventions.

## Considering the Interplay Between Researcher and Researched

Proximal scholarship suggests interdependence of actors involved in a research project and includes interpretations of the researched participants, rather than assuming an objective and neutral authority of the researcher. The traditional *emic* perspective, referring to ideas and behaviors that are culturally specific (Berry, 1969), identifies concepts that are closely linked to local, indigenous processes of discursive signification (Morris, Leung, Ames, & Lickel, 1999). That is, analysis of these processes may be perceived, interpreted, and convey meaning differently to the researcher (who is outside the studied culture) and the researched population (who are deeply embedded within their culture). As the preconceived notions held by the researchers in regards to the meaning of teamwork ended up being quite different from those held by the participants, the importance of this variation is very clearly illustrated in the meaning of teamwork analysis.

This principle indicates that cross-cultural comparative accounts might rely on locally bonded concepts and may, in fact, not be open to direct comparison. Gibson and Zellmer-Bruhn (2001) were able to identify categories (or aspects) of teamwork metaphorical mappings that had implications for what participants expected of their teams. The categories were comparable, but the content of the categories varied across cultures. This layered complexity of analysis need not be as daunting as it may seem, as a proximal approach suggests a way by which to approximate comparison by engaging the voice of those who are being studied. This voice was understood as a result of the interplay between the researchers and the researched—that is, the dialogue, the steps taken to ensure mutual understanding, and the probing analyses in which the researchers attempted to step out of their perspectives and incorporate the perspective of the participants. Specifically, early interviews conducted by Gibson and Zellmer-Bruhn helped to uncover the metaphors. As it became clear that the metaphors had important practical implications, subsequent interviews were used to probe the mappings onto expectations for team management and implementation. By including the perspective of those who are researched, the researchers were able to make better sense of the true meaning of what was being examined.

## OPPORTUNITIES AND CHALLENGES FOR FUTURE RESEARCH

We emphasize that it is not the case that a proximal approach is necessarily better than a distal approach. Both can yield rich findings, and both modes of thinking may be appropriate for different research questions, may serve different purposes, and may be valid within different contexts. We are advocates of matching the approach to the research question and remaining open to the process of discovery. As so aptly stated by Szkudlarek and McDaniel (2010), "One should dare to explore the world in diverse and unpredictable ways" (p. 24).

Such openness was illustrated in the Implementation of Teams Project: The meaning of teamwork analysis illustrated the proximal approach, and several of the other analyses conducted on the survey data illustrated a distal approach. By applying multiple research lenses, the collection of studies emanating from the project reveal insights that could have not been gained through a single lens. This was possible because the researchers remained alert to unexpected occurrences, they explored rather than eliminated the paradoxes, and they nurtured a skeptical attitude toward the established models and theories (Lewis & Kelemen, 2002). A similar approach illustrated in numerous other instances, including by Brannen and Peterson (2009) and by Knight, Holdsworth, and Mather (2007), has successfully combined the distal and proximal perspectives.

Further, we acknowledge that although most multinational organizational scholars recognize the need for expanding research toolboxes (Sullivan, 1998), introducing a proximal worldview is not without challenge. First, researchers need to consider the paradigmatic divides and incommensurability of different approaches (Burrell & Morgan, 1979; Deetz, 1996). The proximal perspective, grounded in the social construction paradigm and qualitative methodology, might be considered by many as detached and alien to the dominant functionalist philosophy (Szkudlarek & McDaniel, 2010). It is difficult to alter an entire set of established norms within an academic field—norms that currently tend to favor distal approaches and quantitative methodologies. Our hope is that this edited volume will help to establish a new norm of greater inclusivity with openness to more diverse research methodologies, particularly qualitative research.

Second, there are logistical concerns that relate to the incorporation of both distal and proximal perspectives into research projects. Such inclusion encourages researchers to be familiar with multiple methodologies, and to feel comfortable working with what may be unfamiliar approaches (Szkudlarek & McDaniel, 2010). The recognition and inclusion of research accounts rooted in the proximal tradition will likely be a time-consuming and tempestuous process, compared with a more distal and linear research design. Though this presents a challenge, the proximal perspective may encourage researchers to engage in a more proactive approach to their own development. For example, one way to facilitate this openness would be to seek out training in methodologies that may be outside of one's current expertise or instructional reach. Another means by which to address this need could be to partner with scholars who have the needed expertise. We encourage scholars to actively choose coauthors who may help fill knowledge gaps, with the goal of increasing the agility with which proximal research questions can be incorporated into research designs.

Finally, including both distal and proximal approaches into scholarly work will significantly increase the time needed for completing research endeavors. The length of time it takes to engage in high-quality qualitative research has been noted (Lofland, Snow, Anderson, & Lofland, 2006), inclusive of both the time spent in the field as well as qualitative data analysis. This temporal duration is a particular concern for junior researchers, who are concerned with tenure clocks. Although we advocate (and the Big Surprise illustrates) that the time spent would expectantly be paid off with the resultant insights, the extended time span of a research project can result in delayed reporting of emergent and time-bonded findings. We hope that this chapter helps to demonstrate why, for multinational researchers, this may be time well spent.

We believe the proximal approach to be a lucrative opportunity for scholars of multinational organizational research. As demonstrated by the Implementation of Teams Project and particularly the Big Surprise, remaining open to the unexpected, accepting uncertainty, and maintaining an appreciation for multiple orientations toward the world can reveal otherwise undiscoverable conceptual treasures. These treasures can be found only if researchers are willing to extend from the traditional mode of thinking in terms of end states and linearity. We hope this chapter prompts readers to similarly appreciate and consider incorporating the proximal approach, and to share with us the continued excitement for experiencing the joys and sorrows of multicultural research.

**Best Practice Recommendations**

- Because no interpretation is culture free, use self-awareness when collecting and making sense of the data.
- Reflect on your own background (e.g., academic training) to understand what methodological biases you might be bringing into the research process and how you could broaden your current analytical lenses.
- Rather than narrowing, use doubt as a broadening device to explore multiplicity of interpretations.
- Encourage a wealth of possible explanations and research outcomes instead of searching for one-dimensional, deterministic solutions.
- Explore paradoxes and embrace discomfort as mechanisms generating new interpretative avenues.
- Engage your respondents in the data examination process to assure the soundness and accuracy of the analysis.

## REFERENCES

Bartunek, J. M., & Seo, M. G. (2002). Qualitative research can add new meanings to quantitative research. *Journal of Organizational Behavior, 23*, 237–242. doi:10.1002/job.132

Berry, J. W. (1969). On cross-cultural comparability. *International Journal of Psychology, 4*, 119–128. doi:10.1080/00207596908247261

Bird, A., Mendenhall, M. E., Stevens, M. J., & Oddou, G. (2010). Defining the domain of intercultural competence for global leaders. *Journal of Managerial Psychology, 25*, 810–828.

Blair, I. V., & Banaji, M. R. (1996). Automatic and controlled processes in stereotype priming. *Journal of Personality and Social Psychology, 70*, 1142–1163. doi:10.1037/0022-3514.70.6.1142

Brannen, M. Y., & Peterson, M. F. (2009). Merging without alienating: Interventions promoting cross-cultural organizational integration and their limitations. *Journal of International Business Studies, 40*, 468–489. doi:10.1057/jibs.2008.80

Burrell, G., & Morgan, G. (1979). *Sociological paradigms and organisational analysis: Elements of the sociology of corporate life*. London, England: Heinemann Educational.

Cohen, S. G., & Bailey, D. E. (1997). What makes teams work: Group effectiveness research from the shop floor to the executive suite. *Journal of Management, 23*, 239–290. doi:10.1177/014920639702300303

Cooper, R. (1992). Systems and organizations: Distal and proximal thinking. *Systems Practice*, 5, 373–377. doi:10.1007/BF01059829

Cooper, R., & Law, J. (1995). Organization: Distal and proximal views. In S. B. Bacharach, P. Gagliardi, & B. Mundell (Eds.), *Research in the sociology of organizations: Studies of organizations in the European tradition* (pp. 275–)301. Greenwich, CT: JAI Press.

Deetz, S. (1996). Describing differences in approaches to organization science: Rethinking Burrell and Morgan and their legacy. *Organization Science*, 7, 191–207. doi:10.1287/orsc.7.2.191

Earley, P. C., & Gibson, C. B. (2002). *Multinational work teams: A new perspective*. Mahwah, NJ: Erlbaum.

Edmondson, A. C., & McManus, S. E. (2007). Methodological fit in management field research. *The Academy of Management Review*, 32, 1155–1179. doi:10.5465/AMR.2007.26586086

Eisenberg, E. (1984). Ambiguity as strategy in organizational communication. *Communication Monographs*, 51, 227–242. doi:10.1080/03637758409390197

Gannon, M. J., & Associates. (1994). *Understanding global cultures: Metaphorical journeys through 17 countries*. Thousand Oaks, CA: Sage.

Gibson, C. B. (2001). From accumulation to accommodation: The chemistry of collective cognition in work groups. *Journal of Organizational Behavior*, 22, 121–134. doi:10.1002/job.84

Gibson, C. B., Conger, J., & Cooper, C. (2001). Perceptual distance: Impacts of differences in team leader and member perceptions across cultures. In W. H. Mobley & M. McCall (Eds.), *Advances in global leadership* (Vol. 2, pp. 245–276). Greenwich, CT: JAI Press.

Gibson, C. B., Cooper, C., & Conger, J. (2009). Do you see what I see? The complex effects of perceptual distance between leaders and teams. *Journal of Applied Psychology*, 94, 62–76. doi:10.1037/a0013073

Gibson, C. B., & Kirkman, B. L. (1999). Our past, present, and future in teams: The role of human resource professionals in managing team performance. In A. I. Kraut & A. K. Korman (Eds.), *Changing concepts and practices for human resource management: Contributions from I/O psychology* (pp. 90–117). San Francisco, CA: Jossey-Bass.

Gibson, C. B., & Vermeulen, F. (2003). A healthy divide: Subgroups as a stimulus for team learning. *Administrative Science Quarterly*, 48, 202–239. doi:10.2307/3556657

Gibson, C. B., & Zellmer-Bruhn, M. (2001). Metaphor and meaning: An intercultural analysis of the concept of teamwork. *Administrative Science Quarterly*, 46, 274–303. doi:10.2307/2667088

Gibson, C. B., & Zellmer-Bruhn, M. (2002). Minding your metaphors: Applying the concept of teamwork metaphors to the management of teams in multicultural contexts. *Organizational Dynamics*, 31, 101–116. doi:10.1016/S0090-2616(02)00095-5

Gibson, C. B., Zellmer-Bruhn, M., & Schwab, D. S. (2003). Team effectiveness in multinational Organizations: Development and evaluation across contexts. *Group & Organization Management, 28,* 444–474. doi:10.1177/1059601103251685

Jack, G. A., Calas, M. B., Nkomo, S. M., & Peltonen, T. (2008). Critique and international management: An uneasy relationship. *The Academy of Management Review, 33,* 870–884. doi:10.5465/AMR.2008.34421991

Kirkman, B. L., Gibson, C. B., & Shapiro, D. (2001). "Exporting" teams: Enhancing the implementation and effectiveness of work teams in global affiliates. *Organizational Dynamics, 30,* 12–29. doi:10.1016/S0090-2616(01)00038-9

Knight, J. G., Holdsworth, D. K., & Mather, D. W. (2007). Country-of-origin and choice of food imports: An in-depth study of European distribution channel gatekeepers. *Journal of International Business Studies, 38,* 107–125. doi:10.1057/palgrave.jibs.8400250

Lakoff, G. (1993). The contemporary theory of metaphor. In A. Ortony (Ed.), *Metaphor and thought* (pp. 202–251). Cambridge, England: Cambridge University Press.

Lee, T. W., Mitchell, T. R., & Sablynski, C. J. (1999). Qualitative research in organizational and vocational psychology, 1979–1999. *Journal of Vocational Behavior, 55,* 161–187. doi:10.1006/jvbe.1999.1707

Lewis, M. W., & Kelemen, M. L. (2002). Multiparadigm inquiry: Exploring organizational pluralism and paradox. *Human Relations, 55,* 251–275. doi:10.1177/0018726702055002185

Locke, K., Golden-Biddle, K., & Feldman, M. S. (2008). Making doubt generative: Rethinking the role of doubt in the research process. *Organization Science, 19,* 907–918. doi:10.1287/orsc.1080.0398

Lofland, J., Snow, D. A., Anderson, L., & Lofland, L. H. (2006). *Analyzing social settings: A guide to qualitative observation and analysis* (4th ed.). Belmont, CA: Wadsworth.

McGrath, J. E. (1984). *Groups: Interaction and performance.* Englewood Cliffs, NJ: Prentice Hall.

Miles, M. B., & Huberman, A. M. (1994). *Qualitative data analysis: An expanded sourcebook.* London, England: Sage.

Morris, M. W., Leung, K., Ames, D., & Lickel, B. (1999). Views from inside and outside: Integrating emic and etic insights about culture and justice judgments. *The Academy of Management Review, 24,* 781–796.

Sullivan, D. P. (1998). The ontology of international business. A comment on international business: An emerging vision. *Journal of International Business Studies, 29,* 877–885. doi:10.1057/palgrave.jibs.8490057

Szkudlarek, B., & McDaniel, D. (2010, August). *Qualitative as proximal: Accelerating international business scholarship through proximal theorizing and qualitative methodology.* Paper presented at the annual meeting of the Academy of Management Meetings, Montreal, Canada.

Zellmer-Bruhn, M. (1999). *Breaking team routines: The effects of time pressure and interruptions on external acquisition of work routines.* (Unpublished doctoral dissertation). University of Wisconsin, Madison.

Zellmer-Bruhn, M. E. (2003). Interruptive events and team knowledge acquisition. *Management Science, 49,* 514–528. doi:10.1287/mnsc.49.4.514.14423

Zellmer-Bruhn, M., & Gibson, C. B. (2006). Multinational organizational context: Implications for team learning and performance. *Academy of Management Journal, 49,* 501–518. doi:10.5465/AMJ.2006.21794668

# 2

# CULTURAL INTELLIGENCE: A REVIEW, REFLECTIONS, AND RECOMMENDATIONS FOR FUTURE RESEARCH

KOK-YEE NG, LINN VAN DYNE, AND SOON ANG

The challenges of working with people from different cultures are well-documented in management research. Although these challenges were largely constrained within the expatriate population 1 to 2 decades ago, rapid globalization has resulted in a much larger group of employees being faced with cross-cultural issues in daily work. Kanter (1995) argued that for organizations to become world class in today's global economy, they must develop a new breed of managers who can see beyond surface-level cultural differences.

Despite the need to better understand and operationalize the abilities this new breed of managers should possess, up until the turn of the 21st century very little systematic research had addressed this gap. Even in the research on adult intelligence, which increasingly recognizes that there are multiple forms of intelligence critical for solving different kinds of problems (beyond the traditional focus on academic and cognitive problems; Gardner, 1993, 1999), there was no focus on the ability to solve problems specifically in the cultural realm. For instance, considerable research attention has been focused on social intelligence (Thorndike & Stein, 1937) targeted at interpersonal relations, emotional intelligence (EQ; Mayer & Salovey, 1993) targeted at understanding one's and others' emotions, and practical intelligence (Sternberg, 1997) targeted at solving practical problems. Yet, none of these nonacademic intelligences focus on the ability to solve cross-cultural problems. This gap prompted Earley and Ang's (2003) work on cultural intelligence (CQ), which draws on Sternberg and Detterman's (1986) integrative theoretical framework on multiple loci of intelligences, to propose a set of capabilities comprising mental, motivational, and behavioral components that focus specifically on resolving cross-cultural problems.

In the history of research on cross-cultural competency, the construct of CQ has been described as a "new kid on the scientific block" (Gelfand, Imai, & Fehr, 2008, p. 376). Despite its relatively short history, CQ has undergone a remarkable journey of growth. The concept was first formally introduced by Earley and Ang in 2003 in their book *Cultural Intelligence: Individual Interactions Across Cultures*. In 2004, we organized the first symposium on CQ at the Academy of Management annual meeting. In 2006, we published a special issue devoted to the conceptualization and empirical investigation of CQ in *Group and Organization Management*. In the same year, we organized the first Global Conference on Cultural Intelligence, which started a diverse network of researchers from different cultures and different disciplines who continue to exchange ideas and work collaboratively to advance the research on CQ to this day.

In 2007, Ang et al. published the first article on the measurement and predictive validity of CQ in *Management and Organization Review*. By offering a validated scale to assess individuals' CQ, this article triggered exponential growth in empirical studies on CQ across diverse disciplines, including cross-cultural applied linguistics (Rogers, 2008), military operations (Ang & Ng, 2005; Ng, Ramaya, Teo, & Wong, 2005; Selmeski, 2007), United Nations peacekeeping operations (Seiler, 2007), immigrants (Leung & Li, 2008), international missionary work (Livermore, 2006, 2008), and mental health counseling (Goh, Koch, & Sanger, 2008). In 2008, Ang and Van Dyne published the *Handbook of Cultural Intelligence: Theory, Measurement, and Applications*, which comprises 24 conceptual and empirical contributions from scholars from different cultural and disciplinary backgrounds. In 2009, Livermore wrote *Leading With Cultural Intelligence: The New Secret to Success*, a practical book that translated academic research on CQ to easily accessible materials and useful recommendations for business leaders and students alike. More recently, Livermore (2011) wrote a new book, *The Cultural Intelligence Difference: Master the One Skill You Can't Do Without in Today's Global Economy*, that focuses on practical ways to increase CQ capabilities.

To sum up the journey of the past 7 years, we have witnessed the development of CQ from a theoretical concept to a measurable construct with strong psychometric properties and construct validity evidence, from theoretical expositions of its practical significance to empirical evidence of its predictive validity, and from an academic construct to a practical framework for multicultural and global education and development. This extraordinary growth of CQ research can be attributed to the theoretical foundation of the construct, rigorous psychometric properties of the Cultural Intelligence Scale (CQS; Ang et al., 2007; Van Dyne, Ang, & Koh, 2008), unprecedented globalization throughout the world, and increasing cultural tensions that followed the September 11th tragedy in 2001 (Ang, Van Dyne, & Tan, 2011).

More important, the innovative integration of research on intelligence and culture offers a novel and elegant theoretical framework for thinking about intercultural competencies (Ang et al., 2007; Gelfand et al., 2008; Ng & Earley, 2006). Anchored on the intelligence research, CQ offers at least three conceptual contributions to a field that was fragmented with a myriad of intercultural competencies that lacked clarity and coherence (Ang et al., 2007; Gelfand et al, 2008). First, CQ is theoretically precise. Drawing from Sternberg and Detterman's (1986) multiple-loci-of-intelligence arguments, CQ is explicit on what it is (it consists of metacognitive, cognitive, motivational, and behavioral elements) and what it is not (it is not personality and not values; Gelfand et al., 2008). Second, the theoretical basis of CQ offers a cohesive and comprehensive framework for considering the multifaceted nature of intercultural capabilities. Because existing intercultural competency models typically focus on only one or two of the four CQ dimensions, CQ provides an integrative framework that helps to organize and integrate the disparate research on intercultural competencies (Ang et al., 2007; Gelfand et al., 2008). Third, through its connection with intelligence research, CQ opens up a wide range of important and interesting phenomena that can be studied in relation to cultural adaptation that were not particularly salient in the past (Gelfand et al., 2008). For instance, cognitive processes such as self- and other awareness, analogical reasoning, and pattern recognition become significant issues to examine in intercultural interfaces (Earley & Ang, 2003; Gelfand et al., 2008). This not only has the potential to enrich understanding of effective adaptation but also promotes interdisciplinary research.

This chapter offers a review of and reflections on our journey, which started almost a decade ago. Our aim is to take stock of what we have learned about CQ as a construct, as well as what we have learned about conducting research on CQ. The former entails an up-to-date review of the research on CQ, and the latter involves a reflection on the process and journey thus far. We then use insights from the review and reflections to suggest ways to move forward and advance the science and practice of CQ. Accordingly, we organize this chapter into three parts. The first section offers a comprehensive review of the existing CQ research. The second section describes our reflections on the rewards and challenges of conducting CQ research. The third section concludes the chapter with key areas for future research and suggestions for how to conduct the research.

## REVIEW OF EXISTING CULTURAL INTELLIGENCE RESEARCH

In this section, we review the existing literature on CQ. We begin by describing the conceptual definition and basis of CQ. Next, we discuss research on the measurement of CQ. We then review empirical studies of CQ and its correlates, antecedents, and outcomes.

### Conceptualization of Cultural Intelligence

CQ, defined as an individual's capability to function and manage effectively in culturally diverse settings (Earley & Ang, 2003), is consistent with Schmidt and Hunter's (2000) definition of *general intelligence* (IQ) as "the ability to grasp and reason correctly with abstractions [concepts] and solve problems" (p. 3). It is built on the growing interest in real-world intelligence, which has yielded several types of intelligence that focus on specific content domains, such as social intelligence (Thorndike & Stein, 1937), EQ (Mayer & Salovey, 1993), and practical intelligence (Sternberg, 1997). CQ contributes to this research by emphasizing the specific domain of intercultural settings, which has not been examined in prior research despite the practical realities of globalization.

The CQ framework is based on Sternberg and Detterman's (1986) integration of the various loci of intelligence residing within the person. According to Sternberg and Detterman, metacognition, cognition, and motivation are mental capabilities that reside within the head, whereas overt actions are behavioral capabilities. *Metacognitive intelligence* refers to control of cognition: the processes individuals use to acquire and understand knowledge. *Cognitive intelligence* refers to knowledge structures and is consistent with Ackerman's (1996) intelligence-as-knowledge concept, which argues for the importance of knowledge as part of intellect. *Motivational intelligence* refers to the mental capacity to direct and sustain energy on a particular task or situation and recognize that motivational capabilities are critical to real-world problem-solving (Ceci, 1996). *Behavioral intelligence* refers to outward manifestations or overt actions: what a person does rather than what he or she thinks (Sternberg & Detterman, 1986).

Applying Sternberg's (1986) multiple-loci-of-intelligence framework, Earley and Ang (2003) conceptualized CQ as comprising metacognitive, cognitive, motivational, and behavioral dimensions with specific relevance to functioning in culturally diverse settings. *Metacognitive CQ* reflects mental processes that individuals use to acquire and understand cultural knowledge, including knowledge of, and control over, individual thought processes (Flavell, 1979) relating to culture. Relevant capabilities include planning, monitoring, and revising mental models of cultural norms for countries or groups of people. Those with high metacognitive CQ are consciously aware of others' cultural preferences before and during interactions; they also question cultural assumptions and adjust their mental models during and after interactions (Brislin, Worthley, & MacNab, 2006; Triandis, 2006).

Whereas metacognitive CQ focuses on higher order cognitive processes, *cognitive* CQ reflects knowledge of norms, practices, and conventions in different cultures acquired from education and personal experiences. This includes knowledge of economic, legal, sociolinguistic, and interpersonal systems of different cultures and subcultures (Triandis, 1994) and knowledge of basic frameworks of cultural values (e.g., Hofstede, 2001). Those with high cognitive CQ understand similarities and differences across cultures (Brislin et al., 2006).

*Motivational* CQ reflects the capability to direct attention and energy toward learning about and functioning in situations characterized by cultural differences. Kanfer and Heggestad (1997) argued that such motivational capacities "provide agentic control of affect, cognition and behavior that facilitate goal accomplishment" (p. 39). According to the expectancy value theory of motivation (Eccles & Wigfield, 2002), the direction and magnitude of energy channeled toward a particular task involves two elements—expectations of success and value of success. Those with high motivational CQ direct attention and energy toward cross-cultural situations based on intrinsic interest (Deci & Ryan, 1985) and confidence in their cross-cultural effectiveness (Bandura, 2002). In addition, Cattell's (1971) investment theory of intelligence would argue that motivational CQ is critical in facilitating the growth of cognitive and metacognitive CQ.

*Behavioral* CQ reflects the capability to exhibit appropriate verbal and nonverbal actions when interacting with people from different cultures. As Hall (1959) emphasized, mental capabilities for cultural understanding and motivation must be complemented with the ability to exhibit appropriate verbal and nonverbal actions, based on cultural values of specific settings. This includes having a wide and flexible repertoire of behaviors. Those with high behavioral CQ exhibit situationally appropriate behaviors based on their broad range of verbal and nonverbal capabilities, such as exhibiting culturally appropriate words, tone, gestures, and facial expressions (Gudykunst, Ting-Toomey, & Chua, 1988).

Ang et al. (2007) further clarified that the four dimensions of CQ are qualitatively different aspects of the overall capability to function effectively in culturally diverse settings. This suggests that CQ is best described as an aggregate multidimensional construct with two distinguishing features: (a) the four dimensions exist at the same level of conceptualization as the overall construct, and (b) the dimensions make up the overall construct (Law, Wong, & Mobley, 1998). In other words, metacognitive, cognitive, motivational, and behavioral CQ are different types of capabilities that together form the overall CQ construct.

The theory of CQ is specific on what CQ is and what CQ is not (Ang & Van Dyne, 2008; Ang et al., 2007; Earley & Ang, 2003). As a form of intelligence, CQ clearly refers to an individual's capabilities, as opposed to personality traits or interests. Ang et al. (2007) further described CQ as a specific individual difference that targets culturally relevant capabilities and, hence, is distinct from broad individual differences, such as personality. CQ is also distinct from other types of intelligence, such as general cognitive ability (Schmidt & Hunter, 1998) and EQ (Mayer & Salovey, 1993), which focus on the ability to solve problems of a different nature. General cognitive ability focuses on the ability to learn and perform across many jobs and settings, whereas EQ focuses on the general ability to perceive and regulate emotions. Both cognitive ability and EQ do not take into account the abilities required of individuals to deal with culturally diverse others, which is the focus of CQ. At the same time, CQ is not specific to any particular culture (i.e., CQ does not refer to one's capability to function in specific cultures) but is a culture-free construct that transcends cultural boundaries. Finally, CQ is a malleable state construct that can be developed over time.

## Measurement of Cultural Intelligence

A significant milestone in the CQ research journey was the development and validation of the 20-item CQS. The process began with a literature review of relevant intercultural competencies and intelligence scales. Specifically, educational and cognitive psychology operationalizations of metacognition (e.g., O'Neil & Abedi, 1996) formed the basis of items for metacognitive CQ. Items for cognitive CQ were developed on the basis of existing cultural domains identified by Triandis (1994) and Murdock's (1987) Human Relations Areas Files. Motivational CQ items were drawn from Deci and Ryan's (1985) work on intrinsic motivation and Bandura's (2002) work on self-efficacy, applied to intercultural settings. Items for behavioral CQ were based on inter-cultural communication research focusing on verbal and nonverbal flexibility (Gudykunst et al., 1988; Hall, 1959). In addition, we conducted interviews to obtain input from eight global executives.

Our initial item pool consisted of 53 questions, with approximately 13 items assessing each CQ dimension. All items were positively worded to avoid methodological artifacts. A panel of subject matter experts (three faculty members and three international executives with significant global experience) independently reviewed the items for clarity, readability, and definitional fidelity. From this process, we retained the 10 best items for each dimension.

We began a large-scale data collection consisting of five studies to validate the CQS. In Study 1, business school undergraduates in Singapore ($N = 576$) completed the 40-item scale. From this study, we deleted items with small standard deviations or extreme means, low item-to-total correlations, high residuals, and low factor loadings. This resulted in a 20-item scale with four items assessing metacognitive CQ; six items for cognitive CQ; five items for motivational CQ, and five items for behavioral CQ. Confirmatory factor analysis (CFA) using maximum likelihood estimation demonstrated that the four-factor correlated model was a good fit to the data.

We then conducted four more studies to validate the 20-item scale across samples, time, methods, and two different countries. In Study 2, CFA results of a nonoverlapping cross-validation sample of undergraduate students in Singapore ($N = 447$) confirmed the four-factor structure. In Study 3, we used a subset of respondents in Study 2 to assess the temporal stability of the scale. Results demonstrated evidence of test–retest reliability. In Study 4, we used a sample of undergraduates from the United States ($N = 337$) to assess the cultural equivalence of the scale. Multigroup tests of invariance using CFA showed that the four-factor structure held across the Singapore and the U.S. samples. In Study 5, we validated an observer version across methods of measurement. The 142 managers who participated in an executive MBA program in the United States completed the 20-item scale and also reported on their interactional adjustment. Each participant was also rated by a randomly assigned peer from his or her MBA team to report on his or her CQ and interactional adjustment. Multitrait, multimethod (MTMM) analyses provided evidence of convergent, discriminant, and criterion validity of the scale across self- and peer ratings.

Taken together, our studies have demonstrated that the 20-item CQS possesses good psychometric properties across samples, time, countries, and methods. The validated scale greatly enhances the "empirical potential" of CQ (Gelfand et al., 2008) and has been instrumental in stimulating much research in the past 3 years that has advanced understanding of CQ and its relationships with other constructs, as we describe in the next section.

### Empirical Research on the Nomological Network of Cultural Intelligence

Our current review builds on and adds to the recent comprehensive review of CQ by Ang et al. (2011) with new studies conducted in 2010 and 2011. We organize our review as follows: (a) discriminant validity of CQ from

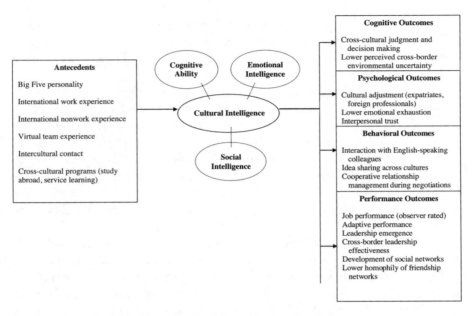

*Figure 2.1.* Summary of cultural intelligence research findings.

other types of intelligence; (b) antecedents of CQ; and (c) consequences of CQ, which can be categorized into cognitive, psychological, behavioral, and performance outcomes. Figure 2.1 summarizes our review described in the following sections.

*Discriminant Validity of Cultural Intelligence From Other Types of Intelligence*

In establishing the construct validity of CQ, one of the earliest questions we addressed was how CQ is different from other forms of intelligence. Using CFA and Fornell and Larcker's (1981) procedures for assessing discriminant validity, Ang et al. (2007) provided the first evidence that CQ is distinct from (a) EQ (Mayer & Salovey, 1993; Schutte et al., 1998) in both their U.S. and Singapore samples and (b) general mental ability as assessed by the Wonderlic Personality Test (Wonderlic, 1999).

Several recent studies have corroborated these results using different measures of EQ and general cognitive ability, data from different source and from different cultures. In a study conducted in Switzerland, Rockstuhl, Seiler, Ang, Van Dyne, and Annen (in press) assessed CQ and EQ with peer ratings, and general cognitive ability. CFA results showed that all three types of intelligence are distinct and had differential relationships with general versus cross-border leadership effectiveness. In a study conducted in South Korea using self-reports of CQ and EQ, Moon (2010a) demonstrated through

CFA that both types of intelligence are distinct. K. Kim, Kirkman, and Chen (2008) assessed CQ and EQ using both self- and observer ratings in a U.S. sample, and showed that CFA results consistently demonstrated discriminant validity of the two forms of intelligence across both sets of ratings. Results of their MTMM analyses further showed that self-ratings of CQ correlated more strongly with observer ratings of CQ ($r = .43$) than with observer ratings of EQ ($r = .26$), thus demonstrating convergent validity of CQ across different methods and divergent validity of CQ from EQ. In another study, Crowne (2009) assessed the discriminant validity of CQ, EQ, and social intelligence, and found all three types of intelligence to be distinct but correlated.

Overall, empirical research has strongly supported the distinctiveness of CQ from other forms of intelligence that focus on different domains of problem solving, such as general cognitive ability, EQ, and social intelligence. Next, we review research on the antecedents of CQ.

*Antecedents of Cultural Intelligence*

Personality traits, which describe what a person typically does across time and situations (Costa & McCrae, 1992), are broad and relatively stable individual difference constructs that influence choice of behaviors and experiences that should shape CQ (Ang, Van Dyne, & Koh, 2006; Earley & Ang, 2003). The first study on personality and CQ (Ang et al., 2006) demonstrated that CQ is distinct from, and has meaningful relationships with, the Big Five personality traits. As expected, Openness to Experience—the tendency to be creative, imaginative, and adventurous (Costa & McCrae, 1992)—was positively related to all four CQ factors, providing further construct validity evidence, because both CQ and Openness to Experience involve elements of novel situations. Likewise, Moody (2007) also found Openness to Experience to be the most significant predictor of CQ, followed by Conscientiousness. In a study conducted in New Zealand, Oolders, Chernyshenko, and Stark (2008) investigated the relationships between six subfacets of Openness to Experience (intellectual efficiency, ingenuity, curiosity, aesthetics, tolerance, and depth) and CQ, and found all subfacets to relate significantly to CQ. Of the six subfacets, tolerance ($r = .44$) and curiosity ($r = .39$) related most strongly to an overall measure of CQ.

Another important antecedent to CQ is international experience. Situated learning theory (Lave & Wenger, 1991) suggests that international experiences provide individuals with the social contexts and authentic activities to learn how to manage cross-cultural differences. Hence, individuals with greater international experience are more likely to acquire greater CQ. Drawing from Takeuchi, Tesluk, Yun, and Lepak's (2005) differentiation of work versus nonwork experience, several studies have examined how international work and nonwork experience relate to CQ. Although these studies demonstrated relationships between international experience and CQ, findings were not consistent across the four factors of CQ.

For international work experience, Shannon and Begley (2008) found that international work experience, as assessed by the number of countries individuals worked in, predicted metacognitive and motivational CQ. Crowne (2008), however, found that international work experience predicted all CQ factors except motivational CQ. Tay, Westman, and Chia (2008) measured the length of international work experience and found it related only to cognitive CQ. It is interesting to note that they found that the positive relationship between international work experience and CQ was stronger for individuals with lower need for control, and they argued that those with low need for control capitalized more on their previous work experiences because they did less pretrip preparations. In a recent study based on Kolb's (1984) experiential learning theory, Li and Mobley (2010) demonstrated a main effect of international experience on CQ. More important, they found learning style moderated the relationship between international experience and CQ, such that the relationship was stronger for those with divergent learning styles, and weaker for those with convergent learning styles.

For international nonwork experience, Tarique and Takeuchi (2008) showed that the number of countries visited predicted all four CQ factors, although the length of stay predicted cognitive CQ and metacognitive CQ. On the other hand, Crowne (2008) showed that number of countries visited for educational purposes predicted cognitive CQ and behavioral CQ, although number of countries visited for vacation predicted motivational CQ. In a study of Korean expatriates, Choi, Moon, and Jung (2010) found that expatriates' international nonwork experience, rather than their work experience, predicted CQ. In addition, expatriates' goal orientation moderated the relationship, such that those high in mastery goal orientation and low in performance avoidance orientation were more likely to develop CQ from their international nonwork experience.

Other studies have examined the impact of international experience gained through specific programs on the development of CQ. For instance, Shokef and Erez (2008) found that participants of virtual multicultural teams comprising members from five different countries and lasting for 4 weeks demonstrated a significant increase in their metacognitive CQ, motivational CQ, and behavioral CQ. In a study using a pre- and postintervention design, MacNab (2011) demonstrated that a systematic program design based on experiential learning and social contact principles had a positive impact on participants' development of CQ. It is not surprising that the amount of time spent interacting with people from other cultures during programs affected the rate of CQ development. Crawford-Mathis (2010) showed that volunteers in a service project in Belize who spent more time interacting with locals demonstrated higher increases in CQ. Likewise, Crowne (2007) found that individuals who stayed in hostels and ate with local residents developed greater CQ than those who stayed in expatriate compounds, where opportunities for contact with locals were significantly lower. Studies have also found that individual differences affect the rate of CQ development. For instance, Wilson and Stewart (2009) examined international service programs and showed that those who had experienced overseas service learning for the first time demonstrated the greatest development in their CQ. This finding suggests that cross-cultural experiences and development programs have more impact on the CQ development of individuals with lower CQ. A recent study by MacNab and Worthley (2011) of a group of managers and management students found that individuals high in general self-efficacy were more likely to improve in their CQ after attending an experiential cross-cultural training program. Drawing on the contact hypothesis and distinctiveness theory, Y. J. Kim and Van Dyne (2010) demonstrated, across two field studies of working adults, that the relationship between contact and CQ was stronger for majority members than for minorities.

In summary, research on antecedents of CQ has focused primarily on personality and international experience. There is less research on situational and environmental predictors. For instance, Ng, Tan, and Ang (2011) proposed that a firm's global cultural capital, including global mind-set and organizational routines that promote a global mind-set, should promote the development of employee CQ. It is also noteworthy that results show that the relationship between international experience and CQ is not straight-forward. Although the quantity of international experience is important for CQ development, there is little research on the quality of the experience. This is an important gap because quality of experience could be as important, if not more critical, than quantity. Individual differences are also likely to affect how international experiences translate into CQ. For example, Ng, Van Dyne, and Ang (2009) theorized that CQ moderates the extent to which individuals can transform their international experiences into experiential learning to enhance their global leadership effectiveness. Thus, CQ can be viewed as a critical learning capability that enhances the benefits of inter-national experience.

*Cognitive Outcomes of CQ*

Several studies have examined the effects of CQ on cognitive and psychological outcomes. An important cognitive outcome is *cultural judgment and decision making* (CJDM), which refers to the quality of decisions regarding intercultural interactions (Ang et al., 2007). Ang et al. (2007) proposed and found that cognitive CQ and metacognitive CQ predicted individuals' quality of decisions across a series of cross-cultural scenarios adapted from Cushner and Brislin (1996). Consistent with expectations, motivational CQ and behavioral CQ did not affect CJDM effectiveness because judgment and decision making emphasize analytical, rather than motivational or behavioral, abilities. Another cognitive outcome examined with important implications for cross-cultural decision making is perceived cross-border environmental uncertainty (Prado, 2006). In a study of 120 managers from 27 countries, Prado (2006) found that cognitive and metacognitive CQ positively predicted managers' perceived cross-border environment uncertainty, which has important implications for accurate risk assessment in international business ventures.

*Psychological Outcomes of Cultural Intelligence*

A key outcome in psychological research on sojourners and expatriates is cultural adjustment (Church, 1982). Cultural adjustment can be further delineated into *general adjustment* (general living conditions in the new culture), *work adjustment* (work culture in the new environment), and *interaction adjustment* (socializing and getting along with locals). *Psychological adjustment* refers to the general well-being when living in another culture.

A number of studies have found that CQ affects individuals' adjustment in a foreign environment. In a study of global professionals, Templer, Tay, and Chandrasekar (2006) demonstrated that motivational CQ predicted work and general adjustment over and above realistic job previews and realistic living conditions previews. Likewise, Ang et al. (2007) demonstrated in multiple studies that individuals with higher motivational and behavioral CQ reported better general, work, interactional, and psychological adjustment. In a study of American expatriates in China, Williams (2008) found that cognitive CQ predicted sociocultural adjustment and motivational CQ predicted both sociocultural and psychological adjustment. In a very recent study involving multisource and multilevel data, Chen, Kirkman, Kim, Farh, and Tangirala (2010) showed that motivational CQ influenced work adjustment of expatriates and that the effect was stronger when cultural distance and subsidiary support were lower. This study is noteworthy because it advances CQ research by focusing on boundary conditions that accentuate or attenuate the effects of CQ.

Given the increased demands placed on employees in the global workplace, an increasingly important psychological outcome examined in the CQ research is emotional exhaustion. In a study involving international business travelers, Tay, Rossi, and Westman (2010) found a negative relationship between CQ and emotional exhaustion (see also Tay et al., 2008). More important, the authors demonstrated that CQ buffered the effects of family demands interfering with work such that the effect of family demands on emotional exhaustion was weaker for those with higher CQ.

Interpersonal trust is another psychological outcome that has received growing attention. In a study of dyads within multicultural teams, Rockstuhl and Ng (2008) found that focal persons were more likely to trust their partners when (a) focal persons had higher metacognitive CQ and cognitive CQ; (b) partners had higher behavioral CQ; and, it is important to note, (c) when both parties were from different cultural backgrounds. In other words, the effects of CQ on interpersonal trust were evident only in culturally diverse dyads and not in culturally homogeneous dyads, thereby demonstrating that CQ matters only in culturally diverse settings. Chua and Morris's (2009) study of executives from diverse backgrounds produced similar results. They showed that overall CQ increased affect-based trust (but not cognitive-based trust) only among culturally diverse members of multicultural professional networks.

## Behavioral Outcomes of Cultural Intelligence

In a study of the interactions between native-English-speaking and non–native-English-speaking employees in a large French multinational firm, Beyene (2007) found that non–native-English-speaking employees with higher CQ had more frequent interactions with native-English-speaking employees, after controlling for employees' ability to speak multiple languages. Chua and Morris (2009) demonstrated that executives' CQ indirectly affected the frequency of idea sharing in intercultural ties through increasing affect-based trust. As expected, CQ did not affect idea-sharing behaviors in intracultural ties.

In a study of intercultural negotiations between East Asian and American negotiators, Imai and Gelfand (2010) found that negotiators with higher CQ demonstrated more integrative information behaviors and cooperative relationship management behaviors. These behaviors, in turn, positively predicted joint profits of the negotiation pairs. Individual differences in cognitive ability, EQ, Openness to Experience, Extraversion, and international experience did not affect negotiation behaviors.

## Performance Outcomes of CQ

Research to date has accumulated important findings on the effects of CQ on individual-level outcomes. We broadly classify these outcomes into general job performance (comprising task and adaptive performance) and performance in specific domains, such as negotiation and leadership.

For general work performance outcomes, Ang et al. (2007) demonstrated that foreign professionals with higher metacognitive CQ and behavioral

CQ were rated by their supervisors as more effective in meeting performance expectations at work. This finding suggests that individuals who are more aware of their environment (metacognitive CQ) and who are able to adapt their behaviors accordingly (behavioral CQ) are better at understanding and enacting role expectations that are culturally appropriate. In a study of expatriates, Chen et al. (2010) found that motivational CQ positively predicted expatriates' job performance. This relationship was fully mediated by their work adjustment. Further, the indirect effect of motivational CQ on performance via work adjustment was significant when subsidiary support and cultural distance were low, thereby highlighting important contextual factors surrounding CQ's effects on performance.

In another multilevel study focusing on real estate sales performance, Chen, Liu, and Portnoy (2011) demonstrated a positive relationship between motivational CQ and agents' cultural sales, defined as the number of sales transactions involving a client from a different culture. Specifically, results based on 305 agents from 26 real estate firms demonstrated that individuals' motivational CQ was positively related to their cultural sales, and this relationship was enhanced by high firm-level motivational CQ and diversity climate.

As the business environment gets increasingly complex and dynamic, *adaptive performance*, defined as modifying behaviors to meet the changing demands of the environment (Pulakos, Arad, Donovan, & Plamondon, 2000), is another practically and conceptually relevant outcome of CQ. In a study on adaptive performance, Oolders et al. (2008) positioned CQ as a more proximal individual difference that mediated the effect of the more distal trait of Openness to Experience on adaptive performance. Results confirmed that CQ positively predicted adaptive performance and mediated the effects of five of the six subfacets of Openness to Experience on adaptive performance.

Global leadership is another domain that has received increasing research attention in relation to CQ. Several qualitative studies involving in-depth interviews with global leaders provide rich accounts and empirical support to the importance of leaders' CQ in managing subordinates of different cultural backgrounds (Dean, 2007; Deng & Gibson, 2008). In a notable quantitative study of senior expatriate leaders, Elenkov and Manev (2009) found that CQ moderated the positive relationship between visionary–transformational leadership and organizational innovation, such that leaders with higher CQ magnified the positive effect of leadership on innovation. In another study, Groves and Feyerherm's (2011) analysis of a highly diverse sample of working adults demonstrated that after controlling for demographic characteristics and EQ, leader CQ was more strongly related to leader performance and team performance in more heterogeneous groups compared with less heterogeneous groups.

In a quantitative study of multicultural teams, Rockstuhl, Ang, Ng, Van Dyne, and Lievens (2009) demonstrated that self-reported CQ positively predicted leadership emergence as rated by team members, after controlling for IQ, EQ, Openness to Experience, and international experience. In another study involving Swiss military leaders, Rockstuhl et al. (in press) contrasted domestic and cross-border leadership effectiveness, and elucidated the role of multiple intelligences (IQ, EQ, and CQ) on both types of leadership outcomes. Results demonstrated an interesting pattern: After controlling for experience and the Big Five personality traits, IQ predicted both domestic and cross-border leadership effectiveness; EQ was a stronger predictor of domestic leadership effectiveness; and CQ was a stronger predictor of cross-border leadership effectiveness. This study highlights the unique and additional challenges faced by global leaders as compared with domestic leaders, and it underscores the role of CQ in enhancing the effectiveness of leaders who operate in diverse cultural contexts. Using polynomial regression and response surface methodology on a sample of graduate students from 35 different nationalities, Lee, Masuda, and Cardona (2010) demonstrated that CQ mediated the effects of three-way interactions between home identity, host identity, and global identity on perceptions of leadership.

Research has also begun to examine the impact of CQ on social networks. Fehr and Kuo (2008) demonstrated, in a culturally diverse sample of students studying and living in the United States and in a sample of American students in a study-abroad program, that CQ predicted the development of social networks, after controlling for international experience, host country language fluency, and cultural distance. In a study of 87 engineers from 12 countries in a multinational company in Singapore, Gjertsen, Torp, Koh, and Tan (2010) found that CQ negatively predicted homophily in friendship networks, after controlling for age, gender, rank, and organization tenure. It is interesting to note that CQ did not predict homophily in advice networks. Instead, individuals' rank and tenure were more predictive of advice ties. This pattern of result is significant because it illustrates another boundary condition of CQ. For more formal, instrumental ties (e.g., advice networks), heterophily was influenced more by indicators of competency such as rank and tenure than by CQ. This could indicate that work-related communication may be governed by strong corporate and professional norms that place less demand on individuals' CQ capability.

In summary, there is a growing body of empirical evidence on predictors and consequences of CQ. Although recent research has begun to examine more complex models, there is little research on cross-level predictors of CQ from the group or firm level. Also, although some research has begun to consider mediating mechanisms that explain the CQ–performance link, there is still relatively little research on more proximal outcomes of CQ. This could include liking, attraction, emotional states, time spent working together, and helping.

# REFLECTIONS ON OUR CULTURAL INTELLIGENCE JOURNEY

Our journey over the past 10 years has been rewarding in several aspects. From a research standpoint, we have seen burgeoning scholarly interest and attention on CQ. This not only demonstrates the recognition and acceptance of CQ in the scientific community but also offers momentum to push the boundaries of CQ research to generate more cutting-edge knowledge to help develop culturally intelligent individuals and organizations. As our review indicates, the research to date has addressed basic construct validity questions, such as what is CQ, what is not CQ, and what CQ predicts. Although we now have some answers to these basic questions, we have also uncovered issues that offer exciting avenues of research. Further, the applicability of CQ to practically any disciplinary area promises many opportunities for creative interdisciplinary research. As such, the journey has been, and will continue to be, intellectually stimulating.

The tight link between CQ research and practice is another reason our journey has been extremely rewarding. Besides research, we have continuously sought to apply our insights to teaching and executive development programs. The Nanyang Business School, Singapore, for instance, offers courses on CQ at both the undergraduate and MBA levels to develop students' CQ capabilities. The CQ concept and instrument have also been used extensively in executive programs for multinational, profit, and nonprofit organizations in more than 40 countries in Asia, Australia/Oceania, Eastern and Western Europe, the Middle East, and North America. We recently conducted a highly successful program with the International Air Transport Association (IATA) headquartered in Geneva, Switzerland, and Montreal, Canada. Every year, IATA selects 20 high-potential leaders from different country offices to participate in their elite Intercultural Leadership Engagement and Development (ILead) program. Beginning in 2009, a CQ training module was incorporated in the ILead program to raise participants' self-awareness of their CQ and to identify opportunities and ways to apply and to develop their CQ during the 5-month ILead program. Feedback from participants was extremely positive. Even though all the participants were experienced and well-traveled executives with immense cross-cultural experiences, the CQ concept provided them with a simple framework to organize their personal insights and strategies for interacting with people from different cultures. Having a measurement tool for obtaining feedback on CQ from others also helped to stimulate personal reflection, awareness, and further development.

At the same time, as with most research on new constructs, we experienced several growing pains. One of the earliest challenges we faced stemmed from the *intelligence* label, given the ongoing controversy and debate on what constitutes intelligence (Weinberg, 1989). As with EQ research, our initial work on CQ was challenged for using the term *intelligence*. Similar to proponents of EQ, we have used the term *cultural intelligence* because it is consistent with the broader definition of *intelligence* as a capability to adapt to the environment (Sternberg & Detterman, 1986). Furthermore, the nature of CQ meets the three criteria of intelligence proposed by Mayer, Caruso, and Salovey (2000). First, CQ reflects abilities rather than personality traits or typical tendencies. Second, existing research shows that CQ correlates with, yet is distinct from, other types of intelligences, such as IQ, EQ, and social intelligence (Ang et al., 2007; Crowne, 2009; K. Kim et al., 2008; Moon, 2010a). Third, CQ can be improved and developed over time (Choi et al., 2010; Crawford-Mathis, 2010; MacNab, 2011; MacNab & Worthley, 2011; Shokef & Erez, 2008; Wilson & Stewart, 2009).

Another challenge related to developing a new construct was the immense construct validation efforts required, particularly in the initial phase of our research. For instance, to convince reviewers of the conceptual distinctiveness of CQ, we had to cull through the large and unsystematic body of literature on intercultural competencies and to compare and contrast CQ with other intercultural competency models and instruments (see Ang et al., 2007).

We also had to be comprehensive in our research design to ensure we measured as many relevant constructs as possible to demonstrate the convergent, divergent, and incremental predictive validity of CQ vis-à-vis these constructs (e.g., IQ, social intelligence, EQ, personality, other cross-cultural competencies). At the same time, we had to consider and manage respondent motivation and fatigue associated with long surveys. This required us to be systematic in prioritizing research questions and constructs to assess, as well as in identifying multiple relevant samples to address different research questions.

To have face validity and to make sure CQ would be relevant, we had to make sure that study participants had prior exposure to cultural diversity. Thus, we were faced with an additional consideration when we designed our studies. We also had to collect data from different countries and to conduct additional analyses to demonstrate the cross-cultural measurement equivalence of the CQS. Fortunately, the multicultural composition of the team facilitated the data collection.

In short, the construct validation process was intense and long drawn. It was undoubtedly an important process that cannot, and should not, be short circuited. Nonetheless, it was a journey that required great perseverance, a strong passion, and deep conviction that CQ is important both theoretically and practically. Fortunately, we worked in a team that shared that conviction, thus making the process much more enjoyable and fulfilling.

The next challenge concerns differential predictions for the four CQ capabilities. The four dimensions of CQ are critical and useful because (a) they are based on theory (Sternberg & Detterman, 1986); (b) they highlight four different capabilities that, taken together, provide an integrative framework to synthesize the disparate intercultural competencies; and (c) they are supported by empirical data using confirmatory factor analyses. However, they also present a challenge. For very specific criterion outcomes, such as cultural judgment and decision making, which essentially involve only cognitive processes, we were able to develop arguments for precise links for cognitive CQ and metacognitive CQ (and not for motivational CQ and behavioral CQ; Ang et al., 2007). However, for broader criterion outcomes, such as adjustment and performance, that are more complex, it is difficult to theorize a priori how the four CQ dimensions will exert different effects, and research to date does not show a clear pattern.

Some studies have used an aggregated representation of CQ as opposed to the four dimensions. We suggest that future research consider the nature of the criterion variable more carefully when deciding whether to use one specific dimension, several dimensions, all four dimensions, or overall aggregation of the four CQ dimensions. Consistent with bandwidth-fidelity arguments (Cronbach & Gleser, 1957), we recommend that broad criteria should be matched with overall CQ, and specific and narrowly defined criteria can be matched with specific, relevant CQ dimensions. For instance, broad criterion outcomes, such as job performance, may be better predicted by the aggregate construct of CQ, which allows for contextual variations in performance requirements (e.g., in some contexts, metacognitive CQ may be more important than motivational CQ in driving performance, or vice versa). In contrast, specific outcomes, such as cultural judgment and decision making, may be better predicted by specific CQ dimensions—in this case, cognitive and metacognitive CQ (Ang et al., 2007). Further, specifying and measuring mediating mechanisms hypothesized to effect the criterion will strengthen theoretical development and help advance understanding of why specific factors and/or overall CQ influence outcomes.

We have also learned that it is critically important to be explicit in defining *culture* for participants because *culture* can mean different things in different contexts and to different people. The CQS items ask about interactions with people from different cultural backgrounds. Depending on the context and framing, the questions can be applied to those from different national cultures, different racial/ethnic backgrounds, different regions of the country, or different subgroups based on age, gender, religion, sexual preference, or functional background, and so on. Each of these interpretations is legitimate. The key is specifying the conceptualization of culture based on the research question and study context. To ensure that participants respond to questions with a consistent mental model, it is important to provide an explicit explanation of *culture* in the instructions of each study.

Another issue is the use of reported measures of CQ versus performance-based tests of CQ. This is similar to the debate faced by EQ scholars (e.g., self-report of EQ vs. ability-based measures of EQ). However, a recent meta-analysis on EQ demonstrated that both self-report and performance-based measures of EQ predict job performance equally well (O'Boyle, Humphrey, Pollack, Hawver, & Story, 2011). Drawing from their findings, O'Boyle et al. (2011) concluded that the method to assess EQ should depend "on the purposes of the project, the feasibility of administering the tests or surveys, and similar factors" (p. 808). For instance, reported measures of intelligence are often more feasible to administer and can be adapted to particular work settings without difficulty. This may enhance the predictive validity of the measure. On the other hand, performance-based tests are useful for high-stakes decisions such as promotion and selection, given that they are objective and less susceptible to faking. In sum, we argue that reported measures (self- or other report) and performance-based measures are complementary approaches to assessing CQ. We elaborate on this point in the recommendations for future research that follow in the next section.

## RECOMMENDATIONS FOR FUTURE RESEARCH

Our review of the CQ literature highlights several key areas in which future research can significantly advance current understanding. We discuss four broad areas below.

First, we concur with Gelfand et al. (2008) that although factor analyses have supported the multidimensionality of CQ, very little is known about how the four different factors function and whether the different theoretical mechanisms account for their effects on specific outcomes. Hence, more precise theorizing and research on the nomological networks of each of the CQ factors can help researchers better understand the nature and functioning of the four CQ dimensions, and how they interact with one another to affect the outcomes of interest.

Second, existing empirical research has relied on self- and other reports of CQ using the CQS (Van Dyne et al., 2008). As reviewed earlier, existing research demonstrates that the CQS is reliable and predicts a variety of criterion outcomes. Nonetheless, developing complementary measures of CQ based on different assessment methodologies can strengthen research, allow triangulation of findings, and offer researchers and practitioners more assessment alternatives. For instance, Gelfand et al. (2008) suggested implicit measures of cultural knowledge using priming techniques, objective tests of cultural knowledge, and cognitive mapping to assess complexity of cultural knowledge. Rockstuhl et al. (2009) recently developed a performance-based measure of CQ using a multimedia situational judgment test methodology. Comparisons of self-reported CQ using the CQS and the performance-based measure of CQ showed the value of both approaches. Self-report CQ predicted cross-cultural leader emergence over and above IQ, EQ, Openness to Experience, and international experience. Performance-based CQ explained variance in cross-cultural leader emergence over and above the self-report measure. This finding suggests that future research should consider complementary approaches to assessing CQ, depending on the research question and research design. For instance, a performance-based measure of CQ may be more appropriate when predicting criteria that rely heavily on cognitive processes, whereas a reported measure of CQ may be more appropriate for predicting outcomes that involve interpersonal interactions such as work performance in team contexts and suitability for positions with global responsibilities. Performance-based measures of CQ may be more appropriate for high-stakes settings, such as selection, transfer, and promotion decisions, where it is important to minimize social desirability and rating biases.

Third, existing empirical research on CQ is predominantly at the individual level of analysis, suggesting opportunities for future research that considers CQ at and from other levels of conceptualization and analyses. As cultural neuroscience becomes increasingly popular in management research, examining CQ at the brain level is one example of a novel unit-of-analysis approach that offers exciting research opportunities (Earley & Ang, 2003; Rockstuhl, Hong, Ng, Ang, & Chiu, 2010). Approaching CQ from this biological perspective can reveal intriguing insights on how different CQ factors map onto different regions of the medial frontal cortex and how individuals tune their neural activity to varying cultural contexts. These findings will complement existing knowledge of CQ from a psychological perspective and offer a more comprehensive understanding of why some individuals are more effective in culturally diverse situations than others.

Firm-level CQ is an example of a higher level of analysis that remains relatively unexplored and presents many exciting research opportunities for organizational behavior and strategy scholars. The recent study by Chen et al. (2011) operationalized firm-level motivational CQ using a reference-shift approach, replacing the individual-level focus in Ang et al.'s (2007) CQ scale with firm-level analysis. Their results demonstrated that the firm-level motivational CQ measure was reliable, with a significant portion of the total variance explained by firm membership.

Alternatively, firm-level CQ could be defined and operationalized using a qualitatively different framework and measure. Ang and Inkpen's (2008) conceptual framework offers a starting point for developing such a measure of firm-level CQ (see also van Driel, 2008). Likewise, Moon (2010b) argued that firm-level CQ can be viewed as comprising processes, positions, and paths capabilities. Future research could operationalize these models and test how firm-level CQ affects firm-level outcomes, such as firm performance and international joint venture performance. For instance, with the growing interest in emerging markets, studies could examine how firm CQ affects success in new markets.

Fourth, understanding of how individuals develop CQ is still relatively limited. Several studies reviewed in this chapter have demonstrated that international experiences contribute to individuals' CQ and that CQ can improve as a result of cross-cultural training interventions and international assignments. These studies, however, have relied on two waves of data to assess change in CQ and thus cannot reveal the nature of changes (Chan, 1998). Research has yet to adopt a multiwave assessment of CQ over time with latent growth modeling focused on factors that affect growth parameters. Future research that systematically tracks and analyzes the development of CQ over time using latent growth modeling will offer great insights to both CQ research and practice. This stream of research can also shed light on how different CQ factors may develop differently by examining their growth trajectories.

Moving forward, our reflections on the past 10 years of CQ research suggest that two factors are key to sustaining this journey. First, finding research partners with similar passion and commitment to the topic is critical, particularly when the area of research is novel and the likelihood of a quick publication is lower than when conducting research on established topics. At the same time, finding collaborators with complementary core competencies is instrumental, given that the research process is highly complex and requires distinctive capabilities at various stages: conceptualization, research design and implementation, analyses, interpretation, and writing.

Second, strengthening the linkage between academic research with management practice and education is instrumental in sustaining, as well as enriching, the journey. We have been fortunate that our research addresses the heart of many challenges faced by managers and organizations in today's global environment. As a result, there is great interest and demand for CQ assessment and development programs. This not only provides opportunities for data access but also provides platforms for testing proposed relationships and identifying new research questions based on inputs from a broad spectrum of people, ranging from undergraduate students to senior executives. In short, we have adopted two guiding principles to sustain and guide our research journey: (a) an emphasis on gathering systematic empirical research to examine our theories, or what is widely termed *evidence-based practice* (Rousseau, 2006), and the equally important but sometimes neglected objective of (b) developing theories and interventions that are relevant and appropriate for real-world settings, termed *practice-based evidence* (Simons, Kushner, Jones, & James, 2003). Intertwining the two has enabled us to develop rigorous research that is being advanced by numerous academic research teams throughout the world and is also being used by practitioners across a diverse array of cultural contexts.

# CONCLUSION

A journey of a thousand miles begins with a single step.
— Lao-tzu, Chinese philosopher (604 BC–531 BC)

A decade ago, we took a step toward developing a program of research on CQ to address the growing challenges and opportunities presented by globalization. Notwithstanding the challenges we faced, the journey has been extremely rewarding because of the tight link we have built between our basic research and applied practice.

As the importance of CQ becomes increasingly salient in people's daily lives, interest in enhancing the scientific understanding as well as the practical application of CQ should continue to grow. This ongoing journey offers many exciting opportunities for researchers to develop more precise and sophisticated models of CQ that should translate into useful practical recommendations for organizations and individuals. It is our hope that the lessons and insights we have gained from our journey thus far will trigger research and practical application by others as we collectively advance our understanding of the science and practice of CQ.

---

**Best Practice Recommendations**

- Select appropriate samples when cultural diversity is salient to study participants.
- Provide an explicit definition of *culture* and *cultural diversity* to participants to ensure common understanding of the CQ items.
- Formulate research questions that focus on criterion variables that are relevant to culture and cultural diversity.
- Consider the breadth of the criterion variables when deciding whether to use multidimensional conceptualizations and measures of CQ or aggregated CQ.
- Specify the measurement source and type of CQ (self-report, observer report, performance based) on the basis of the research question and research design.
- Identify the appropriate level of analysis of CQ (individual, dyadic, group, organization) and operationalize accordingly.
- Specify and measure theoretical mechanisms that explain relationships between CQ and outcomes.
- Consider the development of CQ over time as a function of specific experiences.

---

# REFERENCES

Ackerman, P. L. (1996). A theory of adult intellectual development: Process, personality, interests, and knowledge. *Intelligence, 22,* 227–257. doi:10.1016/S0160-2896(96)90016-1

Ang, S., & Inkpen, A. C. (2008). Cultural intelligence and offshore outsourcing success: A framework of firm-level intercultural capability. *Decision Sciences, 39,* 337–358. doi:10.1111/j.1540-5915.2008.00195.x

Ang, S., & Ng, K.-Y. (2005). Cultural and network intelligences: The twin pillars in leadership development for the 21st century era of global business and institutional networks. In K. Y. Chan, S. Singh, R. Ramaya, & K. H. Lim (Eds.), *Systems and spirit* (pp. 46–48). Singapore Armed Forces Military Institute Monograph.

Ang, S., & Van Dyne, L. (2008). Conceptualization of cultural intelligence: Definition, distinctiveness, and nomological network. In S. Ang & L. Van Dyne (Eds.), *Handbook of cultural intelligence: Theory, measurement, and applications* (pp. 3–15). New York, NY: Sharpe.

Ang, S., Van Dyne, L., & Koh, C. (2006). Personality correlates of the four-factor model of cultural intelligence. *Group & Organization Management, 31,* 100–123. doi:10.1177/1059601105275267

Ang, S., Van Dyne, L., Koh, C., Ng, K.-Y., Templer, K. J., Tay, C., & Chandrasekar, N. A. (2007). Cultural intelligence: Its measurement and effects on cultural judgment and decision making, cultural adaptation and task performance. *Management and Organization Review, 3,* 335–371. doi:10.1111/j.1740-8784.2007.00082.x

Ang, S., Van Dyne, L., & Tan, M. L. (2011). Cultural intelligence. In R. J. Sternberg & S. C. Kaufman (Eds.), *Cambridge handbook on intelligence* (pp. 582–602). Cambridge, England: Cambridge University Press.

Bandura, A. (2002). Social cognitive theory in cultural context. *Applied Psychology, 51,* 269–290. doi:10.1111/1464-0597.00092

Beyene, T. (2007). *Fluency as a stigma: Implications of a language mandate in global work* (Unpublished doctoral dissertation). Stanford University, CA.

Brislin, R., Worthley, R., & MacNab, B. (2006). Cultural intelligence: Understanding behaviors that serve people's goals. *Group & Organization Management, 31,* 40–55. doi:10.1177/1059601105275262

Cattell, R. B. (1971). *Abilities: Their structure, growth, and action.* Boston, MA: Houghton Mifflin.

Ceci, S. J. (1996). *On intelligence: A bioecological treatise on intellectual development.* Cambridge, MA: Harvard University Press.

Chan, D. (1998). Functional relations among constructs in the same content domain at different levels of analysis: A typology of composition models. *Journal of Applied Psychology, 83,* 234–246. doi:10.1037/0021-9010.83.2.234

Chen, G., Kirkman, B. L., Kim, K., Farh, C. I. C., & Tangirala, S. (2010). When does cross-cultural motivation enhance expatriate effectiveness? A multilevel investigation of the moderating roles of subsidiary support and cultural distance. *Academy of Management Journal, 53*, 1110–1130. doi:10.5465/AMJ.2010. 54533217

Chen, X. P., Liu, D., & Portnoy, R. (2011). A multilevel investigation of motivational cultural intelligence, organizational diversity climate, and cultural sales: Evidence from U.S. real estate firms. *Journal of Applied Psychology*. Advance online publication. doi: 10.1037/a0024697

Choi, B. K., Moon, H. K., & Jung, J. S. (2010, August). *Previous international experience, cross-cultural training, and CQ: The role of goal orientation.* Paper presented at the annual meeting of the Academy of Management, Montreal, Canada.

Chua, R. Y., & Morris, M. W. (2009). *Innovation communication in multicultural networks: Deficits in intercultural capability and affect-based trust as barriers to new idea sharing in intercultural relationships.* Unpublished manuscript, Harvard Business School, Cambridge, MA.

Church, A. (1982). Sojourner adjustment. *Psychological Bulletin, 91*, 540–572. doi:10.1037/0033-2909.91.3.540

Costa, P. T., & McCrae, R. R. (1992). *Revised NEO-Personality Inventory (NEO-PI-R) and NEO Five-Factor Inventory (NEO-FFI) professional manual.* Odessa, FL: Psychological Assessment Resources.

Crawford-Mathis, K. (2010, August). *Cultural intelligence and international service learning.* Paper presented at the annual meeting of the Academy of Management, Montreal, Canada.

Cronbach, L. J., & Gleser, G. C. (1957). *Psychological tests and personnel decisions.* Urbana: University of Illinois.

Crowne, K. (2007). *The relationships among social intelligence, emotional intelligence, cultural intelligence, and cultural exposure.* Unpublished doctoral dissertation, Temple University, Philadelphia, PA.

Crowne, K. (2008). What leads to cultural intelligence? *Business Horizons, 51*, 391–399. doi:10.1016/j.bushor.2008.03.010

Crowne, K. (2009, August). *Social intelligence, emotional intelligence, cultural intelligence, and leadership: Testing a new model.* Paper presented at the annual meeting of the Academy of Management, Chicago, IL.

Cushner, K., & Brislin, R. W. (1996). *Intercultural relations: A practical guide* (2nd ed.). Thousand Oaks, CA: Sage.

Dean, B. P. (2007). *Cultural intelligence in global leadership: A model for developing culturally and nationally diverse teams.* Unpublished doctoral dissertation, Regent University, Virginia Beach, VA.

Deci, E. L., & Ryan, R. M. (1985). *Intrinsic motivation and self-determination in human behavior.* New York, NY: Plenum.

Deng, L., & Gibson, P. (2008). A qualitative evaluation on the role of cultural intelligence in cross-cultural leadership effectiveness. *International Journal of Leadership Studies, 3*, 181–197.

Earley, P. C., & Ang, S. (2003). *Cultural intelligence: Individual interactions across cultures*. Palo Alto, CA: Stanford University Press.

Eccles, J. S., & Wigfield, A. (2002). Motivational beliefs, values, and goals. In S. T. Fiske, D. L. Schacter, & C. Zahn-Waxler (Eds.), *Annual review of psychology* (Vol. 53, pp. 109–132). Palo Alto, CA: Annual Reviews.

Elenkov, D. S., & Manev, I. M. (2009). Senior expatriate leadership's effects on innovation and the role of cultural intelligence. *Journal of World Business, 44,* 357–369. doi:10.1016/j.jwb.2008.11.001

Fehr, R., & Kuo, E. (2008, April). *The impact of cultural intelligence in multicultural social networks*. Paper presented at the 23rd Annual Conference of the Society for Industrial and Organizational Psychology, San Francisco, CA.

Flavell, J. H. (1979). Metacognition and cognitive monitoring: A new area of cognitive inquiry. *American Psychologist, 34,* 906–911. doi:10.1037/0003-066X.34.10.906

Fornell, C., & Larcker, D. R. (1981). Evaluating structural equation models with unobservable variables and measurement error. *Journal of Marketing Research, 18,* 39–50. doi:10.2307/3151312

Gardner, H. (1993). *Multiple intelligences: Theory in practice*. New York, NY: Basic Books.

Gardner, H. (1999). *Intelligence reframed*. New York, NY: Basic Books.

Gelfand, M. J., Imai, L., & Fehr, R. (2008). Thinking intelligently about cultural intelligence: The road ahead. In S. Ang & L. Van Dyne (Eds.), *Handbook of cultural intelligence: Theory, measurement, and applications* (pp. 375–387). New York, NY: M. E. Sharpe.

Gjertsen, T., Torp, A. M., Koh, C. K., & Tan, M. L. (2010, August). *The impact of cultural intelligence on homophily in intraorganizational multinational networks*. Paper presented at the annual meeting of the Academy of Management, Montreal, Canada.

Goh, M., Koch, J. M., & Sanger, S. (2008). Cultural intelligence in counseling psychology: Applications for multicultural counseling competence. In S. Ang & L. Van Dyne (Eds.), *Handbook of cultural intelligence: Theory, measurement, and applications* (pp. 257–270). New York, NY: Sharpe.

Groves, K., & Feyerherm, A. (2011). Leader cultural intelligence in context: Testing the moderating effects of team cultural diversity on leader and team performance. *Group & Organization Management, 36,* 535–566. doi:10.1177/1059601111415664

Gudykunst, W. B., Ting-Toomey, S., & Chua, E. (1988). *Culture and interpersonal communication*. Newbury Park, CA: Sage.

Hall, E. T. (1959). *The silent language*. New York, NY: Doubleday.

Hofstede, G. (2001). *Culture's consequences: Comparing values, behaviors, institutions, and organizations across nations*. Thousand Oaks, CA: Sage.

Imai, L., & Gelfand, M. J. (2010). The culturally intelligent negotiator: The impact of cultural intelligence (CQ) on negotiation sequences and outcomes.

*Organizational Behavior and Human Decision Processes, 112*, 83–98. doi:10.1016/j.obhdp.2010.02.001

Kanfer, R., & Heggestad, E. D. (1997). Motivational traits and skills: A person-centered approach to work motivation. *Research in Organizational Behavior, 19*, 1–56.

Kanter, R. M. (1995). *World class: Thriving locally in the global economy.* New York, NY: Simon & Schuster.

Kim, K., Kirkman, B. L., & Chen, G. (2008). Cultural intelligence and international assignment effectiveness. In S. Ang & L. Van Dyne (Eds.), *Handbook of cultural intelligence: Theory, measurement, and applications* (pp. 71–90). New York, NY: Sharpe.

Kim, Y. J., & Van Dyne, L. (2010, April). *Majority–minority status and the development of cultural intelligence.* Paper presented at the 25th Annual Conference of the Society for Industrial and Organizational Psychologists, Atlanta, GA.

Kolb, D. A. (1984). *Experiential learning: Experience as the source of learning and development.* Englewood Cliffs, NJ: Prentice-Hall.

Lave, J., & Wenger, E. (1991). *Situated learning: Legitimate peripheral participation.* Cambridge, England: Cambridge University Press.

Law, K. S., Wong, C. S., & Mobley, W. H. (1998). Toward a taxonomy of multi-dimensional constructs. *Academy of Management Review, 23*, 741–755.

Lee, Y., Masuda, A. D., & Cardona, P. (2010, April). *Multiple cultural identities in cultural intelligence and leadership in multicultural teams.* Paper presented at 25th Annual Conference of the Society for Industrial and Organizational Psychologists, Atlanta, GA.

Leung, K., & Li, F. (2008). Social axioms and cultural intelligence: Working across cultural boundaries. In S. Ang & L. Van Dyne (Eds.), *Handbook of cultural intelligence: Theory, measurement, and applications* (pp. 332–341). New York, NY: Sharpe.

Li, M., & Mobley, W. H. (2010, August). *The role of experiential learning in the development of cultural intelligence.* Paper presented at the annual meeting of the Academy of Management, Montreal, Canada.

Livermore, D. (2006). *Serving with eyes wide open: Doing short-term missions with cultural intelligence.* Grand Rapids, MI: Baker Books.

Livermore, D. (2008). Cultural intelligence and short-term missions: The phenomenon of the fifteen-year-old missionary. In S. Ang & L. Van Dyne (Eds.), *Handbook of cultural intelligence: Theory, measurement, and applications* (pp. 271–285). New York, NY: M. E. Sharpe.

Livermore, D. (2009). *Leading with cultural intelligence: The new secret to success.* New York, NY: AMACOM.

Livermore, D. (2011). *The cultural intelligence difference: Master the one skill you can't do without in today's global economy.* New York, NY: AMACOM.

MacNab, B. R. (2011). An experiential approach to cultural intelligence education. *Journal of Management Education*. Advance online publication. doi: 10.1177/1052562911412587

MacNab, B. R., & Worthley, R. (2011). Individual characteristics as predictors of cultural intelligence development: The relevance of self-efficacy. *International Journal of Intercultural Relations*. Advance online publication. doi:10.1016/j.ijintrel.2010.12.001

Mayer, J. D., Caruso, D. R., & Salovey, P. (2000). Emotional intelligence meets traditional standards for an intelligence. *Intelligence, 27*, 267–298. doi:10.1016/S0160-2896(99)00016-1

Mayer, J. D., & Salovey, P. (1993). The intelligence of emotional intelligence. *Intelligence, 17*, 433–442. doi:10.1016/0160-2896(93)90010-3

Moody, M. C. (2007). *Adaptive behavior in intercultural environments: The relationship between cultural intelligence factors and Big Five personality traits.* Unpublished doctoral dissertation, The George Washington University, Washington, DC.

Moon, T. (2010a). Emotional intelligence correlates of the four-factor model of cultural intelligence. *Journal of Managerial Psychology, 25*, 876–898. doi:10.1108/02683941011089134

Moon, T. (2010b). Organizational cultural intelligence: Dynamic capability perspective. *Group & Organization Management, 35*, 456–493. doi:10.1177/1059601110378295

Murdock, G. P. (1987). *Outline of cultural materials* (5th rev. ed.). New Haven, CT: Human Relations Area Files.

Ng, K.-Y., & Earley, P. C. (2006). Culture + intelligence: Old constructs, new frontiers. *Group & Organization Management, 31*, 4–19. doi:10.1177/1059601105275251

Ng, K.-Y., Ramaya, R., Teo, T. M. S., & Wong, S. K. (2005, November). *Cultural intelligence: Its potential for military leadership development.* Paper presented at the 47th International Military Testing Association Conference, Singapore.

Ng, K.-Y., Tan, M. L., & Ang, S. (2011). Culture capital and cosmopolitan human capital: The effects of global mindset and organizational routines on cultural intelligence and international experiences. In A. Burton & J. C. Spender (Eds.), *The Oxford handbook of human capital* (pp. 96–120). Oxford, England: Oxford University Press. doi:10.1093/oxfordhb/9780199532162.003.0004

Ng, K.-Y., Van Dyne, L., & Ang, S. (2009). From experience to experiential learning: Cultural intelligence as a learning capability for global leader development. *Academy of Management Learning & Education, 8*, 511–526. doi:10.5465/AMLE.2009.47785470

O'Boyle, E. H., Jr., Humphrey, R. H., Pollack, J. M., Hawver, T. H., & Story, P. A. (2011). The relation between emotional intelligence and job performance: A meta-analysis. *Journal of Organizational Behavior, 32*, 788–818. doi:10.1002/job.714

O'Neil, H. E., & Abedi, J. (1996). Reliability and validity of a state metacognitive inventory: Potential for alternative assessment. *The Journal of Educational Research, 89*, 234–245. doi:10.1080/00220671.1996.9941208

Oolders, T., Chernyshenko, O. S., & Stark, S. (2008). Cultural intelligence as a mediator of relationships between Openness to Experience and adaptive performance. In S. Ang & L. Van Dyne (Eds.), *Handbook of cultural intelligence: Theory, measurement, and applications* (pp. 145–158). New York, NY: Sharpe.

Prado, W. H. (2006). *The relationship between cultural intelligence and perceived environmental uncertainty.* Unpublished doctoral dissertation, University of Phoenix, AZ.

Pulakos, E. D., Arad, S., Donovan, M. A., & Plamondon, K. E. (2000). Adaptability in the workplace: Development of a taxonomy of adaptive performance. *Journal of Applied Psychology, 85,* 612–624. doi:10.1037/0021-9010.85.4.612

Rockstuhl, T., Ang, S., Ng, K.-Y., Van Dyne, L., & Lievens, F. (2009, August). *Cultural intelligence and leadership emergence in multicultural teams.* Paper presented at the annual meeting of the Academy of Management, Chicago.

Rockstuhl, T., Hong, Y. Y., Ng, K.-Y., Ang, S., & Chiu, C. Y. (2010). The culturally intelligent brain: From detecting to bridging cultural differences. *NeuroLeadership Institute, 3,* 22–36.

Rockstuhl, T., & Ng, K.-Y. (2008). The effects of cultural intelligence on interpersonal trust in multicultural teams. In S. Ang & L. Van Dyne (Eds.), *Handbook of cultural intelligence: Theory, measurement, and applications* (pp. 206–220). New York, NY: Sharpe.

Rockstuhl, T., Seiler, S., Ang, S., Van Dyne, L., & Annen, H. (in press). Cultural intelligence and cross-border leadership effectiveness: Leadership competencies in a globalized world. *Journal of Social Issues.*

Rogers, P. S. (2008). The challenge of behavioral cultural intelligence: What might dialogue tell us? In S. Ang & L. Van Dyne (Eds.), *Handbook of cultural intelligence: Theory, measurement, and applications* (pp. 243–256). New York, NY: Sharpe.

Rousseau, D. M. (2006). Is there such a thing as "evidence-based management?" *The Academy of Management Review, 31,* 256–269. doi:10.5465/AMR.2006. 20208679

Schmidt, F. L., & Hunter, J. E. (1998). The validity and utility of selection methods in personnel psychology: Practical and theoretical implications of 85 years of research findings. *Psychological Bulletin, 124,* 262–274. doi:10.1037/0033-2909.124.2.262

Schmidt, F. L., & Hunter, J. E. (2000). Select on intelligence. In E. A. Locke (Ed.), *The Blackwell handbook of organizational principles* (pp. 3–14). Oxford, England: Blackwell.

Schutte, N. S., Malouff, J. M., Hall, L. E., Haggerty, D. J., Cooper, J. T., Golden, C. J., & Dornheim, L. (1998). Development and validation of a measure of emotional intelligence. *Personality and Individual Differences, 25,* 167–177. doi:10.1016/ S0191-8869(98)00001-4

Seiler, S. (2007). Determining factors of intercultural leadership: A theoretical framework. In C. M. Coops & T. S. Tresch (Eds.), *Cultural challenges in military operations* (pp. 217–232). Rome, Italy: NATO Defence College.

Selmeski, B. R. (2007). *Military cross-cultural competence: Core concepts and individual development* (Occasional Paper Series, Number 1, pp. 1–42). Royal Military College of Canada, Center for Security, Armed Forces, and Society.

Shannon, L. M., & Begley, T. M. (2008). Antecedents of the four-factor model of cultural intelligence. In S. Ang & L. Van Dyne (Eds.), *Handbook of cultural intelligence: Theory, measurement, and applications* (pp. 41–55). New York, NY: Sharpe.

Shokef, E., & Erez, M. (2008). Cultural intelligence and global identity in multi-cultural teams. In S. Ang & L. Van Dyne (Eds.), *Handbook of cultural intelligence: Theory, measurement, and applications* (pp. 177–191). New York, NY: Sharpe.

Simons, H., Kushner, S., Jones, K., & James, D. (2003). From evidence-based practice to practice-based evidence: The idea of situated generalization. *Research Papers in Education, 18*, 347–364. doi:10.1080/0267152032000176855

Sternberg, R. J. (1986). A framework for understanding conceptions of intelligence. In R. J. Sternberg & D. K.Detterman (Eds.), *What is intelligence? Contemporary viewpoints on its nature and definition* (pp. 3–15). Norwood, NJ: Ablex.

Sternberg, R. J. (1997). *Successful intelligence: How practical and creative intelligence determine success in life.* New York, NY: Plume.

Sternberg, R. J., & Detterman, D. K. (1986). *What is intelligence?* Norwood, NJ: Ablex.

Takeuchi, R., Tesluk, P. E., Yun, S., & Lepak, D. P. (2005). An integrative view of international experience. *Academy of Management Journal, 48*, 85–100. doi:10.5465/AMJ.2005.15993143

Tarique, I., & Takeuchi, R. (2008). Developing cultural intelligence: The roles of international nonwork experiences. In S. Ang & L. Van Dyne (Eds.), *Handbook of cultural intelligence: Theory, measurement, and applications* (pp. 56–70). New York, NY: Sharpe.

Tay, C., Rossi, A. M., & Westman, M. (2010, August). *International business travelers: Inter-role conflicts and moderating effects on emotional exhaustion.* Paper presented at the annual meeting of the Academy of Management, Montreal, Canada.

Tay, C., Westman, M., & Chia, A. (2008). Antecedents and consequences of cultural intelligence among short-term business travelers. In S. Ang & L. Van Dyne (Eds.), *Handbook of cultural intelligence: Theory, measurement, and applications* (pp. 126–144). New York, NY: Sharpe.

Templer, K. J., Tay, C., & Chandrasekar, N. A. (2006). Motivational cultural intelligence, realistic job preview, realistic living conditions preview, and cross-cultural adjustment. *Group & Organization Management, 31*, 154–173. doi:10.1177/1059601105275293

Thorndike, R., & Stein, S. (1937). An evaluation of the attempts to measure social intelligence. *Psychological Bulletin, 34*, 275–285. doi:10.1037/h0053850

Triandis, H. C. (1994). *Culture and social behavior.* New York, NY: McGraw Hill.

Triandis, H. C. (2006). Cultural intelligence in organizations. *Group & Organization Management, 31*, 20–26. doi:10.1177/1059601105275253 van Driel, M. (2008). *Cultural intelligence as an emergent organizational level construct.* Unpublished doctoral dissertation, Florida Institute of Technology, FL.

Van Dyne, L., Ang, S., & Koh, C. (2008). Development and validation of the CQS: The cultural intelligence scale. In S. Ang & L. Van Dyne (Eds.), *Handbook of cultural intelligence: Theory, measurement, and applications* (pp. 16–38). New York, NY: Sharpe.

Weinberg, R. A. (1989). Intelligence and IQ: Landmark issues and great debates. *American Psychologist, 44,* 98–104. doi:10.1037/0003-066X.44.2.98

Williams, M. E. (2008). *Individual differences and cross-cultural adaptation: A study of cultural intelligence, psychological adjustment, and sociocultural adjustment.* Unpublished doctoral dissertation, Trident University International University, Cypress, CA.

Wilson, C. E., & Stewart, A. C. (2009, August). *Developing ethically and culturally-intelligent leaders through international service experiences.* Paper presented at the annual meeting of the Academy of Management, Chicago.

Wonderlic, E. F. (1999). *Wonderlic personnel test user's manual.* Libertyville, IL: Author.

# 3

# STABILITY OF OPQ32 PERSONALITY CONSTRUCTS ACROSS LANGUAGES, CULTURES, AND COUNTRIES

DAVE BARTRAM

Consider a client organization with staff across the world that wishes to evaluate talent using a personality assessment tool. The client wants to use this in selection assessment to help in drawing applicants from one set of countries (e.g., France, Germany, the United Kingdom, Sweden, Australia) for expatriate assignments in some other set of countries (e.g., Brazil, China). The client also wants to carry out an audit of current managers to assess developmental needs globally. Finally, they are planning to put in place a succession management process for which they need to audit top talent across the world and establish a portfolio of the capabilities that such an audit would yield.

All these activities involve making comparisons between people from different countries and cultures who may be using different languages. Such cross-group comparisons are challenging because differences between groups can arise from real cultural differences, other group-related differences, or biases.

In this chapter, I consider the challenges posed by needing to compare people from diverse cultural, linguistic, and national backgrounds (Bartram, 2008b; Oswald, 2008; van de Vijver, 2008). In so doing, I discuss the need to establish that the constructs being used to compare people have similar meanings across all the groups being considered. Only where this is the case does it then become sensible to ask what differences in raw scores on common constructs might imply. The differences can either be "real" (i.e., reflect differences in the average trait levels associated with different countries, cultures, or other groups) or be due to systematic bias (as one might find if people in one country always tend to rate themselves higher than those in other countries when using Likert scales).

This chapter and the examples provided focus on the use of personality assessment in work-related settings, more specifically in job selection. However, the concepts and conclusions are applicable to any other area of practice or research when one is involved in measurement and comparison. With the domain of work-related assessment, the chapter has relevance for the assessment of training needs, work engagement, leadership development, succession planning, and employee survey attitude measures.

For the purposes of test interpretation, researchers typically convert raw scores into standard scores (e.g., sten scales) using a norm reference group. Mean raw score differences between such reference groups can, of course, be removed by group-related norming (i.e., the raw scores for Group A are normed using Group A's data, and those for Group B, using Group B's data). Alternatively, such differences can be preserved by the use of an aggregate norm (i.e., raw scores from both groups are normed using the combined Group A and B samples). The appropriate course of action should depend on whether one has evidence to support the raw score differences as being either real or bias. However, it is common practice to use country-specific norms regardless of the reasons for differences, if any, in between-countries comparisons.

Thus, the question of what raw score differences occur between countries and whether those should or should not be controlled for raises the practical question of how to use norms and what function raw score conversion through norming serves. In particular, I consider the appropriateness of differentially adjusting scores using local norm groups, as this practice acts to remove potentially meaningful between-groups effects.

These issues are considered here in the light of analyses of large international data sets of an occupational personality questionnaire: OPQ32 (SHL, 1999, 2006, 2009). OPQ32 is a multidimensional personality inventory that has evolved over the past decades into its current form, in which it uses a multidimensional item response theory (IRT) scoring model to recover normative scale data from forced-choice item formats (SHL, 2009).

In the data analyses, I first consider a general analysis of 11 European countries and then more detailed analyses of within-country, as well as between-countries, effects for the United Kingdom, South Africa, and China. The key questions are:

1. Can researchers assume that the 32 scales measured by OPQ32 are the same constructs across these various countries (or between diverse cultural groups within the same country)?

2. If they are, what can researchers conclude from an examination of mean scale score differences between countries (or between diverse cultural groups within the same country)?

Before I seek to answer these, I first consider some more basic questions: Can biases be corrected, and if so, how? Why do researchers use norms? What is *culture* and when does it matter?

## CAN BIASES BE CORRECTED, AND IF SO, HOW?

I noted above that making comparisons between people from different countries and cultures who may be using different languages is challenging because differences between groups can arise from real cultural or other group-related differences or from biases. Some biases are correctable; others are not.

The main noncorrectable bias is construct nonequivalence. If the construct measured in Country A does not exist in the same form in Country B, then no amount of careful translation or adaptation will make a scale based on the Country A construct work in Country B. As a consequence, where global assessment is concerned, it is necessary to restrict instruments to those constructs that are globally meaningful. This does not mean that every country and culture has to give the same value to such constructs, merely that they have the same meaning. Thus, a construct like "respect for one's elders" may have a much higher value associated with it in a country with a traditional family culture than in one with a more individualistic culture. However, people in both cultures will understand what the construct is and what it means. Within the world of the global organization and global economy, it is doubtful whether there are any particularly important local constructs that have no global counterpart. The Global Leadership and Organizational Behaviour Effectiveness (GLOBE) project (House, Hanges, Javidan, Dorfman, & Gupta, 2004) distinguished between characteristics of leadership that were regarded as universally important and those that varied from country to country. However, those that varied were universally understood. They simply did not have the same universal values. Correctable effects include translation issues, sampling biases, and response bias effects.

### Translation Issues

A specific item may simply not make sense when translated into another language or applied to a different culture. This is why the International Test Commission (ITC) *Guidelines on Test Adaptation* (Hambleton, 2005) uses the term *adaptation* and not *translation*. The key to good adaptation is to ensure that items tap into the same constructs. Accurate literal translation is not the goal and can often result in poor adaptation. The most effective way of ensuring good translation is to have agreed-upon construct definitions available in both the source and target language and for relevant experts in the target language to review content against those construct definitions. Bartram (2008a) described a procedure in which items are originated in multiple languages in parallel after the construct definitions have been agreed across all the target countries. In this work, a large item set (for assessing work-related behavioral competency constructs) was created using item writers in China, Germany, and the United Kingdom, with items then being reviewed and cross-translated into the non-source languages. Items were trialed and IRT calibrated. The result was a bank of items that provide great breadth of construct coverage and that are truly international.

## Sample Bias

The particular demographics mix within samples may differ between countries. For example, the data from one country might come mainly from sales personnel, whereas another might be biased toward financial services managers. Differences between these groups may be inappropriately attributed to the country they are from. This is controlled by trying as far as possible to match or reweight samples in terms of demographic variables that are known to affect mean scale score levels. For personality inventories, this tends to vary as a function of scale, but researchers typically find effects on at least some scales of age, gender, job level, and business function.

## Cultural- or Language-Based Response Bias

These types of bias arise when there is a culturally related tendency to show systematic bias in how rating scales are used (Harzing, 2006; Smith, 2004). Such effects may manifest themselves in avoidance of extreme scale scores (central tendency), acquiescence (bias toward agreeing with statements), and social desirability responding (agreeing with socially desirable statements and disagreeing with socially undesirable ones). When these effects are known, it is possible to adjust for them after the fact, by making raw score corrections (see, e.g., Hanges, 2004), or to avoid them in the first place by using forced-choice item formats (I discuss this option in more detail later in the chapter).

## WHY DO RESEARCHERS USE NORMS?

Norms provide a basis for comparing the scores of an individual with those of some well-defined reference group. Hence, norms are useful in the interpretation of test scores. Users sometimes confuse norms and validity, and take high scores to mean "good" scores. However, scoring in the top 10% of graduate applicants on trait X is only good to know if trait X is positively correlated with criterion behavior. Norms provide a method for transforming "arbitrary" raw scores into "standard" scores: Standard scores have properties independent of the raw score scale they are based on: For example, the OPQ32 uses sten scores for purposes of score profiling in interpretation ($M = 5.5$, $SD = 2.0$). Other common standard scales used in employment testing include Stanines ($M = 5$, $SD = 2$) and $T$ scores ($M = 50$, $SD = 10$). A norm group reflects a particular profile of four types of variable:

1. endogenous characteristics of people (biological variables, e.g., gender, age, race);
2. exogenous characteristics of people (environmental variables, e.g., educational level and type, job level and type, organization, industrial sector, labor market, language);
3. situational aspects, such as examination setting (paper and pencil vs. computer) and whether the stakes are high or low (e.g., prescreening, selection, development, research); and
4. temporal aspects (e.g., generation effects; when data were collected).

## WHAT IS CULTURE, AND WHEN DOES IT MATTER?

There are many different definitions of *culture*. For example, Hofstede (1980) defined *culture* as "the collective programming of the mind which distinguishes the members of one human group from another" (p. 25). For the present purposes, I say that *culture* is a set of exogenous variables relating to shared values, cognitions, knowledge, language, and standards, or cultural norms. In practical assessment terms, culture matters only when it is related to a group of people for whom within-group variability on relevant constructs is relatively small compared with variability between them and other groups.

To get some feeling for how much impact culture may have on personality trait level scores, it is necessary to review some of the research on cultural differences. In doing this, one should keep in mind that much cross-cultural research focuses on group-level norms and standards set for behavior rather than actual individual behaviors. It is, therefore, quite possible for two cultures to have quite different espoused standards and sets of values, although individuals in those cultures exhibit little, if any, differences in their mean levels of trait scores.

Culture may operate like a set of situational variables that act to constrain or facilitate certain aspects of behavior while not changing a person's actual repertoire of potential ranges of behavior that are determined by their traits. If so, this implies that people may have a high degree of flexibility in moving from one culture to another and in being able to learn what the new constraints and facilitators are to adjust their behavior to fit the new situation. If, on the other hand, cultural effects were embedded in people at the level of individual traits, there would not be such flexibility.

Hofstede (1980, 2001) developed one of the dominant cultural values frameworks by using survey data from IBM employees from 40 countries (originally, 88,000 employees in 72 countries were surveyed, but small country samples were excluded). Although based on one organization, this work has had an enormous impact on thinking in cross-cultural research and has tended to overshadow other frameworks (e.g., Trompenaars, 1993). Hofstede (1994) defined four main dimensions:

1. *Individualism* (IDV) is "the degree to which people in a country prefer to act as individuals rather than as members of groups" (p. 6). This dimension is often referred to as *individualism–collectivism*.
2. *Power Distance Index* (PDI) relates to the extent to which it is accepted that the power vested in institutions and organizations is distributed unequally. This is reflected in the degree to which people feel free to disagree with their superiors and the degree to which their superiors feel the need to consult with their subordinates.
3. *Masculinity* (MAS), often referred to as *masculinity–femininity*, contrasts valuing assertiveness, success, and competition over personal relationships, caring for the weak, and cooperation. In high MAS cultures, men tend to be more assertive and competitive than women, whereas in low MAS cultures, both genders are relatively more cooperative and caring.
4. *Uncertainty Avoidance Index* (UAI) reflects a preference for clear formal rules and guidance. High scores are associated with intolerance for deviant behaviors and a belief in absolute truths.

Later, on the basis of work by Hofstede and Bond (1988), Hofstede (1994) added a fifth dimension, called *Confucian Dynamism* or *Long-Term Orientation* (LTO) versus short-term orientation. Values associated with LTO are thrift and perseverance, whereas short-term orientation focuses on respect for tradition, fulfilling social obligations, and protecting one's "face."

Gelfand, Nishii, and Raver (2006) expanded on Hofstede's (1994) dimensions by adding the construct of *cultural tightness–looseness*, defined as the degree to which institutions in society promote narrower limits on socialization and have higher levels of constraint and systems for monitoring and sanctioning behavior. Although there may be some overlap between Hofstede's constructs and the construct of tightness, Gelfand et al. (2006) proposed that variance in individual attributes would be lower in tight cultures than in loose cultures. In other words, the tighter the cultural constraints, the more the behavior of individuals will be predicted by the cultural norms rather than by individual differences. This is important, as it implies that the variability of individual behavior may be subject to change, as well as the norm for that behavior. By implication, the tighter the cultural control, the less validity measures of individual difference will have as predictors of workplace behavior (even if the variability in the predictors is not constrained).

Until recently, research on Hofstede's (1994) dimensions has been subject mainly to qualitative review (e.g., Kirkman, Lowe, & Gibson, 2006). A relatively limited quantitative review was carried out by Oyserman, Coon, and Kemmelmeier (2002) of the individualism–collectivism dimension, along with other cultural value frameworks (e.g., from the GLOBE project), which looked at 83 studies carried out between 1980 and 2000. Taras, Kirkman, and Steel (2010), however, recently examined the relationships between Hofstede's original four cultural dimensions and organizationally relevant outcomes through a meta-analysis of 598 studies.

Kirkman et al. (2006) noted "a general trend of relatively low amounts of variance explained by the cultural values" (p. 313). A quantitative analysis was needed to assess in more detail just how much variance is accounted for and what the moderators of this are. It was also important to consider the impact of values other than individualism–collectivism (e.g., Gelfand, Erez, & Aycan, 2007; Tsui, Nifadkar, & Ou, 2007), which seems to have been the main focus for much of the research. The focus of Taras et al.'s (2010) analysis was not just to determine effect sizes for cultural values but also to determine when cultural values matter most so that practitioners can know when cultural values are likely to have an impact on organizationally relevant outcomes and when they will not.

Taras et al. (2010) focused on two research questions: First, do significant differences exist in the overall predictive power of the four Hofstede (1994) dimensions? Second, and in many ways, more important, "Do cultural values have significantly different predictive power than other individual-level predictors (i.e., personality traits, general mental ability, and demographics) on organizationally relevant outcomes (i.e., emotions, attitudes and perceptions, behaviors, and job performance)?" (p. 408).

Overall effects of culture ($\rho = .18$) across outcome measures are comparable to demographics ($\rho = .10$) and personality ($\rho = .15$). General mental ability (GMA) is higher ($\rho = .48$). However, as one moves from broader outcomes (e.g., emotions and attitudes) to more specific outcomes (behavior and performance), the effects of culture tend to decrease. For behavior, moreover, culture, demographics, and personality, had much the same predictive power

($\rho = .15$, $.14$, and $.13$, respectively), with general mental ability the strongest predictor ($\rho = .25$). Taras et al. (2010) noted that

> Culture was found to be the weakest predictor of performance, with the direct effect of cultural values being close to zero ($\rho = .03$). Demographics and personality showed comparatively better results ($\rho = .12$ and $\rho = .09$ respectively), and general mental ability stood out as a remarkably good predictor ($\rho = .54$) of performance. (p. 415)

There are indications of exceptions to this. For example, individualism is associated with behaviors like organizational citizenship ($\rho = -.21$), helpfulness ($\rho = -.20$) and conflict resolution styles (up to $\rho = .30$) at levels comparable to that of general mental ability. Uncertainty avoidance is quite strongly negatively related to innovation ($\rho = -.41$).

In relation to cultural tightness, Taras et al. (2010) found some evidence to support the role of this construct as a moderator of the effects of cultural value. They found that cultural values had stronger effects on outcomes in culturally tighter ($\rho = .28$) rather than looser countries.

In terms of limitations, Tara et al.'s (2010) meta-analysis, like all meta-analyses, is limited by the quality and quantity of the studies it reviews. Such studies also take an approach that identifies culture with country. As Chao and Moon (2005) noted, geography may not be the best way to cluster culture, and nations may not be the best units of analysis. The study has also been based on data that used self-report measures of culture and of personality, which are likely to have used Likert-type scale item formats. These are subject themselves to cultural bias effects, which tend to reduce their validity (Harzing, 2006; Smith, 2004).

The implications of Taras et al.'s (2010) research for managerial practice are important. Hofstede's (1994) dimensions are well known in the business world and have spawned a large body of research. In assessing the balance of importance between individual differences measures, such as personality and ability tests, on the one hand, and cultural values, on the other, this research provides some important indicators. It shows clearly that in terms of behavior and performance, GMA is by far the most important predictor. Broad personality traits (the Taras et al., 2010, study considered only the Big Five level of analysis) have impacts as great as, or greater than, culture on behavior and performance. The same is true of demographics (e.g., age, gender). Research has shown that narrow personality scales are associated with higher levels of predictive validity than broader ones (Rothstein & Goffin, 2006; Warr, Bartram, & Martin, 2005). However, very little research has directly examined the impact of cultural values in employee selection settings. It is possible that in the case of cultural variables, as well as for personality ones, narrower measures may have greater effects than broader ones, especially when such measures are directly relevant to some very specific criterion behavior.

The results suggest that cultural values will have a greater impact on people who are older, male, and have relatively more years of education. However, one must be careful not to confuse group effects with individual effects. It is not appropriate to attribute a cultural norm profile to an individual from that culture and then infer that the individual will behave and perform in accordance with that norm. There is a danger that culture is treated like blood type, and there is an assumption that everyone in Culture A shares the same cultural values and differs from those in Culture B. Better multilevel design studies are needed to look at the impact group-level effects have on individual-level outcomes (e.g., selection decisions).

There will always be a range of individual differences in values within cultures, as well as variation in personality and ability. Cultural factors may act to constrain the range of this variation or at least the range of expression through behavior, but it will not remove all variation even in very tight cultures. At the individual level, one would expect variations in values to be highly related to variations in personality attributes, motives, and interests.

## HOW CAN RESEARCHERS CONTROL CULTURAL RESPONSE BIAS?

Triandis (1994) recommended computing an individual's mean score and standard deviation across all items in a survey. Assuming the survey measures many constructs, differences in these overall means and standard deviations will have no construct-specific means and reflect response bias. When averaged across individuals within cultures, these reflect cultural bias effects. If an individual's item responses are then corrected by subtracting their overall average score and dividing this difference by their standard deviation, the resulting scores will be free from any general response bias in terms of either spread or location.

Hanges (2004) criticized Triandis's (1994) method of correcting for differential response bias, stating that if people had responded to anchored scale points, the corrected scores could no longer have been related back to those scale points. More important, he argued against it because it creates ipsative scale scores, and he cited the issues relating to using ipsative scale scores to make comparisons between individuals. He went on to describe a modified procedure aimed at avoiding this problem.

However, such procedures all start from an item format that provides the opportunity for bias—Likert rating scales. This can be avoided by the use of forced-choice item formats, whereby people choose between statements rather than provide ratings. This controls for all forms of systematic bias and removes any halo effects but does not control for differential cultural valances associated with different constructs. For example, in some cultures, Extraversion may be more highly valued than Agreeableness. In such cultures, there may be a tendency to choose Extraversion items over Agreeableness items in a forced choice. Depending on one's point of view (cross-cultural vs. individual assessment), such effects may be treatment effects or error effects.

The use of forced-choice formats has in the past been associated with ipsative scaling. Technically, there are differences between the procedures described by Hanges (2004) and Triandis (1994; i.e., ipsatization) and the scales produced from forced-choice format items (see Meade, 2004). However, recent developments in multidimensional IRT modeling (Brown & Maydeau-Olivares, 2011) mean that it is now possible to recover normative theta scores from forced-choice item format data. Despite being derived from forced-choice item data, these theta values are normative. Not only do they not have the properties of ipsative scales, but they are also free from the systematic forms of bias that affect the use of Likert item scales when these are used to create normative scales. For future cross-cultural research, this IRT-based approach provides a means of controlling for general cultural response bias effects without having to resort to a posteriori correction methods. Brown and Maydeu-Olivares (2011) provided details of the methodology and instrument construction guidelines.

## MEASUREMENT PROPERTIES OF OPQ32

OPQ32 is one of the most widely used occupational styles questionnaire in the world. As its name implies, OPQ32 measures 32 aspects of work-related personality. Building on this, a wide range of secondary measures have been validated, including competency potential, leadership, team impact, and sales potential. Until 2009, OPQ32 was available in two forms: OPQ32n, or the normative version; and OPQ32i, or the ipsative version. OPQ32n required candidates to rate each of a number of statements on a 1-to-5 scale, and OPQ32i required them to choose from sets of statements which one was most like them and which one was least like them—forced-choice format. Although these two forms each had their particular strengths, SHL (the test developer) carried out research into IRT score modeling to develop a way of combining the response bias resistance of forced-choice formats with the normative properties of traditional Likert-based scale scores. Although traditional scoring methods produce ipsative scales from forced-choice item formats, researchers can now use a different scoring approach to recover normative latent trait scores from OPQ32i using a multidimensional IRT model (Brown & Bartram, 2008; SHL, 2009). Based on this new scoring methodology, OPQ32i was relaunched in October 2009 with 104 item triplets (i.e., 104 items were dropped from the original instrument) as OPQ32r. This new version is only available as an IRT-scored instrument, producing 32 normative theta scales.

The first three studies reviewed below report the results of analyses of normative IRT scale scores computed from OPQ32i forced-choice item data. OPQ32i responses were recoded as pairwise comparisons, and only responses relating to the triplets used in the new OPQ32r were considered. The responses were scored using the IRT model with fixed parameters established for the OPQ32r instrument (as they would be scored online). This scoring was performed in Mplus (Muthén & Muthén, 1998–2007), and scale-level theta scores were saved for further analysis. Study 1 provides a comparison between construct equivalence evaluated using analysis of ipsative scale score data and normative theta scores for the same data set. Study 2 explores some within-country effects of native language and ethnicity for a large set of South African English data, and finally, Study 3 compares Chinese (Traditional and Simplified), with South African and UK English samples.

Study 4 looks at OPQ32i ipsative scale data from more than one million people from 29 countries involving more than 20 languages in terms of average scale scores and considers how variations in average country scale scores relate to national-level cultural dimensions.

## CONSTRUCT EQUIVALENCE OF OPQ32 BETWEEN AND WITHIN COUNTRIES

In this section, the results from Studies 1 through 3 are examined in relation to the evidence they provide for construct equivalence between countries (Study 1), as well as between groups within South Africa (Study 2) and China (Study 3). Finally equivalence across the United Kingdom, China, and South Africa is examined.

### Assessing Construct Equivalence Between Countries

OPQ32 is not a factor model, so one cannot compare the fit of a factor model with the 32 scales across samples. Big Five scales can be generated from subsets of the 32 scales, but a stronger test of construct equivalence comes from requiring invariance in scale variances and correlation matrices. For practical purposes, one can argue that construct invariance requires that correlation matrices are invariant across groups: The hypothesis being tested is that in any comparison of two samples, both correlation matrices are drawn from the same population (Bentler, 2005). The goodness-of-fit criteria used are as listed below.

- Comparative fit index (CFI; Bentler, 1990) should be greater than .95.
- Root mean square error of approximation (RMSEA) should be less than .08 for a reasonable fit and less than .05 for a good fit (Byrne, 2006).

Scale level invariance would also require that raw score means are invariant. One would not expect this to be the case. There are many cultural stereotypes that reflect personality differences (e.g., the notion that Southern Europeans are more outgoing than Northern Europeans) that imply there may be differences in country-level scale means. It is of interest to examine such difference if and where they occur, but researchers should do so only when construct invariance has been established. The results of the construct equivalence analyses are presented first for all three studies, and then scale score differences are examined covering the same countries examined in Studies 1 to 3 and some additional ones.

**Study 1: 49,792 Working Adults From 11 European Countries**

European OPQ32i data that had been extracted and analyzed using the ipsative scale scores (Brown, 2006) were reanalyzed with the new IRT-based scoring technique when item-level data were available. Each language group was compared with a UK English reference group ($N = 3,978$). Equivalence of correlation matrices based on the 32 IRT-estimated scales was examined. EQS software was used to test two groups at a time, constraining the correlation matrices to be the same. This analysis is the same as the one originally performed for OPQ32i ipsative scale scores (Brown, 2006), except that now all 32 scales were entered in the analysis, as no ipsative constraints exist in the data. For the analysis of the ipsative data, it was necessary to drop one scale from the set of 32 to remove the constraints on the correlation matrix.

As Table 3.1 shows, the tests revealed good fit indices for all languages compared with UK English. The results are very similar for both the ipsative scale data from 2006 and for the rescored IRT theta score data. This implies that the constructs being assessed are comparable across the samples we have examined and that we can, therefore, consider aggregation across these groups for the purposes of norm creation.

For the IRT theta scale data, the worst case CFI is .982 and the worst case RMSEA is .029. For the ipsative scale data the worst case CFI is .960, and worst case RMSEA is .028. All countries show good fits to the UK correlation matrix.

TABLE 3.1
## European Construct Equivalence Comparisons for 10 Countries
### (N = 49,792)

| Language | N | IRT theta normative scales | | Ipsative scales | |
|---|---|---|---|---|---|
| | | CFI | RMSEA | CFI | RMSEA |
| English | 3,978 | | | | |
| Belgian Dutch | 2,109 | .989 | .024 | .983 | .019 |
| Danish | 8,274 | .991 | .022 | .990 | .014 |
| Dutch | 5,499 | .988 | .024 | .989 | .015 |
| Finnish | 1,943 | .985 | .028 | .979 | .022 |
| French | 3,806 | .988 | .025 | .981 | .020 |
| German | 4,733 | .982 | .029 | .981 | .019 |
| Italian | 1,758 | .988 | .024 | .968 | .025 |
| Norwegian | 7,622 | .989 | .024 | .989 | .015 |
| Portuguese | 1,026 | .990 | .023 | .960 | .028 |
| Swedish | 9,044 | .991 | .021 | .990 | .014 |

*Note.* IRT = item response theory; CFI = comparative fit index; RMSEA = root mean square error of approximation.

## Study 2: Construct Equivalence of OPQ32i Within South Africa

The study included 32,020 people, to assess construct invariance, as well as scale mean differences, between ethnic and first-language groups on the OPQ32i. OPQ32i was administered in English. All candidates were proficient in English to at least Grade 12. As with the earlier European data, the OPQ32i was scored using the multidimensional IRT model to recover latent normative scores. Comparison of the samples was carried out using SEM with EQS on the normative IRT theta scale scores.

The sample details are important here to understand the rationale for the comparisons that were carried out. The candidates came from various industry sectors, collected over the period from 2006 to 2009. Women composed 52.10% of the sample, and men, 47.90%. The mean age was 30.67 years ($SD = 8.23$). In terms of educational level, 37.39% had completed Grade 12; 16.316% had some form of school-leaving certificate; 30.99% had undergraduate degrees; and 15.31%, postgraduate degrees. In terms of ethnicity, 47.60% were African; 13.50%, Colored; 9.60%, Indian; and 29.10%, White. The first (i.e., native) language was known for 25,094 of the candidates: Afrikaans (25.90%), English (27.10%), Venda (2.10%), Tsonga (2.20%), Nguni (Zulu, Xhosa, Swati, and Ndebele; 21.90%), and Sotho (North Sotho, South Sotho, Tswana; 20.80%).

Two types of group comparisons were performed. First, I looked at similarity between correlation patterns for the major ethnic groups (see Table 3.2,

## TABLE 3.2
### Comparisons Between Ethnic Groups and Native Language Groups Within South Africa ($N = 30,020$)

| | N | CFI | RMSEA |
|---|---|---|---|
| *Ethnic group (White vs. others)* | | | |
| White | 9,318 | | |
| African | 15,255 | .972 | .035 |
| Colored | 4,308 | .992 | .020 |
| Indian | 3,083 | .997 | .012 |
| *Native language (English vs. others)* | | | |
| English | 6,793 | | |
| Afrikaans | 6,494 | .998 | .011 |
| Nguni | 5,488 | .978 | .031 |
| Sotho | 5,232 | .976 | .032 |
| Tsonga | 555 | .991 | .021 |
| Venda | 532 | .990 | .022 |
| *Native language (Nguni vs. Sotho)* | | | |
| Nguni | 5,488 | | |
| Sotho | 5,232 | .999 | .006 |

*Note.* CFI = comparative fit index; RMSEA = root mean square error of approximation.

top section, "Ethnic group (White vs. others)"). It is important to note that different ethnic groups would generally have different languages as their first (native) language. For example, it is likely to be English and Afrikaans for the White and Colored groups, English for the Indian group, and native African languages for the African group. So comparisons by ethnicity are not independent of comparisons by native language.

Second, groups were formed by the first (native) language. Each language group was compared with the group whose first language was English (see Table 3.2, "Native language (English vs. others)"). The tests revealed good fit indices for all languages as compared with English. Notably, the least-well-fitting models relate to the two large African language groups (Nguni and Sotho).

Finally, the two large African language groups (Nguni and Sotho) were tested for similarity of their correlation matrices (see Table 3.2, bottom section, "Native language (Nguni vs. Sotho)"). The fit indices in this case are remarkably good. Clearly, there are more similarities between personality constructs for the two native African language groups than between English and African language groups. The only two groups that show a similar high level of fit are the English and the Afrikaans groups.

These high levels of fit again support the view that the construct space that is being assessed is invariant across these groups. As noted earlier, this does not imply that they will all show similar profiles of mean scale scores, but it does mean one can look at scale mean differences and interpret these knowing that these are differences on common or shared constructs. Analyses were also carried out to explore profile mean differences between groups. There is not space to review these here, but these are similar in magnitude to those reported in Study 4, below. They are also very stable, as analysis of mean differences between groups showed no changes between 2006 and 2009.

## Study 3: Use of the OPQ32i in China

F. M. Cheung et al. (2001) and S. F. Cheung, Cheung, Howard, and Lim (2006) have suggested that different constructs from those covered by the Big Five are particularly relevant for the Chinese context. Patterns of gender differences in personality vary between Western and non-Western cultures (McCrae & Terracciano, 2005).

The objective of this third study was to compare two versions of the Chinese OPQ32i (Traditional and Simplified Chinese) with each other and then to compare them with matched samples drawn from the English South African data set examined in Study 2 and a sample drawn from a large UK English data set. As before, the main question of interest was whether there is construct level invariance across these samples. The UK sample was drawn from a set consisting of 72,444 people who had completed OPQ32i online for either selection or development purposes. The South African sample was the same ($N = 32,020$) as that used in Study 2. The Chinese sample consisted of 22,481 people: 7,738 who completed the Traditional Chinese version (mainly from Hong Kong and Taiwan), and 14,684 from the People's Republic of China (PRC) who completed the Simplified Chinese version.

OPQ32i data sets were rescored using the IRT-based rescoring technique to recover normative scale data. All language pairs were compared with each other. Equivalence of correlation matrices based on the 32 IRT theta scales was examined using EQS. Two language groups were examined at a time, constraining the correlation matrices to be the same.

*Traditional Versus Simplified Chinese*

Data sets were large but not matched. Excellent model fit indicates construct equivalence across the two different versions of Chinese (see Table 3.3, top section, "Language pair"). In general, the Traditional Chinese version was completed by candidates from Hong Kong special administrative region (SAR) and the Simplified Chinese by candidates from mainland China (i.e., the PRC).

## TABLE 3.3
### Comparisons of Chinese Language Versions and of Chinese With Matched English and South African Samples

| | $N_1$ | $N_2$ | CFI | RMSEA |
|---|---|---|---|---|
| **A. Language pair** | | | | |
| Traditional Chinese ($N_1$) with Simplified Chinese ($N_2$) | 7738 | 14684 | .991 | .022 |
| **B. Country pair** | | | | |
| Data Set 1 | | | | |
|   UK English ($N_1$) with South African English ($N_2$) | 2163 | 1462 | .985 | .027 |
|   UK English ($N_1$) with Chinese ($N_2$) | 2163 | 2763 | .968 | .039 |
|   South African English ($N_1$) with Chinese ($N_2$) | 1462 | 2763 | .963 | .041 |
| Data Set 2 | | | | |
|   UK English ($N_1$) with South African English ($N_2$) | 576 | 395 | .977 | .033 |
|   UK English ($N_1$) with Chinese ($N_2$) | 576 | 735 | .971 | .038 |
|   South African English ($N_1$) with Chinese ($N_2$) | 735 | 395 | .964 | .041 |

*Note.* CFI = comparative fit index; RMSEA = root mean square error of approximation.

### Equivalence Across China, South Africa, and the United Kingdom

Following comparison of the two versions of Chinese, the country samples were matched by gender and age. As age information was not known for many of the people in the sample, matching procedures substantially reduce sample size. Analyses were conducted with two subsets of data. The first larger sample analysis (see Table 3.3, "Country pair," Data Set 1) was matched by gender and age, with approximate matching by industry for UK and South Africa. A subset of this (see Table 3.3, "Country pair," Data Set 2) was more closely matched demographically by gender, age, and industry across all three countries. The analyses were performed for Data Set 1 (matched by age and gender) and repeated for Data Set 2 (matched by age, gender, and industry sector).

In all cases, there is very good model fit, indicating construct equivalence across the three country groups, even when data (Data Set 1) are not well-matched by industry sector. Again, one sees good evidence for commonality of constructs across difference languages and national groups, implying that one can make valid comparisons using these constructs between people from the groups.

## DIFFERENCES IN AVERAGE SCALE SCORE PROFILES ACROSS COUNTRIES

Study 4 focuses on variations between countries in country-level scale means and standard deviations. The focus of interest here is to consider whether, despite their being construct equivalence, there may be variations in scales scores. Furthermore, if such variations can be related to other independently measured country-level variables, this would suggest that the variations are reflections of true score differences and not measurement bias.

### Study 4: Comparing 31 Countries (N = 1,002,907)

The large quantities of data available make it difficult within the confines of the present chapter to examine all possible variations in mean scale score profile patterns across countries, by language and within country by ethnicity or other demographics. For the present, attention is focused on country and language effects, and on establishing, in general, how much variation there is in scale means and what such variance may be attributed to.

This analysis is based on a sample of recent OPQ32i data from 31 different countries, with a mixture of different languages. It is of interest to see whether differences follow language or country (e.g., there are English data from Australia, New Zealand, Malaysia, the United States, India, and South Africa, as well as the United Kingdom). Ipsative raw scale scores were used for the following analysis, as item level data was not available in sufficient quantity to make it possible to use the IRT theta scoring method.

Table 3.4 lists the countries and languages, with their sample sizes. In each case, it also shows the number of scales (out of a possible 32) showing differences with UK English. Two levels of difference are noted. Any difference of less than 0.25 $SD$ would translate into no change in the sten score given for a scale. Thus, I regard effects smaller than 0.25 as small or negligible. Between 0.25 and 0.75, effects would round to a difference of 1 sten score point (note that the sten scale uses 0.5 $SD$ intervals, with a mean of 5.5). These effects are defined as "moderate." Finally, any difference greater than 0.75 $SD$ would round up to a sten difference of two or more points. This is large and could result in differences in profile interpretation.

The average number of moderate differences is 12 out of 32 scales, but there is considerable variance, with a minimum of 1 and maximum of 18 scales showing some difference. In terms of large effects, only eight countries

TABLE 3.4

Number of Moderate and Large Effect Differences Between UK English
and Other Countries ($N = 1,002,907$)

| Country | Language | $N$ | Moderate effects | Large effects |
|---------|----------|-----|------------------|---------------|
| Australia | English | 179,769 | 1 | 0 |
| New Zealand | English | 2,119 | 4 | 0 |
| France | French | 9,075 | 8 | 0 |
| Italy | Italian | 8,605 | 8 | 0 |
| Germany | German | 8,076 | 9 | 0 |
| United States | English | 32,776 | 9 | 0 |
| South Africa | English | 9,338 | 9 | 0 |
| Belgium | French | 6,010 | 9 | 0 |
| Canada | French | 1,274 | 9 | 0 |
| Belgium | Flemish | 8,358 | 9 | 0 |
| Denmark | Danish | 7,773 | 10 | 0 |
| Middle East | Arabic | 2,037 | 10 | 0 |
| Brazil | Portuguese | 12,549 | 11 | 0 |
| Spain | Spanish | 4,770 | 11 | 0 |
| Hong Kong | Traditional Chinese | 7,735 | 12 | 1 |
| Hungary | Hungarian | 1,658 | 12 | 0 |
| Russia | Russian | 336 | 12 | 0 |
| Greece | Greek | 380 | 13 | 1 |
| Portugal | Portuguese | 1,026 | 13 | 0 |
| Sweden | Swedish | 30,863 | 14 | 0 |
| Netherlands | Dutch | 50,104 | 14 | 0 |
| Finland | Finnish | 11,076 | 14 | 0 |
| India | English | 166,823 | 14 | 1 |
| Norway | Norwegian | 24,367 | 15 | 0 |
| Indonesia | Indonesian | 530 | 15 | 1 |
| PRC | Simplified Chinese | 14,835 | 16 | 1 |
| Poland | Polish | 811 | 17 | 0 |
| Malaysia | English | 11,236 | 17 | 1 |
| Argentina | Spanish | 17,300 | 18 | 2 |
| Japan | Japanese | 343 | 18 | 1 |
| United Kingdom | English | 370,955 | — | — |

*Note.* PRC = People's Republic of China.

show any such effects, and in all but one case this is on only one scale. The one exception has large effects on just two scales. Although these differences are highly significant statistically, their practical importance is relatively small. For comparison, one can consider the effects of gender differences within countries (see Table 3.5). Here, there is an average of 10 scales showing moderate gender differences, with the numbers varying between 1 and 16. Only one country shows a large gender difference and then on just one scale.

TABLE 3.5

Number of Moderate and Large Effect Size Differences for Gender
Differences (Male–Female) for Each Country

| Country | Language | N | Moderate effects | Large effects |
|---|---|---|---|---|
| PRC | Simplified Chinese | 14,835 | 1 | 0 |
| Hong Kong | Traditional Chinese | 7,735 | 3 | 0 |
| India | English | 166,823 | 5 | 0 |
| Brazil | Portuguese | 12,549 | 6 | 0 |
| Malaysia | English | 11,236 | 6 | 0 |
| Argentina | Spanish | 17,300 | 7 | 0 |
| Portugal | Portuguese | 1,026 | 7 | 0 |
| South Africa | English | 9,338 | 8 | 0 |
| Spain | Spanish | 4,770 | 8 | 0 |
| United States | English | 32,776 | 9 | 0 |
| Canada | French | 1,274 | 9 | 0 |
| Poland | Polish | 811 | 9 | 0 |
| Russia | Russian | 336 | 9 | 0 |
| Sweden | Swedish | 30,863 | 10 | 0 |
| Australia | English | 179,769 | 10 | 0 |
| Italy | Italian | 8,605 | 10 | 0 |
| France | French | 9,075 | 11 | 0 |
| Japan | Japanese | 343 | 11 | 0 |
| United Kingdom | English | 370,955 | 12 | 0 |
| Denmark | Danish | 7,773 | 12 | 0 |
| Belgium | French | 6,010 | 12 | 0 |
| Netherlands | Dutch | 50,104 | 12 | 0 |
| Norway | Norwegian | 24,367 | 12 | 0 |
| Germany | German | 8,076 | 13 | 0 |
| Finland | Finnish | 11,076 | 13 | 0 |
| Greece | Greek | 380 | 14 | 0 |
| New Zealand | English | 2,119 | 14 | 1 |
| Hungary | Hungarian | 1,658 | 15 | 0 |
| Belgium | Flemish | 8,358 | 15 | 0 |
| Indonesia | Indonesian | 530 | 15 | 0 |
| Middle East | Arabic | 2,037 | 16 | 0 |

*Note.* PRC = People's Republic of China.

It is of interest to find out what factors might explain the variability in these effects. It is well established, for example, that gender has effects on score profiles (Costa, Terracciano, & McCrae, 2001; McCrae & Terracciano, 2005). Costa et al. (2001) noted that gender differences vary with culture and were most pronounced in individualistic cultures, like those found in Europe and North America.

It is possible to match up the 31 countries in the above tables with data for Hofstede's (1994) four dimensions: PDI, IDV, MAS, and UAI

(Hofstede, 2001, Appendix A5, pp. 500–502). Correlations between Hofstede's dimension scores and the number of scales showing moderate or large gender effects are −.36 for PDI, .41 for IDV, −.05 for MAS, and .26 for UAI. Thus, male and female average score profiles differ most in countries that are low in power distance, high in individualism, and high in uncertainty avoidance. The expected relationship with MAS was not found (high MAS cultures are said to be those where the difference between men and women is high, especially with respect to assertiveness and competitiveness).

To summarize some of the main effects of score variation in relation to culture, Big Five scores were calculated for all the people in the data set used for the above analyses (i.e., 31 countries, $N = 1,002,907$). Then the 31 countries' average Big Five scores and the standard deviations of these averages were correlated with the Hofstede (1994) country dimension scores. The results (see Table 3.6) show strong relationships between cultural dimensions and both means and standard deviations of Big Five scores at the country level of aggregation (Table 3.7 provides a complete set of Big Five country means and standard deviations with the Hofstede country dimension scores). These results indicate that a lot of the variance in overall country mean scores can be accounted for by country-level values dimensions. It also shows that the variability in individual scores within countries is related to cultural values. Table 3.8 summarizes the results of regression analyses that show how much variance in the country means for each of the Big Five can be accounted for by the Hofstede dimension values. For both Emotional Stability and

TABLE 3.6

Correlations Across 31 Countries of OPQ32 Big Five Means and Standard Deviations With Hofstede (1994) Dimensions Country Scores

| | Hofstede (1994) dimensions | | | | | | | |
| --- | --- | --- | --- | --- | --- | --- | --- | --- |
| | PDI | | IDV | | MAS | | UAI | |
| OPQ32 Big Five | M | SD | M | SD | M | SD | M | SD |
| Emotional Stability | −.708 | −.269 | .545 | .445 | −.443 | .294 | −.601 | .072 |
| Extraversion | −.647 | −.403 | .391 | .452 | −.542 | −.053 | −.058 | −.287 |
| Openness to Experience | −.064 | −.504 | .112 | .552 | .025 | −.090 | .353 | .085 |
| Agreeableness | −.482 | −.715 | .305 | .754 | −.366 | −.179 | −.208 | −.157 |
| Conscientiousness | −.321 | −.424 | .368 | .537 | −.036 | −.058 | −.217 | .154 |

*Note.* PDI = Power Distance Index; IDV = Individualism; MAS = Masculinity–Femininity; and UAI = Uncertainty Avoidance Index.

TABLE 3.7
Big Five Average Sten Scores and Hofstede (1994) Country Dimension Scores

| Country | Language | Hofstede (1994) dimension | | | | OPQ32 Big Five | | | | |
|---|---|---|---|---|---|---|---|---|---|---|
| | | PDI | IDV | MAS | UAI | Emotional Stability | Extraversion | Openness to Experience | Agreeableness | Conscientiousness |
| Argentina | Spanish | 49 | 46 | 56 | 86 | 5.47 | 5.98 | 5.21 | 4.81 | 5.51 |
| Australia | English | 36 | 90 | 61 | 51 | 5.58 | 5.39 | 5.40 | 5.68 | 5.68 |
| Belgium | French | 67 | 72 | 60 | 93 | 4.87 | 5.53 | 5.59 | 5.67 | 5.73 |
| Belgium | Flemish | 61 | 78 | 43 | 97 | 5.42 | 5.86 | 5.48 | 6.21 | 5.38 |
| Brazil | Portuguese | 69 | 38 | 49 | 76 | 4.91 | 5.63 | 5.12 | 5.58 | 4.75 |
| Canada | French | 39 | 80 | 52 | 48 | 5.83 | 6.39 | 5.24 | 5.68 | 5.64 |
| Denmark | Danish | 18 | 74 | 16 | 23 | 6.38 | 6.37 | 5.60 | 5.76 | 5.51 |
| Finland | Finnish | 33 | 63 | 26 | 59 | 6.22 | 5.94 | 5.01 | 6.08 | 5.44 |
| France | French | 68 | 71 | 43 | 86 | 4.85 | 5.47 | 5.67 | 5.62 | 5.55 |
| Germany | German | 35 | 67 | 66 | 65 | 6.08 | 5.96 | 6.08 | 5.87 | 5.32 |
| Greece | Greek | 60 | 35 | 57 | 112 | 4.32 | 5.76 | 5.54 | 4.97 | 5.87 |
| Hong Kong | Traditional Chinese | 68 | 25 | 57 | 29 | 5.13 | 5.43 | 5.58 | 5.67 | 5.36 |
| Hungary | Hungarian | 46 | 80 | 88 | 82 | 5.73 | 5.21 | 4.97 | 5.52 | 5.43 |
| India | English | 77 | 48 | 56 | 40 | 5.41 | 5.18 | 5.16 | 4.19 | 5.52 |
| Indonesia | Indonesian | 78 | 14 | 46 | 48 | 4.98 | 5.02 | 5.08 | 5.18 | 4.93 |

(continues)

TABLE 3.7
Big Five Average Sten Scores and Hofstede (1994) Country Dimension Scores  *(Continued)*

| Country | Language | Hofstede (1994) dimension | | | | OPQ32 Big Five | | | | |
|---|---|---|---|---|---|---|---|---|---|---|
| | | PDI | IDV | MAS | UAI | Emotional Stability | Extraversion | Openness to Experience | Agreeableness | Conscientiousness |
| Italy | Italian | 50 | 76 | 70 | 75 | 5.09 | 5.70 | 5.86 | 5.00 | 5.02 |
| Japan | Japanese | 54 | 46 | 95 | 92 | 4.46 | 5.16 | 6.45 | 5.62 | 4.15 |
| Malaysia | English | 104 | 26 | 50 | 36 | 4.90 | 4.58 | 5.11 | 5.29 | 5.17 |
| Middle East | Arabic | 80 | 38 | 52 | 68 | 4.98 | 4.86 | 5.33 | 4.96 | 5.18 |
| Netherlands | Dutch | 38 | 80 | 14 | 53 | 6.01 | 5.84 | 6.08 | 5.73 | 4.49 |
| New Zealand | English | 22 | 79 | 58 | 49 | 5.61 | 5.20 | 5.27 | 5.91 | 6.18 |
| Norway | Norwegian | 31 | 69 | 8 | 50 | 6.22 | 6.29 | 5.30 | 6.14 | 5.26 |
| Poland | Polish | 68 | 60 | 64 | 93 | 4.99 | 4.64 | 5.84 | 4.75 | 5.35 |
| Portugal | Portuguese | 63 | 27 | 31 | 104 | 4.77 | 5.88 | 5.79 | 5.81 | 5.12 |
| PRC | Simplified Chinese | 80 | 20 | 66 | 30 | 5.46 | 5.13 | 5.03 | 5.91 | 5.36 |
| Russia | Russian | 93 | 39 | 36 | 95 | 4.76 | 5.27 | 6.19 | 5.10 | 5.02 |
| South Africa | English | 49 | 65 | 63 | 49 | 5.28 | 4.93 | 5.45 | 5.06 | 5.60 |
| Spain | Spanish | 57 | 51 | 42 | 86 | 4.79 | 5.75 | 5.61 | 5.40 | 5.13 |
| Sweden | Swedish | 31 | 71 | 5 | 29 | 6.24 | 6.37 | 5.61 | 6.28 | 5.83 |
| United Kingdom | English | 35 | 89 | 66 | 35 | 5.38 | 5.52 | 5.66 | 5.79 | 5.61 |
| United States | English | 40 | 91 | 62 | 46 | 5.70 | 5.84 | 5.29 | 5.34 | 5.72 |

*Note.* PDI = Power Distance Index; IDV = Individualism; MAS = Masculinity–Femininity; UAI = Uncertainty Avoidance Index; PRC = People's Republic of China.

TABLE 3.8
Prediction of Country Big Five Means Using Hofstede (1994)
Dimension Scores

| OPQ 32 Big Five | R | R² | F | p | Hofstede dimension beta values | | | |
| | | | | | PDI | IDV | MAS | UAI |
|---|---|---|---|---|---|---|---|---|
| Emotional Stability | .872 | .760 | 20.588 | <.001 | −.400 | .201 | −.266 | −.415 |
| Extraversion | .799 | .638 | 11.464 | <.001 | −.676 | −.088 | −.457 | .211 |
| Openness to Experience | .393 | .154 | 1.188 | ns | −.097 | .084 | −.043 | .397 |
| Agreeableness | .557 | .310 | 2.917 | <.05 | −.432 | −.020 | −.272 | −.037 |
| Conscientiousness | .411 | .169 | 1.319 | ns | −.053 | .311 | .020 | −.174 |

*Note.* PDI = Power Distance Index; IDV = Individualism; MAS = Masculinity–Femininity; and UAI = Uncertainty Avoidance Index.

Extraversion, the effects are large and significant. Effects are more modest and, with the current sample size of 31, not significant for two of the other three scales.

When one looks in more detail at the nature of these relationships by considering patterns of relationships with individual OPQ32 scales, however, their meaning is not always obvious. High PDI scores are associated positively with Forward Thinking ($r = .62$), Emotionally Controlled ($r = .59$), and Data Rational ($r = .58$), and negatively with Socially Confident ($r = −.66$) and Relaxed ($r = −.65$). High IDV scores are associated positively with Vigorous ($r = .75$), Socially Confident ($r = .64$), and Relaxed ($r = .57$) and negatively with Forward Thinking ($r = −.72$) and Competitive ($r = −.54$). This pattern implies a strong negative relationship between PDI and IDV. This is supported by the fact that they correlate at $−.73$ in the sample of 31 countries considered here and at $−.60$ for the set of 69 countries listed in Hofstede (2001). For MAS, there is a positive relationship with Modest ($r = .63$), which seems counterintuitive. Similarly, although UAI is positively associated with Worrying ($r = .57$), it is also positively associated with Variety Seeking ($r = .60$), when one might expect the opposite.

As one would expect, countries that are high on collectivism (i.e., low IDV) and high on power distance (PDI) show reduced variation between people in scores. This is consistent with the view that cultural tightness will tend to reduce the amount of individual variation that is expressed. This is a general effect unrelated to the Big Five. The correlations between standard deviations for the Big Five are very high, indicating the presence of a general factor of within-country variability. It is this general factor that varies most clearly with PDI (negative) and IDV (positive). From a practical viewpoint, although these correlations are substantial, the magnitude of the variation in standard deviations is relatively small (see Table 3.9).

## CONCLUSIONS AND PRACTICAL IMPLICATIONS

The various analyses reported here show a remarkable level of invariance in the pattern of correlation between the 32 OPQ scales across countries, languages, and ethnic groups. Many of the comparisons hold language constant and vary by country or ethnicity; others vary by both language and country. It seems that within the pool of samples examined (which was a population of working adults who were either applicants for jobs or being assessed within a work setting, which included both men and women, with ages ranging across the full range of the working population), the relationships the 32 scales have with each other are very stable. Differences on OPQ32i scales scores at the aggregate group level, on the other hand, do occur as do differences in the level of variability found within countries.

Between-countries effects are comparable in size and extent to those found for differences within countries between men and women. Most differences are small, but a substantial number are moderate (i.e., likely to have the effect of shifting a scale score one sten point). Very few are large (i.e., likely to have the effects of shifting a scale score more than one sten point).

The patterns of gender differences within countries and of differences between countries seem to be highly correlated with national cultural factors, as expressed through Hofstede's (1994) dimension scores. There are also substantial relationships between Hofstede's dimensions scores for the countries and the means and standard deviations of at least some of the Big Five personality scores. However, the nature of these relationships is not always consistent with the meanings of the Big Five constructs and the Hofstede constructs.

On the basis of these findings, the forced-choice format version of OPQ32 is very robust in terms of construct equivalence across countries, between different versions of English and Chinese, and for South Africa, between first language and ethnic groups within country. Some differences occur between and within countries in terms of average scale scores. These effects are comparable in magnitude to those associated with demographics, such as gender, but probably smaller than the effects associated with variables such as job level or managerial position (Bartram, 2009). Effect sizes are generally not of substantive significance in terms of impact on individual profile interpretation.

TABLE 3.9
Big Five Country Standard Deviations

| Country | Language | OPQ32 Big Five | | | | |
|---|---|---|---|---|---|---|
| | | Emotional stability | Extraversion | Openness to experience | Agreeableness | Conscientiousness |
| Argentina | Spanish | 1.59 | 1.66 | 1.74 | 1.77 | 1.74 |
| Australia | English | 2.03 | 2.06 | 2.01 | 1.95 | 2.00 |
| Belgium | French | 2.00 | 1.89 | 1.91 | 1.88 | 2.06 |
| Belgium | Flemish | 2.18 | 2.14 | 2.05 | 1.94 | 2.08 |
| Brazil | Portuguese | 1.69 | 1.86 | 1.88 | 1.73 | 1.80 |
| Canada | French | 1.86 | 1.89 | 1.92 | 1.87 | 1.92 |
| Denmark | Danish | 1.82 | 1.98 | 2.01 | 1.86 | 2.06 |
| Finland | Finnish | 2.06 | 2.24 | 2.11 | 1.98 | 2.14 |
| France | French | 2.00 | 1.84 | 1.92 | 1.76 | 2.00 |
| Germany | German | 2.00 | 1.88 | 1.86 | 1.80 | 1.84 |
| Greece | Greek | 1.90 | 1.67 | 1.97 | 1.80 | 2.10 |
| Hong Kong | Traditional Chinese | 2.16 | 2.09 | 1.95 | 1.87 | 1.84 |
| Hungary | Hungarian | 2.08 | 1.96 | 2.07 | 1.81 | 2.12 |
| India | English | 1.72 | 1.74 | 1.79 | 1.69 | 1.74 |
| Indonesia | Indonesian | 1.67 | 1.81 | 1.75 | 1.67 | 1.86 |
| Italy | Italian | 2.00 | 1.85 | 1.93 | 1.82 | 1.89 |
| Japan | Japanese | 2.27 | 1.91 | 1.84 | 1.78 | 1.86 |
| Malaysia | English | 1.81 | 1.92 | 1.74 | 1.78 | 1.93 |
| Middle East | Arabic | 1.51 | 1.44 | 1.68 | 1.67 | 1.69 |
| Netherlands | Dutch | 2.05 | 1.98 | 1.93 | 1.62 | 1.89 |
| New Zealand | English | 1.98 | 1.95 | 1.98 | 1.84 | 2.06 |
| Norway | Norwegian | 1.83 | 1.91 | 1.88 | 1.88 | 1.89 |
| Poland | Polish | 2.01 | 2.03 | 1.81 | 1.91 | 2.07 |
| Portugal | Portuguese | 1.76 | 1.79 | 2.01 | 1.69 | 1.96 |

(continues)

## TABLE 3.9
### Big Five Country Standard Deviations  (Continued)

| Country | Language | OPQ32 Big Five | | | | |
| --- | --- | --- | --- | --- | --- | --- |
| | | Emotional stability | Extraversion | Openness to experience | Agreeableness | Conscientiousness |
| PRC | Simplified Chinese | 1.91 | 1.91 | 1.79 | 1.61 | 1.75 |
| Russia | Russian | 1.96 | 1.76 | 1.98 | 1.78 | 1.86 |
| South Africa | English | 1.89 | 1.94 | 1.89 | 1.82 | 1.97 |
| Spain | Spanish | 1.78 | 1.90 | 1.88 | 1.80 | 1.94 |
| Sweden | Swedish | 1.90 | 1.91 | 1.87 | 1.89 | 2.00 |
| United Kingdom | English | 2.04 | 2.00 | 2.03 | 1.94 | 2.05 |
| United States | English | 2.05 | 2.09 | 2.05 | 1.97 | 2.03 |

To return to the original question, Where there is construct equivalence, should researchers aggregate across samples for norming purposes to preserve the underlying raw score difference effects? Or, should they use national norming to remove these effects? The impact is directly analogous to that associated with gender: Should researchers remove gender differences by using gender norming or retain these effects by using combined male and female norm groups?

The key question in choosing a norm reference group is, "Does the norm group consist of the sort of persons with whom [the candidate] should be compared?" (Cronbach, 1990, p. 127). Cronbach (1990) made clear that this does not necessarily entail comparing people with others from their own demographic group.

The traditional approach of aggregating data within country, but not between countries, is difficult to justify and relates more to the history of test publishers operating within countries than it does to any good psychometric principles. Decisions on data aggregation should be driven by the evidence needed to ensure that the relevant constructs are invariant across the groups concerned. Sometimes this will allow researchers to aggregate across a wide range of demographics, and at other times it may require them to not generalize beyond one fairly restricted case.

The present results can be considered in light of the following guidelines developed for procedures to be followed in data aggregation for the production of multicultural, multinational, and multilingual norms (Bartram, 2008b):

- Aggregation of norms across countries, cultures, and languages should not be automated.
- Correlation matrices should be checked for measurement invariance.
- Norm samples should be checked for comparability of demographics—reweighting adjustments made if necessary.
- Where demographics are associated with score differences, the mix within samples should be weighted to ensure comparability across samples.
- Mix of countries or cultures should be "reasonable," with more caution exercised for mixing more divergent cultures.
- Use country similarity (e.g., through cluster analyses or closeness on the basis of Hofstede's (1994) dimensions or other cultural metrics) as a guide for "reasonableness."
- In combining across countries or cultures, samples should be weighted appropriately for the final mix—for example, equal weights rather than relative to populations or sample sizes.
- Adherence to these guidelines involves the exercise of expert judgement and needs to be dealt with on a case-by-case basis.

- Expert judgment is also needed when aggregation is not possible and people from different countries are being compared.

In practice, these guidelines can be followed to produce virtual norm groups, in which researchers can be sure they are averaging across comparable constructs. They can define a *virtual* norm group as one that has been created by the aggregation of suitably weighted population or user norms for a specific purpose (e.g., the sort of multinational comparisons discussed here):

- A virtual norm group can be produced by covering the countries of origin of the candidates to be compared by calculating the aggregate mean and standard deviation of the weighted means and standard deviations relating to those countries.
- If the country of origin is different from the target country, then a virtual norm group for the target country or countries can be calculated from the aggregate mean and standard deviation of the weighted means and standard deviations relating to those countries.

For international assessments, it is recommended that both local national and relevant multinational aggregations of national norms be used and that areas where these give rise to differences in scores be highlighted and considered by users in light of what is known about possible sample, translation, or cultural effects.

---

**Best Practices Recommendations**

- When an instrument is adapted for use in some other country, language, or culture, determine whether the same constructs are being measured in both versions. If they are not, do not use the instrument for cross-country, -language, or -cultural comparisons.
- If the same constructs are being used, then check the degree of scalar equivalence between the two versions.
- If there is evidence to support scalar equivalence, then make cross-national or cross-cultural comparisons using norms that are based on data aggregated across the populations.
- If differences arise for other reasons, it may be safer to remove such effects by using separate norms for each population.
- When aggregating data sets, be careful of potential bias arising from mismatching demographics.

---

Future research needs to be based on good demographic data so that differences due to gender, culture, language, country, or other factors can be disentangled from each other. At present, test publishers tend to focus on the country-level for the development of norms, even though they know that countries are generally multicultural and multilingual (the present examination of South African data illustrates this point).

## REFERENCES

Bartram, D. (2008a, July). *Extending the ITC guidelines—A case study: Parallel item creation in 3 languages*. Paper presented at invited symposium convened by R. Hambleton on the ITC Guidelines and methodology for adapting educational and psychological tests. *XXIX International Congress of Psychology*, Berlin, Germany.

Bartram, D. (2008b). Global norms: Toward some guidelines for aggregating personality norms across countries. *International Journal of Testing, 8,* 315–333. doi:10.1080/15305050802435037

Bartram, D. (2009). Leadership competencies: Differences in patterns of potential across 11 European countries as a function of gender and managerial experience. In W. H. Mobley, Y. Wang, & M. Li (Eds.), *Advances in global leadership* (Vol. V, pp. 35–64). Bingley, England: Emerald.

Bentler, P. M. (1990). Comparative fit indices in structural models. *Psychological Bulletin, 107,* 238–246. doi:10.1037/0033-2909.107.2.238

Bentler, P. M. (2005). *EQS 6 structural equations program manual*. Encino, CA: Multivariate Software.

Brown, A. (2006, July). *Investigation into measurement equivalence of OPQ32: Comparison of 14 language versions from 19 countries*. Paper presented at the International Test Commission 5th International Conference on Psychological and Educational Test Adaptation across Language and Cultures, Brussels, Belgium.

Brown, A., & Bartram, D. (2008, April). *IRT model for recovering latent traits from ipsative ratings*. Poster presented at the 23rd Annual Conference of the Society for Industrial and Organizational Psychology, San Francisco, CA.

Brown, A., & Maydeu-Olivares, A. (2011). Item response modeling of forced-choice questionnaires. *Educational and Psychological Measurement, 71,* 460–502. doi: 10.1177/0013164410375112

Byrne, B. M. (2006). *Structural equation modeling with EQS: Basic concepts, applications, and programming* (2nd ed.). New York, NY: Routledge.

Chao, G. T., & Moon, H. (2005). The cultural mosaic: A metatheory for understanding the complexity of culture. *Journal of Applied Psychology, 90,* 1128–1140. doi:10.1037/0021-9010.90.6.1128

Cheung, F. M., Leung, K., Zhang, J. X., Sun, H. F., Gan, Y. Q., Song, W. Z., & Xie, D. (2001). Indigenous Chinese personality construct: Is the five-factor model complete? *Journal of Cross-Cultural Psychology, 32*, 407–433. doi:10.1177/0022022101032004003

Cheung, S. F., Cheung, F. M., Howard, R., & Lim, Y. H. (2006). Personality across ethnic divide in Singapore: Are "Chinese traits" uniquely Chinese? *Personality and Individual Differences, 41*, 467–477. doi:10.1016/j.paid.2005.12.023

Costa, P. T., Terracciano, A., & McCrae, R. R. (2001). Gender differences in personality traits across cultures: Robust and surprising findings. *Journal of Personality and Social Psychology, 81*, 322–331. doi:10.1037/0022-3514.81.2.322

Cronbach, L. J. (1990). *Essentials of psychological testing* (5th ed.). New York, NY: Harper & Row.

Gelfand, M. J., Erez, M., & Aycan, Z. (2007). Cross-cultural organizational behavior. *Annual Review of Psychology, 58*, 479–514. doi:10.1146/annurev.psych.58.110405.085559

Gelfand, M. J., Nishii, L. H., & Raver, J. L. (2006). On the nature and importance of cultural tightness–looseness. *Journal of Applied Psychology, 91*, 1225–1244. doi:10.1037/0021-9010.91.6.1225

Hambleton, R. K. (2005). Issues, designs, and technical guidelines for adapting tests into multiple languages and cultures. In R. K. Hambleton, P. F. Merenda, & C. D. Spielberger (Eds.), *Adapting educational and psychological tests for cross-cultural assessment* (pp. 3–38). Mahwah, NJ: Erlbaum.

Hanges, P. J. (2004). Appendix B: Response bias correction procedure used in GLOBE. In R. J. House, P. J. Hanges, M. Javidan, P. W. Dorfman, & V. Gupta (Eds.), *Culture, leadership, and organizations: The GLOBE Study of 62 Societies* (pp. 737–751). Thousand Oaks, CA: Sage.

Harzing, A.-W. (2006). Response styles in cross-national survey research. *International Journal of Cross Cultural Management, 6*, 243–266. doi:10.1177/1470595806066332

Hofstede, G. (1980). *Culture's consequences: International differences in work-related values*. Beverley-Hills, CA: Sage.

Hofstede, G. (1994). Management scientists are human. *Management Science, 40*, 4–13. doi:10.1287/mnsc.40.1.4

Hofstede, G. (2001). *Culture's consequences: Comparing values, behaviors, institutions, and organizations across nations* (2nd ed.). London, England: Sage.

Hofstede, G., & Bond, M. H. (1988). The Confucian connection: From cultural roots to economic growth. *Organizational Dynamics, 16*, 5–21. doi:10.1016/0090-2616(88)90009-5

House, R. J., Hanges, P. J., Javidan, M., Dorfman, P. W., & Gupta, V. (Eds.). (2004). *Culture, leadership, and organizations: The GLOBE Study of 62 Societies*. Thousand Oaks, CA: Sage.

Kirkman, B. L., Lowe, K. B., & Gibson, C. B. (2006). A quarter century of *Culture's Consequences*: A review of empirical research incorporating Hofstede's cultural values framework. *Journal of International Business Studies*, *37*, 285–320. doi:10.1057/palgrave.jibs.8400202

McCrae, R. R., & Terracciano, A. (2005). Universal features of personality traits. *Journal of Personality and Social Psychology*, *88*, 547–561. doi:10.1037/0022-3514.88.3.547

Meade, A. (2004). Psychometric problems and issues involved with creating and using ipsative measures for selection. *Journal of Occupational and Organizational Psychology*, *77*, 531–551. doi:10.1348/0963179042596504

Muthén, L. K., & Muthén, B. (1998–2007). *Mplus 5*. Los Angeles, CA: Authors.

Oswald, F. L. (2008). Global personality norms: Multicultural, multinational, and managerial. *International Journal of Testing*, *8*, 400–408. doi:10.1080/15305050802435201

Oyserman, D., Coon, H. M., & Kemmelmeier, M. (2002). Rethinking individualism and collectivism: Evaluation of theoretical assumptions and meta-analyses. *Psychological Bulletin*, *128*, 3–72. doi:10.1037/0033-2909.128.1.3

Rothstein, M. G., & Goffin, R. D. (2006). The use of personality measures in personnel selection: What does current research support? *Human Resource Management Review*, *16*, 155–180. doi:10.1016/j.hrmr.2006.03.004

SHL. (1999). *OPQ32 manual*. Thames Ditton, England: SHL Group plc.

SHL. (2006). *OPQ32 technical manual*. Thames Ditton, England: SHL Group Ltd., and retrieved from http://www.shl.com/opqtechnicalmanual

SHL. (2009). *OPQ32 development and psychometric properties of OPQ32r (supplement to the OPQ32 technical manual)*. Thames Ditton, England: SHL Group Ltd.

Smith, P. B. (2004). In search of acquiescent response bias. *Journal of Cross-Cultural Psychology*, *35*, 50–61. doi:10.1177/0022022103260380

Taras, V., Kirkman, B. L., & Steel, P. (2010). Examining the impact of *Culture's Consequences:* A three-decade, multilevel, meta-analytic review of Hofstede's cultural value dimensions. *Journal of Applied Psychology*, *95*, 405–439. doi:10.1037/a0018938

Triandis, H. C. (1994). Cross-cultural industrial and organizational psychology. In H. C. Triandis, M. D. Dunnette, & L. M. Hough (Eds.), *Handbook of industrial and organizational psychology* (2nd ed., Vol. 4, pp. 103–172). Palo Alto, CA: Consulting Psychologists Press.

Trompenaars, F. (1993). *Riding the waves of culture: Understanding diversity in global business*. Chicago, IL: Irwin Professional.

Tsui, A. S., Nifadkar, S. S., & Ou, A. Y. (2007). Cross-national, cross-cultural organizational behavior research: Advances, gaps, and recommendations. *Journal of Management*, *33*, 426–478. doi:10.1177/0149206307300818

van de Vijver, F. (2008). Personality assessment of global talent: Conceptual and methodological issues. *International Journal of Testing*, *8*, 304–314. doi:10.1080/15305050802435011

Warr, P., Bartram, D., & Martin, T. (2005). Personality and sales performance: Situational variation and interactions between traits. *International Journal of Selection and Assessment*, *13*, 87–91. doi:10.1111/j.0965-075X.2005.00302.x

# 4

# CROSS-CULTURAL GENERALIZATION: USING META-ANALYSIS TO TEST HYPOTHESES ABOUT CULTURAL VARIABILITY

DENIZ S. ONES, STEPHAN DILCHERT, JÜRGEN DELLER,
ANNE-GRIT ALBRECHT, EMILY E. DUEHR, AND FRIEDER M. PAULUS

Cross-cultural research in work psychology has typically aimed to assess the influence of cultural variables on theoretical and applied questions (Berry, Poortinga, & Pandey, 1997; Heine, 2010). With increased globalization in business operations and human resources applications, establishing both universals and particulars is more important than ever. Our purpose in this chapter is to present meta-analysis as a systematic, quantitative approach for examining generalizability of cross-cultural findings in general and in international industrial and organizational psychology research in particular.

Cross-cultural questions can be addressed at least at three levels: intracultural, intercultural, and transcultural (McCrae, 2001). *Intracultural* research

We acknowledge and extend our thanks to research teams and individuals who supplied some of the data used in this chapter: Members of the project International Generalizability of Expatriate Success Factors (iGOES) and Collaborative International Study of Managerial Stress (CIMS). We are especially thankful to Paul Spector for generously sharing information and data with us. We also thank Frank Schmidt and In-Sue Oh for providing insights regarding second-order sampling error in meta-analysis and sharing their unpublished work.

is concerned with conceptualizations and operationalizations of psychological variables, as well as relationships among them, within specific cultural settings. Relationships among variables and tests of psychological principles are intended to apply within limited cultural boundaries. Thus, cross-cultural generalization cannot be, and often is not, expected or explicitly examined. Most psychological research studies conducted and published in the United States, Canada, and the United Kingdom represent intracultural research. Similarly, psychologists from other parts of the world and other cultures have also conducted research aiming to identify psychological variables, theories, and effects that are relevant only for the cultures they have studied (e.g., Benet-Martínez & John, 2000; Cheung et al., 2001; Newenham-Kahindi, 2009; Weingarten, 2000). Unfortunately, the largest bulk of industrial and organizational psychology research has been conducted in countries from the Anglo cultural cluster and as such represents intracultural research in that context. For example, Shen et al. (2011) found that in the past 10 years, over 85% of the studies published in the *Journal of Applied Psychology* were conducted using U.S. or Canadian samples. (The state of the research literature is similar in other fields of psychology; see, e.g., Quiñones-Vidal, López-García, Peñaranda-Ortega, & Tortosa-Gil, 2004). The generalizability of findings from this body of work to other cultural contexts is generally unknown (Heine, 2001; Heine & Buchtel, 2009).

To address this shortcoming, *intercultural* research has aimed to uncover differences in psychological constructs, measures, effects, relationships, and theories across different cultures and cultural regions of the world. Representative intercultural investigations directly compare findings across cultures. At its most rudimentary, bicultural comparisons are made. That is, parallel studies are conducted in two countries, and results are explicitly compared. For example, for research published in international business journals, more than 30% of international comparisons involve only two or three cultures (Franke & Richey, 2010). Differences observed are attributed to cultural differences between the cultures examined (e.g., Bagozzi, Verbeke, & Gavino, 2003; Cortina & Wasti, 2005; Ghorpade, Hattrup, & Lackritz, 1999; Wasti, Bergman, Glomb, & Drasgow, 2000). Bicultural studies do not lead to unambiguous conclusions about the effects of specific cultural variables on the comparisons undertaken. When only two cultures are examined, specific cultural variables that may be responsible for differences cannot be identified. A vast number of cultural variables and features distinguish each culture at hand. Therefore, more sophisticated intercultural approaches incorporate multiple group comparisons and seek to identify cultural dimensions moderating effects under examination (e.g., Kirkman, Chen, Farh, Chen, & Lowe, 2009). In these studies, investigators aim to systematically document cultural influences on findings. Intercultural generalizability of findings is expressly explored using observations from different cultures.[1]

Finally, *transcultural* research aims to identify universal psychological variables and to uncover universal relationships, effects, and theories. Identifying universals is perhaps the most essential, yet the most difficult, enterprise in cross-cultural research. It is fundamentally important because unless the same construct is demonstrated to exist in different cultures, and unless measures of such constructs are structurally equivalent, even the most basic cross-cultural comparisons cannot be made. Yet, establishing multicultural construct and scalar equivalence amounts to gathering evidence for the null hypothesis that latent differences are interpretable. Even when constructs and their measures are investigated and shown to be equivalent, transnational research continues to be extremely difficult because the objective is to gather evidence for demonstrating lack of cultural differences in research involving such measures. Obtaining conclusive evidence for various relationships, effects, and empirically based theories transcending culture (and language) involves an arduous process. Intercultural comparisons with multicultural samples are treated as replications. Such investigations more often than not wind up documenting cultural particulars, rather than universals.

Many observed relationships vary from culture to culture, even when issues involving construct and scalar equivalence have been established in preceding research. Typically, two major interpretations have flowed from the observation that observed relationships vary across cultures. The first is a substantive conclusion of true cultural influences on relationships under investigation. In this case, as already pointed out in our discussion of intercultural research, the focus of research shifts to identifying the specific cultural moderators that explain inconsistent findings across cultures.

The second interpretation is a cautious one in which researchers try to identify differences in sample representativeness and composition that may

---

[1]We should note that too often in psychological research, the term *culture* is used when researchers actually investigate differences across *countries* (Sawang, Oei, & Goh, 2006). Synonymous use of the two terms is problematic from several perspectives. Countries are geographic and national units that might be considered lower level building blocks making up a cultural context. Hence, the first issue is one of sampling. Cultures are composed of more than one country (Hofstede, 2001; House et al., 2004); thus, comparing across any two countries does not necessarily constitute a representative comparison of the two respective cultures. Comprehensive cross-cultural research thus requires sampling from several countries within each cultural cluster (for examples, see Hofstede, 2001; Project GLOBE, House et al., 2004; and the iGOES project discussed later in this chapter). Second, countries by themselves might be heterogeneous with regard to the cultural background of their nationals. Some such examples are Switzerland (depending on the sample, Germanic or Latin Europe), or South Africa (where White samples are typically considered to belong to the Anglo cluster; see Ashkanasy, Trevor-Roberts, & Earnshaw, 2002). The main objective of this chapter is to illustrate the use of meta-analysis in cross-cultural research, in particular with regard to establishing cross-cultural generalizability. The principles we illustrate, however, can be applied equally successfully to cross-country and true cross-cultural research. For simplicity, we use the term *cross-cultural* even when some of the data we use to illustrate meta-analytic techniques originally compared countries or "geopolitical entities" (e.g., Spector et al., 2002).

be responsible for the varying findings. Here, first, the question of whether individuals constituting a sample are representative of a given culture is of particular relevance. For example, a group of MBA students might not be representative of the typical employee in developing or emerging nations (e.g., Bangladesh, South Africa; see, e.g., Rahim et al., 2002). Second, differences in sampling strategy across cultural samples are a concern, as they can be a source of artificial variability in findings. For example, cross-cultural researchers who rely on easily accessible samples might study employees from particular industries (e.g., oil industry in Northern Africa), which in addition to a lack of representativeness, also might not be easily comparable to samples studied in other cultural contexts. Similar issues exist with regard to sampling from rural versus urban areas or large and small organizations (see, e.g., Findlay, Li, Jowett, & Skeldon, 1996). Finally, researchers have also suggested that ethnocultural identity of study participants should be formally assessed before comparing cross-cultural samples (e.g., Marsella, Dubanoski, Hamada, & Morse, 2000). For example, being a member of a particular country or cultural cluster does not necessarily mean that the individual subscribes to the cultural values and beliefs associated with the given culture or follows predominant traditions and practices. The ethnocultural identity of individuals may differ from dichotomous membership in a group (e.g., country, culture). Thus, overall sample representativeness and parallelism of sample characteristics is accorded high attention in intercultural studies aiming to rule out sample differences as a potential competing explanation to cultural specificity.

When differences are observed across samples in cross-cultural research, true cultural differences (and sample representativeness) are not the only explanations that ought to be considered. A main thesis of this chapter is that when differences are observed, findings can be due to chance (sampling error) as well as other statistical artifacts (see Hunter & Schmidt, 2004). Testing whether cross-cultural variability in findings is due to real effects of culture or such statistical artifacts is an important step that is essential in cross-cultural research. Addressing the biasing influences of statistical artifacts may help reveal cross-cultural universals. The magnitude of cultural variation in results can be empirically examined using approaches of psychometric meta-analysis.

## EFFECTS OF STATISTICAL ARTIFACTS ON STUDY FINDINGS IN CROSS-CULTURAL RESEARCH

Most intercultural research accepts variation of effect sizes across cultural settings at their face value. As we have already noted, researchers seek substantive explanations for study-to-study variation: Various characteristics of samples (e.g., cultural origin, sample representativeness, cultural identity of participants) are invoked as reasons for observed differences. In sophisticated intercultural investigations, culture-based sample characteristics are modeled and tested. For example, correlation and regression approaches use cultural variables to estimate the magnitudes of cultural effects (e.g., Spector et al., 2002). Multiple group comparisons in structural equation models test whether cross-cultural equivalence can be supported and seek to identify sources of cross-cultural inequivalence (e.g., measurement, factor structure; Nye & Drasgow, 2011).

Yet, cross-cultural research is not immune to the effects of statistical artifacts that influence study results (Hunter & Schmidt, 2004). Sampling error influences study findings in all research, including cross-cultural research. *Sampling error* refers to imprecision in estimates of effects examined due to chance variations in sampling individuals into studies (Hedges, 1994, p. 30). It is a function of finite sample sizes and, thus, is always present in real data (Hunter & Schmidt, 1990). Sampling error is a nonsystematic error and can cause observed effects or relationships to be larger or smaller than their true values. Thus, when findings from different cultures are being compared, sampling error results in differences that yield an impression of variability across cultures. If observed findings from cross-cultural research are taken at face value, there is a danger of interpreting chance variability in findings as true cultural effects. It may be particularly important to stress that sample representativeness and similarity in sample composition across cultural samples are different from sampling error. The former represent sampling bias. Even though these sampling biases may also hamper findings and comparisons, their effects are not entirely a consequence of sample size. More important, ensuring representativeness or similarity in sample composition is not a way to prevent sampling error.

There are other statistical artifacts that influence all study findings and create inconsistencies across research studies. Table 4.1 lists additional statistical artifacts that have an impact on cross-cultural studies and describes their effects on cross-cultural generalization of findings. Some of these have systematic influences (e.g., measurement error) and others nonsystematic influences on research findings (e.g., deviations from perfect construct validity [deficiency or contamination]). We focus our discussion on the impact of statistical artifacts, which can be corrected for in psychometric meta-analysis (see Hunter & Schmidt, 1990, 2004).

As is indicated in Table 4.1, these statistical artifacts influence both magnitudes of effect sizes and their variation from study to study, from culture to culture. First, the following statistical artifacts systematically bias effect sizes and relationships downward: measurement error (unreliability), artificial dichotomization of a continuous variable, and range restriction (direct

TABLE 4.1
Additional (Nonsampling Error) Statistical Artifacts Influencing
Cross-Cultural Study Findings and Their Effects

| Artifact | Effect on | |
| | Magnitudes of effect sizes | Variability of effect sizes across cultures |
| --- | --- | --- |
| Measurement error in the dependent variable | Systematically lower than their actual values | Variation in measurement error in dependent variable creates illusory cross-cultural variability. |
| Measurement error in the independent variable | Systematically lower than their actual values | Variation in measurement error in independent variable creates illusory cross-cultural variability. |
| Dichotomization of a continuous dependent variable | Systematically lower than their actual values | Across-cultures differences in arbitrarily chosen dichotomization cutpoints on the dependent variable create illusory cross-cultural variability. |
| Dichotomization of a continuous independent variable | Systematically lower than their actual values | Across-cultures differences in arbitrarily chosen dichotomization cutpoints on the independent variable create illusory cross-cultural variability. |

| Range restriction or enhancement in the dependent variable | For range restriction, systematically lower than their actual values; for range enhancement, systematically higher than their actual values | Both range restriction and enhancement in the dependent variable create illusory cross-cultural variability. |
| Range restriction or enhancement in the independent variable | For range restriction, systematically lower than their actual values; for range enhancement, systematically higher than their actual values | Both range restriction and enhancement in the independent variable create illusory cross-cultural variability. |
| Deviation from perfect construct validity in the dependent variable | Will differ from their actual values; nature of deficiency and contamination in the dependent variable determine whether effects are under- or overestimated. | Creates illusory cross-cultural variability |
| Deviation from perfect construct validity in the independent variable | Will differ from their actual values; nature of deficiency and contamination in the independent variable determine whether effects are under- or overestimated. | Creates illusory cross-cultural variability |
| Reporting errors | Will differ from their actual values | Creates illusory cross-cultural variability |
| Variance due to extraneous factors | Will differ from their actual values | Creates illusory cross-cultural variability |

or indirect). Effect sizes and relationships are artificially depressed because of the influences of these dependent, as well as independent, variables. On the other hand, direct or indirect range enhancement in study variables can artificially magnify effects.[2] Second, study-to-study differences in each of the statistical artifacts listed in Table 4.1 contribute to illusory between-cultures variability in cross-cultural research. That is, degrees of measurement error, range restriction or enhancement, and artificial dichotomization can be different across samples, studies, and cultures examined.

Thus, when multiple studies, cross-cultural replications, or multiple samples are used to evaluate cross-cultural differences in findings, to identify transcultural effects, or both, sampling error and other systematic statistical errors contribute to observed but illusory cross-cultural variability. Fortunately, their influences on cross-cultural studies can be estimated, modeled, and used to clarify the degree of true cross-cultural variability across studies incorporating data from multiple cultures. Psychometric meta-analysis (Hunter & Schmidt, 2004) can be used to accomplish this research objective. Since its formulation more than 30 years ago, psychometric meta-analysis has proven to be a crucial analytic system in the natural and social sciences (Schmidt, 2010). Many research literatures have been transformed through applications of meta-analytic techniques to substantive research questions (see DeGeest & Schmidt, 2010, for a historical overview of meta-analysis in industrial and organizational psychology). By describing and illustrating how psychometric meta-analysis can be used to test for cross-cultural generalizability of findings, we hope to highlight the unique usefulness of the technique for cross-cultural research.

Other scholars have stressed the need for improving the methodological rigor of cross-cultural research (van de Vijver & Leung, 2000, 2001). These articles highlight the typical pattern of cross-cultural data collection, which tends to include small, convenience samples and brief instruments that are only moderately reliable. These problems have resulted in poor cross-cultural reliability of much previous research. Meta-analytic approaches, with their quantitative attention to the degree of sampling error and statistical artifacts influencing effect sizes, can help cross-cultural researchers identify real versus illusory cultural differences.

A major contribution that meta-analytic techniques can make to cross-cultural research is to enable researchers to test the cross-cultural generalizability of relationships. In the remainder of this chapter, we review, illustrate, and discuss three unique applications of meta-analysis to examine cross-cultural effects. First, we review and discuss pooling findings across intracultural studies

---

[2]Range enhancement in variables studied can occur by chance or when individuals from tails of the normal distribution are purposefully oversampled in a research design (e.g., contrasted group studies comparing those high and low on a trait or characteristic).

to examine questions of cross-cultural generalizability. Second, we illustrate the value of applying meta-analysis to carefully conducted intercultural studies to examine the same question. Third, we demonstrate the use of meta-analysis to examine transcultural variability using primary data collected from different cultural settings. For each type of application, we offer a brief background, review and present illustrative findings, and discuss contributions and potential limitations.

## USING META-ANALYSIS WITH INTRACULTURAL STUDIES TO EXAMINE QUESTIONS OF CROSS-CULTURAL GENERALIZABILITY

The most popular approach to examine cross-cultural generalizability is to pool results from investigations conducted within different cultures to examine mean effects and their variability across cultures. The input to such quantitative summary consists of intracultural studies that investigate the relationship between a given dependent and independent variable (or, more generally, the association between a set of variables or a given psychological principle) within a single, relatively homogeneous culture. Pooling within-cultural replications using meta-analytic methods can enable conclusions regarding cross-cultural generalizability of relationships or psychological principles.

The most common way in which intracultural studies are combined is to pool results from studies conducted by different researchers, using different measures of the same constructs, which were administered to samples in different cultures. This approach provides several advantages: The meta-analyst can draw on a sample of studies that are already available, that use the most appropriate measure of each construct in each cultural context, and—in the case of important and frequently investigated relationships—that are numerous enough to constitute a large database of effects that helps reduce second-order sampling error and increase confidence in results observed.

Even though the idea of combining intracultural studies using meta-analysis is not new, it is rarely recognized as a methodology in the cross-cultural psychologist's toolbox. First and foremost, this may be because there is a limited pool of psychological constructs that have well-established transcultural conceptualizations and operationalizations. Second, few psychological principles are of such importance that several intracultural studies have been conducted in each world culture, enabling a quantitative pooling of results using meta-analytic techniques. A third potential reason relates to how psychological researchers tend to think about effects or relationships among variables. Dichotomous thinking typically accompanies null hypothesis testing: Effects or relationships are either confirmed or not. Even when the focus is on learning about the strength of the relationship between two variables, quantitative reviews often examine mean effects and their absolute range. There is often little attempt to quantify the degree of variation in results across studies (and thus cultures). This is despite the fact that a strong focus in the development of meta-analytic techniques was the investigation of generalizabilty of effects—especially for psychometric meta-analysis as a reaction to the situational specificity hypothesis (see Schmidt & Hunter, 1977).

From the cross-cultural psychologist's point of view, however, the degree of true variability in effects or relationships is just as important as the strength of a given relationship across studies from different cultural samples and contexts. For example, Jost, Glaser, Kruglanski, and Sulloway (2003) investigated the relationship between political conservatism and a variety of psychological variables (openness, uncertainty avoidance, fear of threat and loss, among others). The authors did not intentionally study the nature and meaning of conservatism across cultures but were aware of, and cautious about, effects related to cultural variables (e.g., the historical influences of different political systems around the world). The authors thus made their best efforts to include studies from outside the U.S. context and were able to obtain data from other Anglo cultures and Germanic Europe, Nordic Europe, Eastern Europe, Latin Europe, and Africa. Their results revealed moderate to strong mean correlations between conservatism and many of the variables investigated. Because of their efforts to include data from 12 countries from different cultural regions, the authors carefully posited that the "conclusions [they] have reached possess a considerable degree of cultural generalizability" (Jost et al., 2003, p. 369). From a cross-cultural generalizability point of view, merely confirming the existence of relationships is a weak test. In addition to the magnitudes of relationships, the focal interest in this case is the true variability in effects observed across cultures. This effect is quantified by the standard deviation associated with correlations corrected for statistical artifacts ($SD_\rho$; see Hunter & Schmidt, 2004, for the formulae to compute these values). $SD_\rho$ was not examined or reported in Jost et al.

Low values of $SD_\rho$ in meta-analyses of intracultural studies indicate that the variability of effects across cultures is small. That is, once sampling error and other statistical artifacts that create illusory variability (see Table 4.1) are corrected for and cross-cultural variability is found to be negligible or small, it is reasonable to conclude that the true relationships between the variables are similar (or generalize) across cultures. $SD_\rho$ is also used to compute credibility intervals around estimated true mean effects (Hunter & Schmidt, 2004, p. 205). These intervals illustrate the range in which the majority of true effects across the cultures investigated are found. Narrow intervals confirm that the phenomenon investigated varies little across cultures (or that there is only one true effect and little cultural specificity). In short, low $SD_\rho$s, not strong relationships by themselves, allow one to rule out cultural specificity and offer strong evidence of cross-cultural generalizability.[3]

To illustrate the use of meta-analysis in establishing cross-cultural generalizabilty in this manner, we present some examples from the industrial and organizational psychology literature. Table 4.2 summarizes results from two meta-analyses that investigated the relationship between individual differences predictors (Big Five personality dimensions, general mental and specific cognitive abilities) and overall job performance. Salgado (1997) examined the relationships between the Big Five personality dimensions (Emotional Stability, Openness to Experience, Agreeableness, and Conscientiousness) and job performance. Salgado, Anderson, Moscoso, Bertua, and de Fruyt (2003) examined the predictive validity of standardized tests of general mental ability (GMA) and specific cognitive abilities in predicting job performance. Both meta-analyses used intracultural studies, in this case studies conducted in countries of the European Community, as input to investigate the effects of interest. Although many perceive Europe as a relatively homogeneous culture, it is composed of several distinct cultural regions (Anglo, Latin, Germanic, Eastern, and Nordic Europe; see House, Hanges, Javidan, Dorfman, & Gupta, 2004). The studies summarized for illustrative purposes here were conducted with Anglo, Germanic, Latin, and Northern European samples.

Both the Salgado (1997) and the Salgado, Anderson, Moscoso, Bertua, and de Fruyt (2003) meta-analyses investigated the value of a class of predictor measures (personality and cognitive ability) in their focal cultures and thus mainly focused on operational validity (meta-analytic estimates of the mean effect, corrected for unreliability in the criterion and range restriction).

---

[3]Psychometric meta-analysis conceptualizes observed variance to be the sum of true variance and error variance (i.e., variance due to statistical artifacts). In accordance with classical measurement theory, true scores and error are assumed not to covary, and hence there is no covariance term in modeling observed variance as the sum of true and error variances.

One might ask how to interpret variability in cross-cultural effects when error and true effects are potentially correlated. Two possible scenarios exist, both with different but equally persuasive conclusions: First, if all variance in observed effects is accounted for after corrections for statistical artifacts, such as sampling error and unreliability, the conclusion is that error and true effect must be independent (because the sum of true variance and the covariance between true and error equals observed variance minus error variance, which equals zero). In the context of this chapter, if the difference between observed variance and error variance is found to be nonexistent, then both cross-cultural variability and the covariance term can be concluded to be zero. That is, even if statistical artifacts were correlated with the effect sizes being cumulated, a zero difference of observed variance and error variance would indicate cross-cultural generalizability.

In the second scenario, in which a portion of variance remains unexplained after correcting for statistical artifacts, if we were to assume that statistical artifacts covaried with effects being cumulated, the implication for cross-cultural generalizabilty is that we can be more optimistic than $SD_\rho$ would typically suggest. This is because a portion of the variance being interpreted as "true variance" (i.e., cultural specificity) would actually be due to the covariance of error (i.e., statistical artifacts) and the effects sizes meta-analyzed.

## TABLE 4.2
### Findings From Meta-Analyses Testing Generalizability of Individual-Differences–Overall-Job-Performance Relationships on the Basis of Intracultural Studies

| Individual differences predictor | Culture(s) | k | N | $r_{mean}$ | $SD_r$ | $\rho$ | $SD_\rho$ | CI |
|---|---|---|---|---|---|---|---|---|
| Emotional Stability | European Community[a] | 22 | 2,799 | .08 | .11 | .18 | .10 | .05, .31 |
| Extraversion | European Community[a] | 22 | 2,799 | .06 | .15 | .14 | .18 | -.09, .37 |
| Openness | European Community[a] | 11 | 1,629 | .00 | .09 | .02 | .06 | -.06, .10 |
| Agreeableness | European Community[a] | 19 | 2,574 | .00 | .09 | -.02 | .05 | .04, -.08 |
| Conscientiousness | European Community[a] | 18 | 2,241 | .10 | .12 | .26 | .11 | .12, .40 |
| General mental ability | European Community[b] | 93 | 9,554 | .29 | .18 | .62 | .19 | .37, .86 |
| Verbal ability | European Community[b] | 44 | 4,781 | .16 | .16 | .35 | .24 | .04, .66 |
| Numerical ability | European Community[b] | 48 | 5,241 | .24 | .12 | .52 | .00 | .52, .52 |
| Spatial–mechanical | European Community[b] | 40 | 3,750 | .23 | .20 | .51 | .29 | .13, .88 |
| Perceptual | European Community[b] | 38 | 3,798 | .24 | .17 | .52 | .19 | .28, .76 |
| Memory | European Community[b] | 14 | 946 | .26 | .13 | .56 | .00 | .56, .56 |

*Note. k* = number of studies pooled, each from a different culture; $r_{mean}$ = sample size weighted mean correlation; $SD_r$ = standard deviation of $r_{mean}$; $\rho$ = operational validity, corrected for unreliability in the criterion and range restriction (where appropriate); $SD_\rho$ = standard deviation of $\rho$. Confidence interval (CI) = 80% credibility interval: (90% of the estimates for $\rho$ are above the lower bound).
[a]Data from Salgado (1997).
[b]Data from Salgado, Anderson, Moscoso, Bertua, and de Fruyt (2003). Criteria in both meta-analyses were ratings of overall job performance.

However, both analyses also provided estimates of the variability of predictive validities across cultures contributing data to the analyses, as discussed above. In Table 4.2, $SD_\rho$ is the standard deviation of operational validity estimates that is observed across cultures and thus provides a direct indication of how criterion-related validities of tests vary across European cultures. Even though estimates of mean $\rho$ (operational validity) are not corrected for the attenuating effect of predictor unreliability, these effects are corrected for in estimating variability across studies (and thus, cultures).

We first focus on the results for personality–job performance relationships. Several of the Big Five dimensions predict job performance in the European Cultural context, most notably conscientiousness ($\rho = .26$), but also emotional stability ($\rho = .18$) and ($\rho = .14$). It is informative to examine how variable true effects are across European cultures: Although none of the $SD_\rho$s are close to zero, the credibility interval around the mean estimate for conscientiousness indicates that one can expect the true effect to generalize across the majority of cultures included in the analysis, in that it will be positive and significantly above zero. The same cannot be said of E, for example, for which large variability ($SD_\rho = .18$) is observed around a modest mean effect ($\rho = .14$), resulting in a wide credibility interval. This finding, however, does not necessarily imply that the relationship of Extraversion and job performance is subject to cultural specificity—it simply means we cannot yet confirm cross-cultural generalizability.

Triandis (1994) argued that in testing the generality of a psychological law, findings of cultural differences pose the problem of "*rival hypotheses* that must be checked and 'controlled' . . . [and] unless we are able to devote substantial resources to testing them, we should probably not even attempt to show such a difference" (p. 114). This rather pessimistic quote illustrates one of the fundamental difficulties in reviewing cross-cultural research, both in a narrative and in a quantitative fashion: When results are inconsistent and fail to generalize, there is a host of competing explanations, few of which can be conclusively ruled out. As discussed above, meta-analysis of different intracultural studies can establish cross-cultural generalizability in the absence of variability of true effects. But in the presence of such variability, cultural specificity is only one possible explanation for why effects displayed differences across cultures. Other competing explanations include statistical artifacts that are either unaccounted or cannot be corrected for, potential correlations between statistical artifacts and the effects being cumulated, unidentified moderators, and idiosyncrasies and deficiencies in measurement that cannot be corrected because their exact nature is unknown to the meta-analyst summarizing research from a variety of sources. Hence, researchers need to ask themselves how to improve the application of meta-analytic methods in cross-cultural psychology even further. We can think of two such ways, both of which require significant effort on behalf of researchers, and thus only few examples exist in the psychological literature: Meta-analyses of intracultural studies with fully nested investigations of moderators (illustrated below) and meta-analyses of systematic intercultural studies (illustrated in the following section).

## Meta-Analysis With Intracultural Research: Cultural Specificity Versus Moderators

Let us assume that the relationship between two variables has been investigated cross-culturally by quantitatively pooling results from many different intracultural studies. The resulting estimate of the true effect might be large, but significant unexplained variability around the mean effect may also be reported. We know that we cannot conclude that the true effect is the same across studies, but we also cannot conclude that there is any cultural specificity, because there are a host of "rival hypotheses" in the form of unexamined moderators.

To illustrate this case, consider the data summarized in Table 4.3. Here, we present results from several different meta-analyses that examined the relationship between general mental ability and overall job performance in Europe. For the overall results across European cultures presented by Salgado, Anderson, Moscoso, Bertua, and de Fruyt (2003; see row 1 in Table 4.3), the credibility interval around the operational validity estimate indicates that the vast majority of effects is positive, but it also illustrates large variability. Based on this single finding, both cultural specificity (i.e., the relationship differs across European cultures) as well as unexamined moderators (e.g., job complexity) are reasonable explanations. The next logical step is to examine each in isolation. A different meta-analysis by Salgado, Anderson, Moscoso, Bertua, de Fruyt, and Rolland (2003) examined the same relationship and also considered job complexity as a moderator (see rows 2–4 in Table 4.3). The large variability around estimated true effects for each job complexity level suggests that job complexity alone does not account for all variance in effects and that the search for additional moderators (including cultural context) might be justified. One way to do this is to examine the relationship within homogeneous cultural clusters. A third meta-analysis (Salgado & Anderson, 2003) presents meta-analytic results within those cultures for which enough country-level data were available and thus can be used to further disentangle the effects of some moderators. Again there was some variability around true effects, even if operational validities generalize in all countries. The combination of both types of data strongly suggests reasons other than just cultural specificity or job complexity as a moderator of validity— for example, second-order sampling error ($SD_\rho$ is particularly large where

TABLE 4.3

Predicting Job Performance: Comparison of Intracultural
and Cross-Culturally Pooled Analyses and Results

| Predictor | Culture(s) | $k$ | $N$ | $r_{mean}$ | $SD_r$ | $\rho$ | $SD_\rho$ | CI |
|---|---|---|---|---|---|---|---|---|
| General mental ability | European Community[a] | 93 | 9,554 | .29 | .18 | .62 | .19 | .37, .86 |
| | High-complexity jobs[b] | 14 | 1,604 | .23 | .15 | .64 | .24 | .33, .95 |
| | Medium-complexity jobs[b] | 43 | 4,744 | .27 | .18 | .53 | .26 | .21, .86 |
| | Low-complexity jobs[b] | 12 | 864 | .25 | .15 | .51 | .10 | .38, .64 |
| | France[c] | 26 | 1,445 | .48 | .18 | .64 | .15 | .45, .83 |
| | Germany[c] | 8 | 701 | .35 | .19 | .68 | .26 | .35, 1.00 |
| | Low countries[c,d] | 15 | 1,075 | .24 | .20 | .63 | .34 | .20, 1.00 |
| | Spain[c] | 11 | 1,182 | .35 | .15 | .64 | .15 | .45, .83 |
| | United Kingdom[c] | 68 | 7,725 | .26 | .12 | .56 | .08 | .46, .66 |
| Extraversion | Confucian Asia[e] | 124 | 27,408 | .11 | .10 | .16 | .10 | .03, .30 |
| | South Korea[f] | 14 | 3,447 | .06 | .07 | .09 | .04 | .04, .14 |
| | Japan[f] | 100 | 21,371 | .11 | .07 | .16 | .03 | .12, .20 |
| | Taiwan[f] | 3 | 475 | .14 | .11 | .19 | .10 | .06, .32 |
| | China[f] | 3 | 353 | .21 | .19 | .30 | .23 | .01, .59 |
| | Singapore[f] | 4 | 1,762 | .22 | .05 | .31 | .03 | .27, .35 |

*Note.* $k$ = number of studies pooled, each from a different culture; $r_{mean}$ = sample size weighted mean correlation; $SD_r$ = standard deviation of $r_{mean}$; $\rho$ = sample size weighted correlation corrected for sampling error and unreliability in both dependent and independent variable; $SD_\rho$ = standard deviation of $\rho$. Confidence interval (CI) = 80% credibility interval; (90% of the estimates for $\rho$ are above the lower bound). [a]Data from Salgado, Anderson, Moscoso, Bertua, and de Fruyt (2003). [b]Data from Salgado, Anderson, Moscoso, Bertua, de Fruyt, and Rolland (2003). [c]Data from Salgado and Anderson (2003). [d]Low countries include Belgium and The Netherlands. [e]Second-order meta-analytic result computed by the authors; $SD_\rho$ and $SD_\rho$ were computed by taking the square root of the sum of the average sample size weighted within-meta-analysis variances of $r/\rho$ and the variance across $rs/\rho s$ from the contributing meta-analysis. [f]Data from Oh (2009).

$k$s are small).[4] To draw definitive conclusions, more intracultural studies are needed and a fully nested series of meta-analyses needs to be conducted.

Table 4.3 presents a second example of the same approach. Here, we summarize country-level meta-analyses examining the relationship between Extraversion and job performance in Asian countries from Oh (2009). In most instances, the variability around operational validity estimates is low, indicating little room for potential moderators within the homogeneous cultures (with the exception of results for China). If results were to be combined across cultures, any unexplained variability would likely be due to cultural specificity. Oh indeed discusses results of such an analysis and concludes

---

[4]These findings also make salient one of the major fallacies in cross-cultural research, which is to attribute importance to findings of mean differences across cultures without a discussion of variability within cultures (see the discussion in Oyserman, Coon, & Kemmelmeier, 2002). This applies both to findings of mean-score differences across cultures compared with variability within cultures, as well as to differences in correlational effects across cultures compared with variance of such effects within single cultures.

that "the apparent (or observed) between-nations variability is in fact fully artifactual once the second-order sampling error is considered" (p. 136). To illustrate this, we present second-order meta-analytic results computed by us, along with Oh's data, in Table 4.3. One previously used procedure for estimating second-order meta-analytic mean effects is simple and consists of pooling estimates of $\rho$ and weighting by the associated total sample sizes (see Barrick, Mount, & Judge, 2001). The procedure to estimate the second-order $SD_\rho$, however, needs to take into account both within-culture and between-cultures variability of estimated true effects. Hence, the $SD_\rho$s obtained *within* each meta-analysis are converted to variances, sample size weighted and pooled, before adding the variance observed in $\rho$s *across* meta-analyses and subsequently converting back to $SD_\rho$ by computing the square root.[5] In this case, results reveal that even though there might be variability in the validity of , results generalize and variability is mostly driven by a single outlier, overall supporting cross-cultural generalizabilty of the effect in Asian countries.

In sum, to conclusively rule out competing explanations of variability observed across studies conducted in different cultures, large numbers of intracultural studies and a series of nested meta-analytic investigations are needed until the source of any variability can be pinpointed to specific moderators. Cultural specificity is only one potential moderator of relationships between dependent and independent variables, and we caution cross-cultural psychologists to conclude in its favor whenever different results are observed across cultures, unless other rival hypotheses have been investigated using psychometric meta-analysis.

## USING META-ANALYSIS IN INTERCULTURAL STUDIES TO EXAMINE QUESTIONS OF CROSS-CULTURAL GENERALIZABILITY

Another approach to further improve on the use of meta-analysis in cross-cultural research is to eliminate unknowns about methodological artifacts that cannot be corrected for in typical meta-analytic research. One way to do so is to meta-analyze studies conducted by a single research team or multiple, coordinated teams using consistent methods across different cultures, in an effort to ensure consistency, maximize control over, or hold consistent any extraneous variables, as well as generate and use knowledge about statistical artifacts that distort individual study findings.

---

[5]In a recent unpublished manuscript, Schmidt and Oh (2011) presented the equations and optimal methods for conducting second-order meta-analyses. In their approach, second-order sampling error variance is computed directly and subtracted from the variance of corrected population effect sizes across meta-analyses.

Cross-cultural researchers have encouraged larger, more representative samples and better measurement of study variables as vital in examining both cross-cultural specificity and generalizability of findings. A decade ago, lamenting the difficulties of coordinating a cross-cultural research design, McCrae (2001) noted, "In the ideal design, . . . measures of demonstrated scalar equivalence would be administered to stratified representative samples of individuals with the appropriate ethnocultural identity, across a wide range of different cultures" (p. 824). Even when these "ideals" in intercultural studies are met, or at least approximated, meta-analysis has an important role to play.

### Intercultural Application of Meta-Analysis: A Detailed Example

Spector et al. (2001, 2002) conducted a major intercultural data collection, the Collaborative International Study of Managerial Stress (CISMS). The project is a good example of a thoroughly conducted intercultural research effort. We use it to illustrate how to apply meta-analytic techniques to intercultural data and, for this purpose, will focus on CISMS's examinations of relationships among locus of control and well-being. Spector et al.'s (2001, 2002) research provided the first intercultural study on the relationship between locus of control and three aspects of well-being at work: job satisfaction, psychological well-being, and physical well-being. Their goal was to determine whether the relationship between locus of control and well-being generalizes beyond Western cultures and whether the strength of this relationship is moderated by the cultural dimension of individualism–collectivism.

Spector et al. (2001, 2002) collected data from samples in 23 nations and territories, representing 5,185 managers in organizations that were locally owned, either by private owner or the national government. Sample details are provided in Spector et al. (2001, 2002). The same measures were used with each of the 23 samples. Measurement instruments included the Work Locus of Control Scale (WLCS; Spector, 1988), a 16-item measure of generalized control beliefs in the work setting (for ease of illustration, we reversed all relationships such that higher scores reflected internal locus of control). Scale reliabilities in U.S. samples ranged from .75 to .85 (Cronbach's alpha). In the CISMS's cross-cultural data, internal consistency reliability was lower for translated versions of the WLCS despite rigorous independent back translations and retranslations. Reliabilities varied interculturally but remained acceptable, ranging from .65 to .88 (Spector et al., 2001).

CISCMS measured well-being using the Occupational Stress Indicator-2 (OSI2), which contains measures of job satisfaction, psychological-, and physical strain (12, 12, and six items, respectively). Internal consistency reliabilities ranged from .84 to .94 for job satisfaction, from .75 to .87 for psychological well-being, and from .70 to .84 for physical well-being (Spector et al., 2001). For both the WLCS and the OSI2, Spector et al. (2002) used structural equation modeling to test the interitem covariances across cultural samples, which is the most stringent test of factor equality when comparing scales across samples (Lytle, Brett, Barsness, Tinsley, & Janssens, 1995). Based on the results of this test of structural equivalence, Spector et al. (2002) could be reasonably confident that their chosen instruments could appropriately be transported to cultures outside of a Western context. Hence, they investigated relationships among variables using these same scales across cultures.

To reach conclusions about cross-cultural generalizability of the relationships examined, Spector et al. (2002) counted the number of significant relationships. Such a vote-counting approach is problematic, however, as it can lead to serious flaws in research synthesis because of its inattention to sampling error and other statistical artifacts (Hunter & Schmidt, 1990). Vote counting led Spector et al. (2002) to conclude that the relationship between locus of control and job satisfaction was "consistent" and "a little less consistent" for psychological well-being but not generalizable for physical well-being (p. 460).

As discussed above, sampling error and unreliability of measures are potentially important causes of variation across cultures. In this case, internal consistency reliabilities varied considerably across countries (Spector et al., 2001). If the goal is to assess and test the cross-cultural generalizability of the locus-of-control–well-being relationships, then influences of sampling error and other statistical artifacts (including unreliability in measures) need to be taken into account. Otherwise, illusory variation created by these statistical artifacts can be confused with real cross-cultural differences. Meta-analytic techniques can provide more precise estimates of effects and more direct tests of cross-cultural variability.

First, meta-analytic techniques can be used to assess whether the relationship between work locus of control and each of the three measures of well-being (job satisfaction, psychological well-being, and physical well-being) generalizes across cultures. In meta-analysis, generalization can be tested in a nuanced a manner. Meta-analysis pools results across studies; in this case, intercultural studies designed to gather parallel data using equivalent measures in multiple cultures. Effects of statistical artifacts on correlations are then corrected for. Observed variance across studies is computed, but confounds variability due to statistical artifacts, potential correlations between statistical artifacts and effects being cumulated, unexamined moderators, and true cross-cultural variability. Psychometric meta-analysis computes variance due to artifactual sources of variance. Once variance due to statistical artifacts is removed from observed variance, true variance across the pooled effect sizes emerges ($SD_\rho$; Hunter & Schmidt, 2004). When carefully planned intercultural studies, such as those conducted by Spector and colleagues, are pooled and corrected for the biasing influence of statistical artifacts, true variability can give an indication of the upper limit of cultural specificity in the data. Small $SD_\rho$s suggest cross-cultural generalizability. Large $SD_\rho$s can suggest a combination of effects: statistical artifacts that are not corrected for, potential correlations between statistical artifacts and effects being cumulated, unexamined moderators, and cultural specificity.

We used psychometric meta-analysis to correct for sampling error and unreliability in results presented by Spector et al. (2002). The correlations from each country that contributed to the overall estimate of the relationship were individually corrected. In other words, because reliability coefficients were calculated separately for each country, it was possible to correct each correlation individually. This procedure addressed the issue of measurement transportability, rather than ignoring reliability differences across countries. We did not correct for possible range restriction because there was no evidence of mechanisms that would result in direct and indirect restriction or enhancement (e.g., sample selection on study variables). Findings from our analyses are reported in Table 4.4.

Recall that meta-analysis offers a nuanced examination of cultural moderation. Corrected estimates of effect size variance can provide an indication of the magnitude of cultural effects. A less nuanced evaluation, such as whether an effect is consistently positive or negative across studies is also possible. If the lower credibility interval associated with the effect is positive, the inference is a positive relationship across the majority of studies included in the meta-analysis (Hunter & Schmidt, 2004).

Meta-analysis of the Spector et al. (2002) data shows that the mean corrected correlation between locus of control and job satisfaction was .41. The

TABLE 4.4
Findings From Meta-Analyses Testing Generalizability
of Work-Locus-of-Control–Well-Being
Relationships on the Basis of Intercultural Research

| Relationship | $k$ | $N$ | $r_{mean}$ | $SD_r$ | $\rho$ | $SD_\rho$ | CI |
|---|---|---|---|---|---|---|---|
| Internal locus of control–job satisfaction | 23 | 4,910 | .35 | .08 | .41 | .03 | .37, .45 |
| Internal locus of control–psychological well-being | 23 | 4,910 | .31 | .13 | .39 | .11 | .24, .53 |
| Internal locus of control–physical well-being | 23 | 4,910 | .18 | .13 | .23 | .12 | .09, .38 |

Note. $k$ = number of studies pooled, each from a different culture; $r_{mean}$ = sample size weighted mean correlation; $SD_r$ = standard deviation of $r_{mean}$; $\rho$ = sample size weighted correlation corrected for sampling error and unreliability in both dependent and independent variable; $SD_\rho$ = standard deviation of $\rho$. Confidence interval (CI) = 80% credibility interval; (90% of the estimates for $\rho$ are above the lower bound).

mean corrected relationship between locus of control and psychological well-being was .39. The mean relationship between locus of control and physical well-being was slightly smaller at .23. Note that all three lower 90% credibility values indicate that the relationships are consistently positive across cultures. That is, despite variability in point estimates across cultures, the overall pattern of relationships indicates that an internal locus of control is positively related to well-being across cultures. The $SD_\rho$s associated with each meta-analysis differed. The smallest value was for the locus-of-control–job satisfaction relationship ($SD_\rho = .03$). This suggests that there was no evidence of cross-cultural specificity in study findings across the 23 cultures examined. Somewhat larger $SD_\rho$s between work locus of control and psychological well-being as well as physical well-being (.11 and .12, respectively) suggest that there is some, albeit small, room for potential moderators, including cultural ones, to affect relationships. (Duehr & Ones, 2004, investigated individualism as one such potential moderator and did not find evidence supporting it.)

Although the data collected by Spector et al. (2001, 2002) are not perfect, they meet several of the ideal requirements outlined by McCrae (2001) and are one of the best existing examples of intercultural research in an organizational context. First, only managerial samples were compared across cultures. Second, considerable effort was made to collect data from an array of organizations within each culture, rather than relying on any single organization (as Hofstede did with the IBM corporation, for example). Spector et al. (2001, 2002) also attempted to gather fairly large samples in all cultures, but this aim was only met with moderate success. The sample sizes vary widely across cultures, ranging from 60 in France to 513 in Japan. Finally, the same measures were used in all cultures examined. Cross-cultural equivalence of measures was attended to. However, even the best intercultural studies are influenced by statistical artifacts including sampling error and measurement unreliability. As we illustrated in the above example, meta-analysis can be valuable to separate these artifactual sources of cross-cultural variation from the effects of true cultural differences.

The strength of systematic intercultural research lies in the greater attendance to sampling of cultures in researching cross-cultural influences on study findings. The strength of meta-analysis lies in its ability to model and minimize the influences of sampling error and other statistical artifacts. Combining the two approaches in cross-cultural research can offer a potent methodological tool to cross-cultural researchers. Meta-analytic combination of findings from intercultural research enables researchers to separate true and illusory cross-cultural variance. At present, most intercultural studies interpret observed differences in study findings as true cross-cultural effects. But when data from carefully planned and systematically conducted intercultural studies are used as the input for meta-analysis, a number of potential sources of variability can be better controlled for and ruled out. The meta-analytic approach described and illustrated here can move cross-cultural research to test cultural hypotheses in more robust ways. Although hierarchical linear modeling (HLM) can also be used to simultaneously investigate within-country individual-level and country-level relationships (Level 1 and Level 2 variables, respectively), only the meta-analytic approach described above teases apart artifactual and true variation. In HLM, observed relationships (both Level 1 and Level 2) are taken at their face value and interpreted as true effects.

## USING META-ANALYSIS IN INTERCONTEXTUAL STUDIES TO EXAMINE QUESTIONS OF CROSS-CULTURAL GENERALIZABILITY

Systematic intercultural studies such as those described above are an important vehicle for investigating whether psychological principles apply in a similar manner to different world cultures. Intercontextual studies are similar to intercultural studies in that they investigate cross-cultural generalizability of relationships between psychological variables by using consistent measures and methods and applying them to samples across cultures. However, in contrast to intercultural studies, intercontextual studies attempt to hone in on the impact of the cultural context, rather than the cultural composition, of study samples.

Typical intercultural studies collect data from samples that are native to the culture being investigated. Hence, these investigations confound the *culture of the respondents* (i.e., individuals' cultural experiences, language, race, ethnicity, etc.) with the *culture of the context* (i.e., the forces acting on and experiences shared by all individuals in a given culture, regardless of their origin). For example, an intercultural study of personality and its relationship to job performance will answer the question of whether personality traits predict performance in the same manner for Americans, Europeans, Asians, and Africans within their respective home cultures. An intercontextual study would ask the question whether personality relates to job performance in the same manner across cultural contexts by holding constant the cultural background of the samples investigated. Here, the focus is truly on the moderating influence of culture as a context variable, not as an amalgam of experiences collected by study participants over their life span.

To examine the influence of cultural context, the cultural background of study participants needs to be held constant. In this way, the cultural influence that is systematically varied is contextualized as the context shared by participants at a given point in time, not necessarily as a characteristic of the sample. Recall that the latter is the way culture is operationalized in intracultural studies, which confound culture with study, sample, and/or context. Even though systematic intercultural studies (e.g., Spector et al., 2002) address differences across studies (in design and representativeness), they still confound sample and context. Hence, intercontextual studies are important because even though meta-analysis can address differences across studies (see Table 4.1), it cannot disentangle sample and context differences unless they are controlled in the individual primary studies that constitute the meta-analytic input. Investigating cross-cultural differences may benefit from careful theorizing about when and how cultural backgrounds of study participants versus when and how cultural context will influence relationships. Meta-analytic cumulation in intercontextual studies is warranted when hypotheses about culture as context are being examined and intercontextual generalizability is tested.

Intercontextual studies present the same advantages as intercultural studies: It is possible to systematically sample the cultures for which generalization of effects is being investigated. A research team can define clearly, and focus consistently on, the same constructs of interest, including associated factors, such as bandwidth. Similarly, the same measures can be used consistently, eliminating some of the difficulties associated with unknown (and variable) influences of measurement artifacts. Study procedures and operational decisions will be consistent across contexts as well, reducing factors that often create illusory variability in observed effects in less systematic reviews (see Table 4.1). Hence, cumulating results from intercontextual studies using meta-analysis provides the same benefits as doing so for intercultural studies (as illustrated by our analysis of Spector et al., 2002, presented above). With regard to conclusions that can be drawn from such meta-analyses, intercontextual studies allow researchers to more singularly pinpoint the influence of cultural context by itself.

## Intercontextual Application of Meta-Analysis: A Detailed Example

To illustrate the role of meta-analysis in pooling results across cultural contexts, we next present a brief summary of a large-scale intercontextual research project and summarize some preliminary results. International Generalizability of Expatriate Success Factors (iGOES) is an ongoing research project with the goal of examining the cross-cultural generalizability of relationships between various individual differences traits and important job- and life behaviors and outcomes (Deller, 2008). Specifically, our research team (based in both Germany and the United States) investigates the relationships between personality variables (Big Five and related traits), cognitive ability, demographic characteristics, and background variables with job performance, job- and life-satisfaction, as well as several concepts of adjustment in all cultural regions of the world. To this end, we have collected data from 25 countries covering all 10 GLOBE cultural clusters: Anglo (Ireland, United Kingdom, United States), Latin Europe (France, Italy), Nordic Europe (Denmark, Finland, Sweden), Germanic Europe (The Netherlands, Switzerland), Eastern Europe (Czech Republic, Poland, Russia), Latin America (Argentina, Costa Rica, Mexico), Middle East (Egypt, Morocco, Turkey), Sub-Saharan Africa (Ghana), Confucian Asia (China, Singapore), and Southern Asia (India, Malaysia, Thailand). Because one goal of the iGOES project was to examine the influence of cultural context, the cultural background of study participants was held constant. iGOES participants all stem from the Germanic European cultural context (i.e., German-speaking Austrians, Germans, and Swiss nationals), who are on expatriate assignments outside of their home country. We were interested in whether the cultural context that these expatriates were operating in moderated relationships between various individual traits and criteria (e.g., job satisfaction, job performance).

Measures, methods, and operational decisions were held constant across cultural contexts investigated (and, with some adjustments, across duration of the research project). To ensure maximum consistency of study procedures, more than 35 research assistants have been dispatched so far to collect data in person within each of the 25 countries, both by conducting in-depth, standardized interviews with study participants and by administering and overseeing the administration of standardized instruments (e.g., personality and cognitive ability tests).

Table 4.5 presents a selected set of preliminary results from the iGOES project. The analyses summarize the relationships between general mental ability and overseas adjustment and job satisfaction criteria, as well as between openness to experience and job performance. Neither of these were focal relationships of the project, and no strong effects were hypothesized; however, both serve to illustrate the application of the meta-analytic technique and conclusions that can be drawn from the respective results.

First, we observe that the relationship between general mental ability and overseas adjustment is somewhat negative (operational validities ranged from $-.02$ to $-.15$ across adjustment facets). Closer examination of the effects reveals that the relationship with overall and general adjustment was generalizably negative (credibility intervals did not include zero), and the mean effect for work adjustment was small with a large variance in true effects that was unexplained by statistical artifacts. Notwithstanding unexamined moderators and the potential for second-order sampling error, these results lead us to conclude that there may be much variability in true effects across the cultural contexts investigated. Comparing results for the GMA–satisfaction relationships, we notice $SD_\rho$s of zero, suggesting results generalize across cultural contexts examined.

## TABLE 4.5
### Meta-Analysis Aiming to Examine Intercontextual Generalization of Relationships Across Cultures: Findings From an Intercultural Expatriate Study

| Predictor Criterion | k | N | $r_{mean}$ | $SD_r$ | ρ | $SD_\rho$ | CI |
|---|---|---|---|---|---|---|---|
| General mental ability | | | | | | | |
| Adjustment, overall | 20 | 1,556 | −.08 | .13 | −.12 | .08 | −.22, −.02 |
| Adjustment, general | 11 | 831 | −.10 | .14 | −.15 | .11 | −.29, −.01 |
| Adjustment, work | 11 | 825 | −.01 | .17 | −.02 | .17 | −.24, .20 |
| Job satisfaction | 7 | 527 | .07 | .11 | .09 | .00 | .09, .09 |
| Life satisfaction | 5 | 360 | .13 | .09 | .17 | .00 | .17, .17 |
| Openness | | | | | | | |
| Overall job performance | 19 | 707 | .04 | .11 | .07 | .00 | .07, .07 |
| Effort and initiative | 19 | 707 | .01 | .15 | .01 | .00 | .01, .01 |
| Management and supervision | 19 | 707 | .00 | .11 | .00 | .00 | .00, .00 |
| Job specific task proficiency | 19 | 707 | .06 | .12 | .10 | .00 | .10, .10 |
| Nonjob specific task proficiency | 19 | 707 | .04 | .13 | .06 | .00 | .06, .06 |

Note. $k$ = number of studies pooled, each from a different culture; $r_{mean}$ = sample size weighted mean correlation; $SD_r$ = standard deviation of $r_{mean}$; ρ = sample size weighted correlation corrected for sampling error and unreliability in both dependent and independent variable; $SD_\rho$ = standard deviation of ρ. Confidence intervals (CI) = 80% credibility interval; (90% of the estimates for ρ are above the lower bound). Criterion measures for adjustment, job satisfaction, and life satisfaction were based on self-ratings; criterion measures for overall job performance and facets were based on other ratings.

Second, results reveal consistently small relationships between openness and job performance among the expatriate samples studied in the different cultural contexts. Even though these results are in line with the general literature relating overall openness to job performance (Griffin & Hesketh, 2004), they are in conflict with those theories that posit that openness could be a valuable asset to perform in unknown and often uncertain work environments (Ones & Viswesvaran, 1997, 1999).[6] The estimates of $SD_\rho$, which are zero for all openness–performance relationships, suggest that openness does not predict job performance, at least among Germanic European expatriates, regardless of the cultural region of the world they are dispatched to.

### Implications of Intercontextual Applications of Meta-Analysis

The approach we have illustrated in this section is an initial attempt to conceptualize culture strictly as the context individuals experience and in which psychological principles are observed at a given point in time. The approach, of course, is based on the knowledge that individuals, over

---

[6]The full set of results of how Openness and its facets relate to adjustment, life, and work satisfaction among expatriates can be found in Albrecht, Dilchert, Deller, and Paulus (in press).

the course of their lives, are subject to experiences that are both idiosyncratic and unique, and that are an essential component of what psychologists term *culture*. However, by holding the cultural background of the sample constant and thus eliminating it from the equation, we can focus on the impact of cultural context on individuals' behaviors, careers, and lives in general.

In the case of the iGOES project, results from our investigation also answer very important applied questions; for example, we now know which individual differences predictors best predict job performance, adjustment (or a lack thereof), as well as satisfaction of an employee population crucially important to many industries and economies (see Brookfield Global Relocation Services, 2009). In terms of systematic intercontextual, cross-cultural investigations of the focal relationships examined, the iGOES project is only an initial step. Given the necessity to hold constant the home culture of study participants (see above), similar investigations need to be conducted among individuals from other world cultures who, similarly to the Germanic Europeans in our study, are investigated within each of the 10 cultural contexts and many countries around the world.[7] We hope that future research will not only replicate these investigations of individual-differences–criterion relationships among individuals with different cultural backgrounds but will also use the power of psychometric meta-analysis to systematically investigate generalizability of effects across cultural contexts.

## CONCLUSION

In this chapter, we focused on the role that meta-analytic cumulation can play in integrating research findings across cultures. We presented a conceptual basis for using psychometric meta-analysis to examine whether effects and relationships generalize across different cultures. The contribution of meta-analysis to examinations of cross-cultural specificity versus generalizability lies in its systematic quantitative approach to examining questions across multiple studies and samples. Meta-analytically pooling data across multiple investigations and statistically correcting for artifacts such as sampling error and unreliability in measurement, among others, can enable researchers to distinguish between illusory and true variance across

---

[7]Furthermore, to paint the complete picture of cultural influences on psychological variables, we might also conduct studies that reverse these designs and examine cross-cultural effects in intracontextual studies (systematically sampling individuals from different world cultures and observing them within the same cultural context). Such designs may contribute to the understanding of the formative influence of different cultures on individuals subjected to them (cultural background), and how those influences determine behavior even in foreign contexts.

studies. In cross-cultural research, observed differences across individual studies conducted in different cultures and different cultural settings are not only due to cultural differences but also often stem from statistical artifacts. The major advantage of psychometric meta-analysis in cross-cultural research rests on its ability to examine whether differences in research findings are due to statistical artifacts versus psychologically meaningful moderators, including culture, and estimating the relative magnitude of each effect.

We illustrated the methodological approach of using meta-analysis to test hypotheses about cultural variability using three different types of cross-cultural data. The first involved intracultural studies that have been conducted in different cultures. The multiple strengths of this approach include its ability to incorporate all studies that have been conducted across cultures. There is no requirement that research efforts across cultures be coordinated. As long as the same meaningful constructs are assessed across cultures, meta-analysis can be used to pool findings from intracultural studies.[8] In this sense, meta-analysis serves as a vehicle through which cumulative transcultural scientific principles can be established or potentially moderating influences of culture can be examined. Another strength of the meta-analytic approach using intracultural studies from different cultures involves its ability to integrate multiple effect sizes per culture and thus potentially reducing second-order sampling error. That is, the robustness of the approach can be expected to increase as the numbers of studies from each culture increase. On the flipside, a potential weakness of this approach lies in the possible lack of availability of studies for each culture, as well as the sometimes small numbers of different cultures that can be sampled (see Franke & Richey, 2010, for an informative analysis of the typical numbers of cross-cultural samples included in international business research).

A second approach we illustrated was using meta-analysis to assess cross-cultural generalizability by pooling data from a systematic intercultural research study. This approach requires input data from multiple cultures, collected as part of the same study, by the same research team, using the same measures and participant sampling procedures. In most intercultural research, differences observed across cultures have been interpreted as true cultural effects because culture-level sampling had been attended to (i.e., attempts were made to sample cultures in a representative manner). The meta-analytic approach tests whether observed culture-level differences can be explained by the biasing effects of statistical artifacts. Influences of sampling error and culture-level differences in measurement unreliability, among other statistical

---

[8]Demonstrations of scalar invariance are not required or even possible in this approach. Different measures of the same construct used in studying the same relationships within each culture contribute to these meta-analytic efforts.

artifacts, can be modeled and tested for their influences on variation across cultures. Combining meta-analysis with intercultural research capitalizes on the strengths of each approach: systematic sampling of cultures, greater uniformity across features of studies pooled (which in other respects may have biased cross-cultural comparisons), while attending to the influences of statistical artifacts. A potential weakness stems from the typical inclusion of only one effect size per culture in a given meta-analysis. This weakness is easily overcome when multiple replications are undertaken within each culture, which are then meta-analytically pooled within culture before pooling across cultures, thus addressing the problem of second-order sampling error. However, we were not able to find data from intercultural studies that conducted multiple replications within cultures, and therefore did not illustrate this approach.

Finally, we noted that in most cross-cultural investigations, the concepts of study, sample, and contexts are often confounded with (or used as a proxy for) culture. We then illustrated the use of meta-analysis in studying intercontextual cultural effects independently. The strengths and weaknesses of this approach mimic that of using meta-analysis with data from an intercultural research study. However, intercultural research studies typically operationalize culture as the sample's culture (e.g., French, Egyptian, or Russian individuals) or confound culture with both sample and context (e.g., Greeks residing in Greece, Chinese residing in China). An innovative approach to disentangling culture as sample versus context is examining individuals stemming from one cultural region across different cultural contexts. Our third illustration used meta-analysis to examine cross-cultural specificity versus generalizability on the basis of intercultural data that conceptualized culture as context in this manner.

Scientific research is a cumulative enterprise. A large number of studies are needed before effects can be considered well established. Replications are essential to examine the generalizability of findings. Cross-cultural research is no exception. However, in comparing results across studies, researchers need to be cautious not to interpret small or artifactual variation across cultures as indicative of true cross-cultural differences. Meta-analysis offers an important methodology to cross-cultural research, as it enables scholars to test the true degree of cross-cultural generalizability of findings. Future research can advance the conceptual and illustrative ideas offered in this chapter in greater methodological detail. Researchers examining cross-cultural effects can use the illustrations outlined in this chapter as a starting point in applying meta-analysis to their own data. We are confident that meta-analysis will continue to serve a powerful, integrative role in interpreting psychological findings and that the science of psychology will be better for it.

## Best Practices Recommendations

- Cultural specificity is only one possible explanation for why observed effects may differ across cultures. Not all differences observed in cross-cultural research are due to the effect of culture.
- Sampling error and other statistical artifacts create illusory variability across all studies, including cross-cultural studies.
- Consider the role of statistical artifacts (see Table 4.1 when determining whether a relationship has cross-cultural generalizability).
- Conduct quantitative reviews of intercultural, intracultural, and transcultural studies using psychometric meta-analysis to examine the extent of cross-cultural generalizability of effects.
- In cross-cultural meta-analyses, pool studies with psychological constructs that have well-established transcultural conceptualizations and reliable, construct-valid operationalizations.
- In interpreting cross-cultural studies, do not confound the culture of the respondents with the culture of the context. Carefully consider which aspect of culture is of interest before pooling different types of studies.
- Rather than examining only mean effects and their absolute range, quantify the degree of variation in results across studies and cultures.
- When there is large variability in true effects, carefully investigate rival hypotheses of potential substantive moderators before drawing conclusions regarding cultural specificity.
- To conclusively rule out competing explanations, large numbers of intracultural studies and a series of nested meta-analytic investigations are needed until the source of any variability can be pinpointed to specific moderators.
- Once sampling error and other statistical artifacts that create illusory variability (see Table 4.1) are corrected for and cross-cultural variability is found to be negligible or small, it is reasonable to conclude that the true relationships between the variables are similar (or generalize) across cultures.

# REFEFERENCES

Albrecht, A.-G., Dilchert, S., Deller, J., & Paulus, F. M. (in press). Openness in cross-cultural work-settings. *Journal of Personality Assessment.*

Ashkanasy, N. M., Trevor-Roberts, E., & Earnshaw, L. (2002). The Anglo cluster: Legacy of the British empire. *Journal of World Business, 37*, 28–39.doi:10.1016/S1090-9516(01)00072-4

Bagozzi, R. P., Verbeke, W., & Gavino, J. C., Jr. (2003). Culture moderates the self-regulation of shame and its effects on performance: The case of salespersons in the Netherlands and the Philippines. *Journal of Applied Psychology, 88*, 219–233. doi:10.1037/0021-9010.88.2.219

Barrick, L. A., Mount, M. K., & Judge, T. A. (2001). Personality and performance at the beginning of the new millenium: What do we know and where do we go next? *International Journal of Selection and Assessment, 9*, 9–30. doi:10.1111/1468-2389.00160

Benet-Martínez, V., & John, O. P. (2000). Toward the development of quasi-indigenous personality constructs: Measuring *Los Cinco Grandes* in Spain with indigenous Castilian markers. *American Behavioral Scientist, 44*, 141–157.

Berry, J. W., Poortinga, Y. H., & Pandey, J. (Eds.). (1997). *Handbook of cross-cultural psychology: Vol. 1. Theory and method* (2nd ed.). Needham Heights, MA: Allyn & Bacon.

Brookfield Global Relocation Services. (2009). *Global relocation trends: 2009 survey report.* Woodridge, IL: Author.

Cheung, F. M., Leung, K., Zhang, J.-X., Sun, H.-F., Gan, Y.-Q., Song, W.-Z., & Dong, X. (2001). Indigenous Chinese personality constructs: Is the Five-Factor Model complete? *Journal of Cross-Cultural Psychology, 32*, 407–433. doi:10.1177/0022022101032004003

Cortina, L. M., & Wasti, S. A. (2005). Profiles in coping: Responses to sexual harassment across persons, organizations, and cultures. *Journal of Applied Psychology, 90*, 182–192.doi:10.1037/0021-9010.90.1.182

DeGeest, D. S., & Schmidt, F. L. (2010). The impact of research synthesis methods on industrial-organizational psychology: The road from pessimism to optimism about cumulative knowledge. *Research Synthesis Methods, 1*, 185–197. doi:10.1002/jrsm.22

Deller, J. (2008, April). Introduction to the iGOES (International Generalizability of Expatriate Success Factors) project. In D. S. Ones & J. Deller (Chairs), *Expatriate success: Findings from 10 host-cultural clusters around the world.* Symposium conducted at the 23rd Annual Conference of the Society for Industrial and Organizational Psychology, San Francisco, CA.

Duehr, E. E., & Ones, D. S. (2004, April). *Locus of control and well-being: A reexamination of cross-cultural generalizability.* Poster session presented at the 19th Annual Conference of the Society for Industrial and Organizational Psychology, Chicago, IL.

Findlay, A. M., Li, F. L. N., Jowett, A. J., & Skeldon, R. (1996). Skilled international migration and the global city: A study of expatriates in Hong Kong. *Transactions of the Institute of British Geographers, 21,* 49–61.doi:10.2307/622923

Franke, G. R., & Richey, R. G. (2010). Improving generalizations from multicountry comparisons in international business research. *Journal of International Business Studies, 41,* 1275–1293.doi:10.1057/jibs.2010.21

Ghorpade, J., Hattrup, K., & Lackritz, J. R. (1999). The use of personality measures in cross-cultural research: A test of three personality scales across two countries. *Journal of Applied Psychology, 84,* 670–679. doi:10.1037/0021-9010.84.5.670

Griffin, B., & Hesketh, B. (2004). Why openness to experience is not a good predictor of job performance. *International Journal of Selection and Assessment, 12,* 243–251. doi:10.1111/j.0965-075X.2004.278_1.x

Hedges, L. V. (1994). Statistical considerations. In H. Cooper & L. V. Hedges (Eds.), *The handbook of research synthesis* (pp. 29–38). New York, NY: Russell Sage Foundation.

Heine, S. J. (2001). Self as cultural product: An examination of East Asian and North American selves. *Journal of Personality, 69,* 881–905. doi:10.1111/1467-6494.696168

Heine, S. J. (2010). Cultural psychology. In S. T. Fiske, D. T. Gilbert, & G. Lindzey (Eds.), *Handbook of social psychology* (5th ed., Vol. 2, pp. 1423–1464). Hoboken, NJ: Wiley.

Heine, S. J., & Buchtel, E. E. (2009). Personality: The universal and the culturally specific. *Annual Review of Psychology, 60,* 369–394. doi:10.1146/annurev.psych.60.110707.163655

Hofstede, G. (2001). *Culture's consequences: Comparing values, behaviors, institutions, and organizations across nations* (2nd ed.). Thousand Oaks, CA: Sage.

House, R., Hanges, P., Javidan, M., Dorfman, P., & Gupta, V. (2004). *Culture, leadership, and organizations: The GLOBE study of 62 societies.* Thousand Oaks, CA: Sage.

Hunter, J. E., & Schmidt, F. L. (1990). *Methods of meta-analysis: Correcting error and bias in research findings.* Thousand Oaks, CA: Sage.

Hunter, J. E., & Schmidt, F. L. (2004). *Methods of meta-analysis.* Thousand Oaks, CA: Sage.

Jost, J. T., Glaser, J., Kruglanski, A. W., & Sulloway, F. J. (2003). Political conservatism as motivated social cognition. *Psychological Bulletin, 129,* 339–375. doi:10.1037/0033-2909.129.3.339

Kirkman, B. L., Chen, G., Farh, J.-L., Chen, Z. X., & Lowe, K. B. (2009). Individual power distance orientation and follower reactions to transformational leaders: A cross-level, cross-cultural examination. *Academy of Management Journal, 52,* 744–764. doi:10.5465/AMJ.2009.43669971

Lytle, A. L., Brett, J. M., Barsness, Z. I., Tinsley, C. H., & Janssens, M. (1995). A paradigm for confirmatory cross-cultural research in organizational-behavior. *Research in Organizational Behavior, 17,* 167–214.

Marsella, A. J., Dubanoski, J., Hamada, W. C., & Morse, H. (2000). The measurement of personality across cultures: Historical, conceptual, and methodological issues and considerations. *American Behavioral Scientist, 44*, 41–62. doi:10.1177/00027640021956080

McCrae, R. R. (2001). Trait psychology and culture: Exploring intercultural comparisons. *Journal of Personality, 69*, 819–846. doi:10.1111/1467-6494.696166

Newenham-Kahindi, A. (2009). The transfer of Ubuntu and Indaba business models abroad: A case of South African multinational banks and telecommunication services in Tanzania. *International Journal of Cross-Cultural Management, 9*, 87–108. doi:10.1177/1470595808101157

Nye, C. D., & Drasgow, F. (2011). Effect size indices for analyses of measurement equivalence: Understanding the practical importance of differences between groups. *Journal of Applied Psychology.* Advance online publication. doi: 10.1037/a0022955.

Oh, I.-S. (2009). *The five-factor model of personality and job performance in East Asia: A cross-cultural validity generalization study.* Unpublished doctoral dissertation, University of Iowa, Iowa City.

Ones, D. S., & Viswesvaran, C. (1997). Personality determinants in the prediction of aspects of expatriate job success. In D. M. Saunders (Ed.), *New approaches to employee management* (Vol. 4, pp. 63–92). Greenwich, CT: JAI Press.

Ones, D. S., & Viswesvaran, C. (1999). Relative importance of personality dimensions for expatriate selection: A policy capturing study. *Human Performance, 12*, 275–294.

Oyserman, D., Coon, H. M., & Kemmelmeier, M. (2002). Rethinking individualism and collectivism: Evaluation of theoretical assumptions and meta-analyses. *Psychological Bulletin, 128*, 3–72. doi:10.1037/0033-2909.128.1.3

Quiñones-Vidal, E., López-García, J. J., Peñaranda-Ortega, M., & Tortosa-Gil, F. (2004). The nature of social and personality psychology as reflected in JPSP, 1965–2000. *Journal of Personality and Social Psychology, 86*, 435–452. doi:10.1037/0022-3514.86.3.435

Rahim, M. A., Psenicka, C., Polychroniou, P., Zhao, J.-H., Yu, C.-S., Chan, K. A., . . . van Wyk, R. (2002). A model of emotional intelligence and conflict management strategies: A study in seven countries. *The International Journal of Organizational Analysis, 10*, 302–326. doi:10.1108/eb028955

Salgado, J. F. (1997). The five-factor model of personality and job performance in the European Community. *Journal of Applied Psychology, 82*, 30–43. doi:10.1037/0021-9010.82.1.30

Salgado, J. F., & Anderson, N. (2003). Validity generalization of GMA tests across countries in the European Community. *European Journal of Work and Organizational Psychology, 12*, 1–17. doi:10.1080/13594320244000292

Salgado, J. F., Anderson, N., Moscoso, S., Bertua, C., & de Fruyt, F. (2003). International validity generalization of GMA and cognitive abilities: A European Community meta-analysis. *Personnel Psychology, 56*, 573–605. doi:10.1111/j.1744-6570.2003.tb00751.x

Salgado, J. F., Anderson, N., Moscoso, S., Bertua, C., de Fruyt, F., & Rolland, J. P. (2003). A meta-analytic study of general mental ability validity for different occupations in the European Community. *Journal of Applied Psychology, 88,* 1068–1081. doi:10.1037/0021-9010.88.6.1068

Sawang, S., Oei, T. P. S., & Goh, Y. W. (2006). Are country and culture values interchangeable? A case example using occupational stress and coping. *International Journal of Cross-Cultural Management, 6,* 205–219. doi:10.1177/1470595806066330

Schmidt, F. L. (2010). Detecting and correcting the lies that data tell. *Perspectives on Psychological Science, 5,* 233–242. doi:10.1177/1745691610369339

Schmidt, F. L., & Hunter, J. E. (1977). Development of a general solution to the problem of validity generalization. *Journal of Applied Psychology, 62,* 529–540. doi:10.1037/0021-9010.62.5.529

Schmidt, F. L., & Oh, I.-S. (2011). *Second-order meta-analysis: Statistical methods and illustrative applications.* Manuscript submitted for publication.

Shen, W., Kiger, T. B., Davis, S. E., Rasch, R. L., Simon, K. M., & Ones, D. S. (2011). Samples in applied psychology: Over a decade of research in review. *Journal of Applied Psychology.* Advance online publication. doi: 2010.1037/a0023322.

Spector, P. E. (1988). Development of the Work Locus of Control Scale. *Journal of Occupational Psychology, 61,* 335–340. doi:10.1111/j.2044-8325.1988.tb00470.x

Spector, P. E., Cooper, C. L., Sanchez, J. I., O'Driscoll, M., Sparks, K., Bernin, P., . . . Yu, S. (2001). Do national levels of individualism and internal locus of control relate to well-being: An ecological-level international study. *Journal of Organizational Behavior, 22,* 815–832. doi:10.1002/job.118

Spector, P. E., Cooper, C. L., Sanchez, J. I., O'Driscoll, M., Sparks, K., Bernin, P., . . . Yu, S. (2002). Locus of control and well-being at work: How generalizable are Western findings? *Academy of Management Journal, 45,* 453–466. doi:10.2307/3069359

Triandis, H. C. (1994). Cross-cultural industrial and organizational psychology. In H. C. Triandis, M. D. Dunnette, & L. M. Hough (Eds.), *Handbook of industrial and organizational psychology* (Vol. 4, pp. 103–172). Palo Alto, CA: Consulting Psychologists Press.

van de Vijver, F. J. R., & Leung, K. (2000). Methodological issues in psychological research on culture. *Journal of Cross-Cultural Psychology, 31,* 33–51. doi:10.1177/0022022100031001004

van de Vijver, F. J. R., & Leung, K. (2001). Personality in cultural context: Methodological issues. *Journal of Personality, 69,* 1007–1031. doi:10.1111/1467-6494.696173

Wasti, S. A., Bergman, M. E., Glomb, T. M., & Drasgow, F. (2000). Test of the cross-cultural generalizability of a model of sexual harassment. *Journal of Applied Psychology, 85,* 766–778. doi:10.1037/0021-9010.85.5.766

Weingarten, K. (2000). Witnessing, wonder, and hope. *Family Process, 39,* 389–402. doi:10.1111/j.1545-5300.2000.39401.x

# 5

# ADMINISTRATIVE, MEASUREMENT, AND SAMPLING ISSUES IN LARGE-SCALE CROSS-NATIONAL RESEARCH: UN OR NATO APPROACH?

JUAN I. SANCHEZ AND PAUL E. SPECTOR

Not every organizational theory developed in English-speaking countries can be readily transferred to other cultural settings (Boyacigiller & Adler, 1991; Church & Lonner, 1998; Maruyama, 1984; Triandis, 1994a). The cross-cultural transferability of a given organizational theory depends on the researcher's ability to disentangle theoretical elements that are culture general from those that are culture specific (often referred to as the *etic–emic distinction;* Berry, 1969). However, researchers' ability to draw reasonable inferences about culture effects is bounded by sampling and measurement artifacts potentially confounded with culture.

This chapter describes a series of lessons learned in two large-scale studies that were part of a cross-cultural/cross-national (CC/CN) research project, the Collaborative International Study of Managerial Stress (CISMS), in which both of us have participated. Initiated in 1995 by Cary L. Cooper, Manchester Institute of Science and Technology, England, and Paul E. Spector, University of South Florida, CISMS brought together job stress researchers from around the world to collect data with the same instruments in their own countries. Data were then combined to explore country differences. The initial study targeted sources of job stress and personality in managers, and it resulted in numerous publications in a variety of refereed journals (e.g., Sanchez, Spector,

& Cooper, 2000; Spector, Cooper, Sanchez, O'Driscoll, et al., 2002; Spector et al., 2001). CISMS2 focused on work–family issues. In addition to Cooper and Spector, it is headed by Steven Poelmans, Instituto de Estudios Superiores de la Empresa [Institute of Higher Business Studies] Business School, University of Navarra, Spain; Tammy Allen, University of South Florida; Laurent Lapierre, University of Ottawa, Canada; Michael O'Driscoll, University of Waikato, New Zealand; and Juan I. Sanchez, Florida International University. In neither phase of CISMS did the central team have external grant support for the project, although in some cases the individual country research partners supported their own data collection through grants.

Administrative and methodological choices in CC/CN studies are closely interrelated because the manner in which a study is managed often determines the researchers' ability to minimize the potential confounds between culture and third variables that plague CC/CN research. Because such confounds grow exponentially as new countries are added to the study, project administration can be a particularly challenging issue in large-scale CC/CN studies.

In the next sections, we first describe the administrative choices that we made in our large-scale project; we argue that these choices increased our ability to cope with potential confounds that threaten this type of study, facilitated an adequate progression of the research program, and—perhaps more important—resulted in a number of contributions to the literature. We describe our approach, which is accurately described as a relatively centralized one, to the administration of these studies, and contrast it with a less centralized one. Mirroring the difference between a military, possibly more centralized international organization and a civilian, more decentralized organization, we have tongue-in-cheek labeled these as the "NATO" and the "UN" approaches, respectively. Next, we discuss some of the most severe confounds between culture and third variables that threaten these large-scale CC/CN investigations, and we provide a series of recommendations or lessons learned from our experience that we used to minimize such threats to the validity of our studies.

## ADMINISTRATIVE ISSUES IN CROSS-CULTURAL/ CROSS-NATIONAL RESEARCH

In this section, we focus on three specific aspects of the CISMS administration: selection of countries and researchers, prestudy contract, and leadership model. In explaining these aspects of our administrative approach, we do not wish to imply that ours is the best approach, or even better than other approaches; however, we believe that the relatively large number of published works that has resulted from this CN/CC work to date is partly determined by our choices regarding the administration of the project, and therefore, we believe that it is fair to characterize it as a fairly effective model to conduct large-scale CN/CC research. Nevertheless, a more decentralized approach might be more appropriate when researchers are interested in delving deeper into the emic aspects of each country, even though such a culturally tailored approach would create a new set of issues related to standardization of measures and methods, which may also create additional confounds in cross-country comparisons.

## Selection of Researchers

The creation of a central team of seasoned researchers was in our opinion instrumental to the success of CISMS. This project proceeded in two independent phases conducted several years apart. We applied lessons from the first phase to refine our administrative approach in the second phase. In both cases, we began with a central team of researchers who participated in the choice of scales to be included in the survey, the design of the study, the formulation of broad research goals and objectives, and the writing of papers that addressed the objectives of the study. The second, noncentral group of research collaborators primarily handled data collection in a specific country using a protocol provided by the central team. In some cases, these individuals produced papers that involved smaller scale comparisons among subsets of countries, or they conducted smaller scale follow-up studies that involved their own countries.

All members of the central team knew each other relatively well and had considerable contact throughout the project. Subsets of this group had collaborated with one another in the past. In addition, this team of researchers spanned North America, Europe, and Asia. We believe that the culture of trust and the history of prior collaboration that existed among the central team of researchers was a key success factor. The fact that the studies were designed to meet various research agendas simultaneously also prevented conflict, as each researcher had a chance to include those specific variables in which he or she were particularly interested. Counting on well-seasoned researchers also helped smooth the manuscript preparation process, as all researchers in the central team were capable of contributing valuable insights and sharing feedback with each other, especially during the often delicate revise-and-resubmit stage. Still another noteworthy benefit derived from working with experienced and committed researchers was the fact that the primary author of a given manuscript received prompt feedback, typically within a few days and in most cases within a week, from virtually every member of the central team. Such feedback was particularly helpful when coauthors coincided on raising similar concerns. This kind of concordance was interpreted as a clear sign that the manuscript needed to be revised accordingly, because external reviewers would most likely raise the same concerns. In a way, operating within this central team of researchers provided a simulated editorial review process of the kind used in refereed journals but with a larger group of reviewers than the standard of two or three reviewers per submission used by most journals. Undoubtedly, all of these internal reviewers were highly motivated to see the manuscript published, which cannot always be said about external reviewers.

## Prestudy Contract

Because the rules for participation and authorship were clearly delineated up front, CISMS was relatively easy to manage. Before becoming part of the team, all participating researchers agreed to a contract, or set of written rules that specified the obligations and rights of each participant. Potential disputes or conflict within the team were prevented by the rules specifying authorship. Each participating researcher agreed to have their manuscripts reviewed by all the members of the central team and to include their names as coauthors in any resulting manuscripts after incorporating their feedback into the manuscript. The order of authorship was determined according to effort and contribution and, when these were deemed similar in magnitude, by alphabetical order. Partners who were not part of the central team were treated similarly to the central team members. These partners were also invited to have input into papers before they were submitted, although generally this occurred once papers were completed by the central team but prior to submission. Thus they were able to have as much input as they wished, with some being far more active than others in this regard.

## Leadership Model

The impetus for CISMS emanated primarily from two researchers, Paul E. Spector in the United States and Cary L. Cooper in the United Kingdom. They played a critical role as the main liaisons behind the study and were instrumental in recruiting other researchers. Without their ample network of academic contacts in a variety of countries, our large-scale CC/CN studies would not have been possible. Each member of the central team was also instrumental in recruiting other researchers in geographical areas where they enjoyed academic and professional contacts (e.g., Latin America, Eastern Europe). There were times when progress in data collection within specific locations turned out to be slow or problematic. These were dealt with on a case-by-case basis. The issues encountered ran the gamut. For instance, we had a participating researcher from Iran, who upon learning that the study included data from Israel, decided to withdraw from the study, alleging safety concerns. In addition, researchers from mainland China objected to the treatment of Taiwan as a separate nation; this issue was resolved by clarifying that our study dealt with different nations, territories, or both, and as a result, the term *territory* was included in several manuscript titles in lieu of the term *country*. All participating researchers were asked to send the data in electronic form to the central team, but in some cases they sent the questionnaires, and the data were entered by the central team. Templates and instructions regarding data entry were provided to all participating researchers. When issues or questions about the data arose during data entry, the central team was consulted.

## MEASUREMENT AND SAMPLING ISSUES IN CROSS-CULTURAL/ CROSS-NATIONAL RESEARCH

As mentioned, certainty regarding cultural effects in organizational research depends on the extent to which confounds and third-variable effects can be ruled out or at least minimized. These threats are even more relevant in large-scale than in small-scale CC/CN studies because as the number of countries increases, the potential for confounds increases too. In this section, we focus on the different types of confounds that may diminish the researchers' certainty regarding cultural effects. Because large-scale CC/CN studies often require translations of the same measure to a large number of foreign languages, we begin with a discussion of measurement equivalence, followed by discussions of construct and then sample equivalence. Throughout our exposition, we provide a series of suggestions to cope with these potential threats to the validity of CC/CN studies.

### Measurement Equivalence Between Translated Instruments

The Sapir–Whorf, or Whorfian, hypothesis (Werner & Campbell, 1970) conceives language as a filter between individuals and the objective reality that surrounds them. According to this hypothesis, language filters the evaluative, connotative, and affective meaning of scale items, thereby preventing comparisons between linguistically different groups. This notion of language as an insurmountable obstacle in the way of CC/CN comparisons, however, has not been shared by a majority of researchers, who have developed various approaches to study cultural differences despite linguistic differences.

Before any observed differences are attributed to culture as opposed to language, researchers need to rule out linguistic biases in their measures

(Berry, 1969; Brislin, 1986; Geisinger, 1994; Lytle, Brett, Barsness, Tinsley, & Janssens, 1995; Riordan & Vandenberg, 1994; Spirrison & Choi, 1998). The need to sort out linguistic from cultural effects arises from the fact that culture and language are typically confounded, because individuals from different cultures often speak different languages.

Because most of the available research instruments were originally developed using the English language and in countries that are culturally similar (e.g., Canada and the United States), using these instruments within such a limited set of relatively homogeneous countries may not pose serious problems of measurement equivalence. Participants will tend to interpret the words and phrases in each item similarly across countries for the most part. However, the more different the culture, even within the English-speaking world, the less likely it is that interpretations will remain exact (Liu, Borg, & Spector, 2004). A participant from India, for example, might not see an item as representing the exact same degree of the construct than an Australian counterpart. Thus, comparing sample means becomes problematic, because researchers cannot be certain that the degree of the construct represented by the scale values associated with each item is similarly calibrated across countries.

When researchers cross languages, issues of measurement equivalence worsen. English is a language that admits flexible uses of words and phrases. For example, nouns can be easily transformed into verbs (e.g., once there is a *Google*, it does not take long for people to begin *Googling*) or even into adjectives by simply adding a suffix to them. With less morphologically flexible languages, expressing the same idea may require a lengthier stream of words that, in the English language, are condensed into a single term. In the case of a scale anchor, for instance, an exact match that reflects the same scale value might not exist. Even a very good translation may fail to produce an item that closely matches the degree of extremity represented in the original, even though the basic idea underlying the translated item remains the same.

Back-translation procedures have become a widely accepted standard in cross-cultural research to rule out linguistic biases such as those inherent in poorly translated instruments (Brislin, 1986). Back-translation involves translating the measure to the target language first, and then independently translating it back to the source language and comparing the two same language versions to ascertain linguistic problems in the translation. Nevertheless, back-translations do not necessarily guarantee measurement equivalence. For instance, back-translators share knowledge that may lead them to consider terms as if they were synonyms whereas respondents do not see them that way (e.g., *simpático* in Spanish and *friendly* in English may not always mean the same thing, but translators may see them that way because of their learned semantic connection between the two languages).

Many organizational scales ask respondents to appraise tangible conditions of their work environment, such as the extent to which environmental factors are a source of stress (e.g., Lazarus, 1966). Therefore, there may be between-cultures variation in interpretations of the degree of the focal construct represented by an item. Such differing interpretations in the degree of the construct represented by the item may result in flawed attributions of observed differences to culture rather than faulty instruments. Thus, a back-translation might be technically correct, but that does not guarantee that items are sufficiently equivalent for mean comparisons. Even if the same construct is assessed, the different language versions may not be equivalently calibrated. To illustrate this point, consider an item that reads "I love my job." A linguistically correct Spanish translation would be "Yo amo mi trabajo." However, the verb *amar* ("to love") in Spanish is usually confined to people, and it is seldom, if ever, used to refer to things or social constructs such as a job. Thus, monolingual Spanish speakers might find this item puzzling, strange, or even amusing, thus possibly distorting their response over what is intended.

Still another potential problem of back-translations is that they may retain the grammar and idiomatic expressions of the source language, which may be easy to back-translate but may not have the same meaning to monolinguals in the target language. For example, an item developed for a Chinese scale (i.e., "One should not be afraid of the change of heavens"), which measured beliefs of control in China, was successfully back-translated from English to Chinese, but it obviously lacks unambiguous meaning for English-speaking monolinguals (Siu & Cooper, 1998).

The potential for measurement nonequivalence may be exacerbated by the use of closed-ended scales, which are widely used in organizational research. Using such scales, research participants respond to items varying along the continuum of interest. However, some items are more extreme than others, and such differences affect participant responses (Spector, Van Katwyk, Brannick, & Chen, 1997). For example, an individual who agrees with an item, "I am sometimes tense at work," will not necessarily endorse a more extremely worded item such as "I sometimes experience panic at work." The reason is that even though both items reflect anxiety, they symbolize different degrees of the anxiety construct. Individuals or groups who answer the same sets of items can be compared to determine their relative standing on the underlying construct. However, if different samples of individuals interpret the items differently, or if translations modify the extremity to which the item expresses the construct, sample comparisons can be contaminated. Such differences in the extremity or calibration of the items can occur even when back-translation suggests equivalent meanings.

Still another source of potential nonequivalence in closed-ended scales is found in the Likert-type anchors used in many organizational scales. Translators will admit that finding equivalent anchors for the extreme points of the scale is relatively easy, but finding equivalent anchors for the midpoints can be challenging. For instance, a suitable Spanish translation of *very much agree* would be *muy de acuerdo*, but translating the anchor *agree slightly* is not similarly straightforward because the exact degree conveyed by the word *slightly* may differ from language to language (just consider how different the amount of time that needs to pass beyond the previously designated time for an individual or an event to be "slightly late" is in different cultures).

## Disentangling Culture and Language Effects

We have argued that back-translation does not guarantee the absence of language and other extraneous variables on cross-cultural comparisons. For this reason, research designs that either analyze or control extraneous variables may be used to control such threats. These designs include some or all of the following features: (a) between-participants comparisons across languages that hold culture constant, such as comparing the English and French versions of a measure using samples from the same nation (e.g., Canadians; Candell & Hulin, 1986); (b) between-participants comparisons across cultures holding language constant, such as comparing U.S. versus Australian samples or Spaniards versus Mexicans (Ryan, Chan, Ployhart, & Slade, 1999); and (c) within-participant comparisons of responses in different languages provided by bilinguals, such as having bilingual respondents complete an English and a Spanish version of the same measure (Hulin, Drasgow, & Komocar, 1982; Katerberg, Smith, & Hoy, 1977; Rybowiak, Garst, Frese, & Batinic, 1999).

None of these approaches, however, is free of limitations. First, between-participants comparisons across languages that attempt to hold culture constant may not succeed, because of response or self-selection bias. Consider, for instance, the case of a sample of 1,931 Canadians enlisted in the Canadian Armed Forces surveyed by Candell and Hulin (1986). Among 596 participants who identified French as their primary language, 235 chose to complete the English version of a survey. It is likely that the 235 French Canadians who responded in English were more acculturated to the patterns of English-speaking Canada than those who chose the French version. Therefore, it is reasonable to argue that culture was in part confounded with language in this comparison between two groups of French Canadians.

Second, between-participants comparisons across cultures that hold language constant (e.g., Argentina vs. Mexico, Brazil vs. Portugal) may be still influenced by sample differences in third variables that are often confounded with nation. For instance, a notary public typically enjoys a much higher social status in Europe and in Latin America than in the United States, and therefore comparing notaries public across countries may yield differences associated with third variable effects rather than with culture.

Finally, within-participant comparisons that use multilinguals in a repeated measures design do not control for the fact that multilinguals may differ from monolinguals both linguistically and culturally. That is, those who master foreign languages tend to also be bicultural because they were exposed to the cultures of the countries in which such languages are spoken, and therefore they may process and interpret the translated version differently than monolinguals (Hong, Morris, Chiu, & Benet-Martinez, 2000).

Let us now turn to possible strategies that can help in ruling out rival hypotheses arising from the nonequivalence between translated instruments across countries. Note that this potential problem is aggravated by the fact that translation and back-translation often proceed independently of measurement criteria. That is, researchers and translators seldom work together, and therefore psychometric criteria are seldom used to decide when a back-translated scale is sufficiently close to the original version. Instead, this decision is usually left to the translators' professional judgment. The two processes (i.e., back-translation and determination of measurement equivalence) do not feed each other, because translators are seldom apprised of the statistical consequences of their specific translation choices, so that they can modify their translations accordingly.

### Bilingualism Versus Biculturalism of Translators

Although translators may be linguistically competent, their ability to ascertain cultural nuances in the manifestation of a given construct across cultures may be limited. We believe that translators should be carefully selected according to not only their linguistic competence but also to the extent to which they are truly bicultural individuals who are familiar with the subtleties inherent in the ways in which individuals in the two cultures express their attitudes and emotions. In some cases, a linguistically imperfect translation may provide better psychological equivalence than a linguistically perfect one. Let us offer an example of what we mean here. The Spanish expression *¿Como andas?*—which literally means "How do you walk?"—is used in some Spanish-speaking nations to mean "How are you?" Linguistically competent Spanish–English translators do not always realize this and other colloquial usages of certain phrases, thereby rendering a technically correct but nonequivalent translation. Therefore, biculturalism seems more important than even the most impressive academic credentials of bilingual competence for translators in charge of producing equivalently calibrated instruments.

*Studies Involving Monolinguals*

Perhaps the easiest way to explore measurement equivalence is to administer a given scale to monolinguals across different countries. Likely, the scale was developed in one country in a single language, and translation (and back-translation) will be needed for at least some countries. The psychometric properties of the scale across countries can be compared with test for equivalence, and a number of alternatives exist for this purpose. Perhaps the simplest test would be to compare the internal consistencies of the scale across samples. Although this is not a very conclusive test, failure to maintain internal consistency reliability is an early sign that the scale is not functioning well. More complex approaches are often preferred, including those based on structural equation modeling (SEM) and item response theory (IRT). SEM can be used to compare the item variances and covariances across samples to see whether the underlying factor structure of a scale is equivalent (Bollen, 1989; Byrne, 1994; Byrne, Shavelson, & Muthén, 1989; Ghorpade, Hattrup, & Lackritz, 1999; Schaffer & Riordan, 2003; van de Vijver & Leung, 1997; Vandenberg & Lance, 2000). IRT methods can be used to compare item responses for each item across samples from different countries (Raju, Laffitte, & Byrne, 2002). Although both approaches provide a great deal more information than internal consistency analyses, they do not guarantee that scales have equivalent meaning.

*Studies Involving Bilinguals*

Studies involving bilinguals are rare because large samples of bilinguals are not readily available. Although using bilinguals is not a substitute for a rigorous back-translation, it permits a within-participant design that uses a different language in each administration, thereby holding constant the aforementioned extraneous variables that permeate between-participants designs.

Two sets of issues have been raised in relation to the study of bilinguals: (a) issues related to research design and (b) issues related to the manner in which bilinguals process information. The first design-related issue involves the need to address practice effects. *Practice effects* refer to the change in scores obtained in the second administration brought about by taking the test more than once. In studies using bilinguals who take the same measure in two languages, one can gauge practice effects by adding a control group for which the focal measure is also administered twice, but in the same language. Differences across the two administrations index the practice effect.

Order effects in the presentation of the two versions of the same measure are also a potential threat. For instance, individuals may be asked to complete the original English version first, and then they may be asked to complete the Spanish version at a later point in time. Even if the Spanish translation is faulty, respondents may still recall the English version and answer accordingly. Counterbalancing the order of language presentation can remedy this problem.

Still another variable that has remained uncontrolled in research designs involving bilinguals is language proficiency. Differences in the extent to which respondents master either the source or the target language may account for the differences between the two versions of a survey. In the absence of information regarding language mastery, such differences may be erroneously attributed to linguistic biases.

The manner in which bilinguals process information has also been a controversial topic. Some argue that even though responses by bilinguals are comparable across the two languages, such a pattern misleadingly underestimates the number of biased items encountered when comparing monolingual samples (Hulin et al., 1982). Candell and Hulin (1986) argued that bilinguals may use their knowledge of the source language when responding to a translated survey, hence assuming that certain words have equivalent meanings even though they may not. As Hulin (1987) pointed out, *amigo*, *friend*, and *tovarish* are not always synonyms, but bilinguals sharing a number of rules of thumb may interpret them similarly, whereas monolinguals see unique meaning in each one of them.

A second argument regarding how bilinguals process information claims that they adapt to the culture associated with the language used in the measure, so that the same bilingual respondent would give different answers to the two versions of the same measure. This effect has been labeled *cultural accommodation* (Bond & Yang, 1982). Cultural accommodation implies Whorfian thinking about language, which is seen as an evolved cultural pattern intrinsically linked to socialization (Bandura, 1986). Under this approach, the use of a specific language will inevitably lead to culturally biased responses. For example, Ralston, Cunniff, and Gustafson (1995) found differences between bilingual (i.e., Chinese and English) managers in Hong Kong. Specifically, managers using the English version of an attitudinal survey scored higher on important Western values than those answering the Chinese version. The latter, in turn, scored higher on important Eastern values than those using the English version. However, given the high level of power distance in the Chinese culture, if employed students are charged with "snowballing" these surveys to their supervisors, it is conceivable that they might choose to accommodate their superiors' language preference for a Chinese version. In other words, culture and survey version may be partly confounded because those who answer the English version may be more Western-oriented than those who answer the Chinese one.

Between-groups designs do not lend themselves to a true test of the cultural accommodation hypothesis, whose prediction that the same individual would change his or her responses to accommodate the survey's language demands a within-group design. An example of a study that used such a within-participant design was Rybowiak et al. (1999). They found generally higher mean scores in the Dutch than in the English version of their Error Orientation Questionnaire. Rybowiak et al.'s results, however, might have been explained by differences in language proficiency between the two languages, because their Dutch respondents might have been more proficient in their native tongue than in English. It is also possible that the order of scale presentation and the practice effects inherent in any retest might have been confounded with the language effects in their study.

Hulin and Mayer (1986) argued that the Whorfian thinking implied in the cultural accommodation hypothesis seems unlikely when comparing similar languages. That is, although it can be argued that languages such as Cantonese and English may create somewhat discrepant mental worlds that interfere with cross-language comparisons, English has its roots in the larger group of Indo-European languages that also involves the majority of the Western languages. Therefore, English shares at least basic semantic structures with many other languages such as German, and even with Romance languages such as French, Italian, or Spanish.

A key design feature that has been largely neglected in prior research involving bilinguals is the use of relatively long time frames of at least 2 or 3 months, so that participants are unlikely to recall their responses to the first administration. In addition, control for the effects of language proficiency through using bilinguals with similar levels of reading comprehension in both the source and the target language is recommended. For instance, studies of bilinguals whose command of the second language is limited may suggest language effects, but we counter that such effects are more parsimoniously explained by the participants' limited language proficiency.

Counterbalancing and/or analyzing the order of language administration, so that half of the participants receive the English version first and the other half receive the foreign language version first, also helps assess language effects. In other words, manipulating the language order helps rule out that bilinguals' recall of the source (e.g., English) version affects their responses to the target (e.g., Spanish) version.

The cultural accommodation hypothesis predicts that when bilinguals respond to a measurement instrument, the language in which the instrument is taken influences their responses. This type of accommodation effects have been reported when switching between rather different languages, such as English and Chinese (Ralston et al., 1995), but also between more similar languages, such as Dutch and English (Rybowiak et al., 1999). Indeed, when administering the same measure to Dutch bilinguals, the Dutch version tended to yield somewhat higher mean scores, but patterns of correlations with other variables were similar between the two language versions. The mean differences might have been caused by subtle translation differences (both Dutch and English language versions were translated from the original German questionnaire). Smaller differences between languages might be obtained among samples that are bicultural in addition to being bilingual; that is, when participants are used to employing both languages in their interactions with native speakers on a daily basis more so than the Dutch participants were in the Rybowiak et al.'s sample.

Some argue that comparing bilinguals' responses to those from monolinguals overlooks the fact that bilinguals process semantic information differently. There is even brain imaging and eyetracking evidence suggesting different brain structures and centers of activation when processing one's first versus second language (Marian, Spivey, & Hirsch, 2003). However, we would counter that virtually any sample of monolinguals is likely to differ from a sample of bilinguals in not only linguistic but also cultural factors. That is, monolinguals do not typically share the dual familiarity with either culture that bilingual participants typically enjoy. Therefore, comparing bilinguals and monolinguals' answers makes it easier to disentangle potential confounds between language and culture effects.

We expect that research using bilinguals will be more common in the future. That is, worldwide access to the same information through the Internet is, in our opinion, a factor with already visible results that include larger numbers of people who not only understand English but also are familiar with cultural nuances elsewhere. Fluency in a foreign language, however, should not be assumed to imply that the individual is familiar with the culture associated with such foreign language.

**Response Biases**

An additional confound in CC/CN research is the potential for culture/ national differences in response biases or tendencies (Triandis, 1994b; van de Vijver & Leung, 1997). Cheung and Rensvold (2000) suggested that culture influences how individuals use rating scales, especially in regard to the extent to which people either prefer or avoid extreme responses. These tendencies may be complex, however, as Iwata et al. (1998) found that Japanese were less likely than Americans to use extreme responses for positively worded depression items, but there were no differences for negatively worded items. Thus, Japanese avoided reporting extreme positive feelings more so than Americans, but this difference did not exist for extreme negative feelings.

These cultural response tendencies might go beyond how people use response choices in rating scales. Ross (2004) discussed how people in some countries might be more apt to respond in accordance to what they believe the researcher wants, thus being more subject to experimenter effects. This suggests that care must be taken, not only in the translation of scales, but in how instructions are phrased and the mode of presentation. It might not be enough to just standardize procedures, as people in certain cultures might be more inclined to pick up on certain instructions than others.

Response biases and tendencies can make it difficult to compare means across groups. Thus, a given score might not reflect the same level of a construct across people in different groups. Of course, it is not clear than the same score means the same thing between two people within the same group, but the problem is exacerbated when group (e.g., country) is confounded with response tendency. Furthermore, it is not necessarily the case that response tendency differences within a group are equivalent across all scales or even all items within a scale, as shown by Iwata et al. (1998). Finally, researchers cannot be certain that a given difference can be attributable to response tendencies just because one group usually scores higher or lower than others. In other words, do the Japanese in the Iwata et al. study avoid extreme positive reports because of cultural modesty tendencies, or do Japanese accurately report that they experience less positive affect than Americans? The possibility that observed differences might or might not be accounted for by response biases makes it difficult to find simple solutions to this problem.

### Construct Equivalence in Cross-Cultural/Cross-National Research

Measurement equivalence is not a panacea in cross-cultural research. Indeed, there is a theoretically more fundamental issue in large-scale CC/CN research studies than measurement equivalence. That is, the underlying construct of interest may not be equivalent across countries and/or cultures. In other words, a given construct might manifest itself differently across countries or cultures, so that different items would be needed to capture it adequately (Lonner, 1990). This is an important and often forgotten point in CC/CN research; namely, that the same construct can have quite different behavioral manifestations across countries (Lonner, 1990).

As a result, an item that represents a typical behavioral manifestation of the construct in country X may not capture the idiosyncratic way in which the same construct is behaviorally manifested in country Y. Consider, for instance, a comparison of the covariance structures of Spector's (1988) Work Locus of Control Scale between a UK and a Spanish sample (Sanchez, Spector, & Cooper, 2006). An inspection of the correlation matrix of the Spanish sample revealed that the item "If you know what you want out of a job, you can find a job that gives it to you" had practically null correlations with other scale items (median $r = .10$), whereas in the United Kingdom, this item had larger correlations with other items in the scale (median $r = .23$). This differential item functioning should not be surprising to anyone familiar with the high level of unemployment in Spain at the time, which led those countries of the European Union. Thus, "internals" (individuals who believe they can generally control things at work) in Spain were understandably less confident about their ability to find a fulfilling job than were internals in the United Kingdom, where the unemployment rate was lower.

The source scales are often developed in English according to theories developed in English-speaking countries, and therefore, they may fail to capture the nuances of how the focal constructs are manifested in cultures elsewhere (Maruyama, 1984; Weisz, Rothbaum, & Blackburn, 1984). That is, even if a construct exists across countries, its behavioral manifestations could vary considerably (Lonner, 1990). As a result of not being fully aware of the manner in which constructs are manifested across cultures, researchers may build in their cultural biases into the definition and operationalization of constructs (Boyacigiller & Adler, 1991). The answer to whether constructs have different cultural manifestations awaits much-needed research regarding how measures of such constructs developed in other languages fare when they are translated into English (e.g., Spector, Sanchez, Siu, Salgado, & Ma, 2004).

An example of such different behavioral manifestations of the same construct is the type and the degree of the reactions to working conditions across cultures. An aspect of the work environment that might be a powerful stressor for people in one country might not be so for people in a different country. For example, direct disagreements among employees might be more likely to be perceived as interpersonal conflict among Chinese, for whom saving face and group harmony are an important value, than among Americans, who are less sensitive to direct confrontation. In an analysis of stressful work incidents, Liu (2003) found that Americans were more likely to have direct conflicts with others, whereas Chinese were more likely to have indirect conflicts. A different study reported that when asked to describe a stressful incident at work, Americans but not Indians reported instances of lack of control and work overload, whereas Indians but not Americans reported instances of lack of structure and situational constraints (Narayanan, Menon, & Spector, 1999). Most notably, the most frequently cited stressor was different—opposite, in fact—for Americans and Indians (i.e., too little control and too little direction, respectively). This finding suggests the presence of rather different reactions to issues of work autonomy between samples from the two countries, thereby questioning whether the same score reflects the same degree of the underlying construct in each country.

Unfortunately, the theoretically more important notion of construct nonequivalence has received far less attention than the statistical question of measurement nonequivalence. Some of the same approaches can be used to deal with both, but establishing the construct validity of a scale among countries or cultures goes beyond establishing equivalent psychometric properties or equivalent calibration of scores. In our opinion, researchers who are concerned with construct equivalence should not obsess with covariance structure tests to the detriment of more substantive issues. To paraphrase Meehl (1971), statistical procedures are not automatic inference machines and should never replace the researchers' judgment.

In addition, covariance structure tests that rely on large sample sizes appear to be overly sensitive to unique item variance. For instance, Sanchez et al. (2006) spotted measurement nonequivalence even when comparing two administrations, just 3 weeks apart, of the same measure to the same participants and in the same language. If we were to apply the same tests of measurement equivalence that are expected from cross-cultural studies to monocultural research, we are guessing that many studies involving several administrations of the same measure would never pass them.

Establishing construct equivalence clearly goes beyond running covariance structure tests. It demands an accumulation of evidence supporting the interpretation of the construct underlying the measure. For scale development in a single country or culture, this means among other things compiling data to explore the nomological network of relationships of a given scale with other variables. In CC/CN research, this can be more complex, as it is not a foregone conclusion that nomological networks are unaffected by cultural or national differences, and therefore theories of a construct might differ across locations. Therefore, CC/CN research still faces the challenge of simultaneously assessing the equivalence of constructs, of measures, and of theories.

Much CC/CN research largely ignores issues of construct equivalence because it tends to rely on measures that are developed in a single country and to export them elsewhere. Even if the items are successfully translated, there exists the possibility that certain items do not adequately gauge the manner in which the construct is expressed universally because the scale might have been developed ethnocentrically. Multicultural scale development (MCSD) represents an alternative procedure to help minimize ethnocentrism in scale development. MCSD involves enlisting researchers from multiple countries and letting them influence the scale development from its inception.

MCSD begins by assembling a diverse team of research partners from culturally distinct countries. The team then goes through a multistage procedure for scale development that is more complex than the typical process. First, a clear definition of the construct of interest is agreed on so that everyone has a similar understanding of what the items should reflect. Second, each team member independently formulates scale items. Third, the items are mixed up and compiled into a questionnaire that is administered to a pilot sample. This can be done initially in a single country, or it can be done in parallel in multiple countries. Item analysis or more complex analyses such as factor analysis can be applied to help select items for the final scale. Fourth, the final scale should be administered to samples in at least the countries of the research partners to verify its internal consistency reliability and similar underlying factor structure. Fifth, validation studies should be conducted in multiple countries, although it should be kept in mind that relationships between the construct of interest and other constructs might vary across culturally dissimilar countries.

Spector et al. (2004) used a similar approach to develop scales intended to capture cross-national manifestations of control beliefs. Partners from three countries (China, Spain, and the United States) each wrote items that were combined into an initial large item pool that included items written by all coauthors. The final scales were translated into Chinese, back-translated, and then administered to samples in Hong Kong, the People's Republic of China, and the United States. These scales maintained internal consistency reliability across samples, a finding that contrasts to prior studies in which U.S.-developed scales experienced a loss of internal consistency when administered to Chinese samples.

The procedure described above can be used as an initial step in CC/CN research to create scales with the potential to maintain construct equivalence across translation and national borders. It can also be used in combination with other approaches, such as within-participant bilingual studies, to explore how equivalent a scale truly is. A series of studies might be necessary to gain confidence that a scale can be used successfully internationally and that differences in results can be attributed primarily to cultural differences as opposed to measurement issues. This type of pilot-testing research may be critical in the measurement of constructs that require cross-cultural generalizations, such as cultural values, whose generalizability across nations has proven problematic (e.g., Spector, Cooper, Sanchez, Sparks, et al., 2002).

### Sample Equivalence Between Cultures

Still another source of potential confounds in large-scale CC/CN research lies in the availability of equivalent participant samples. Researchers sometimes end up comparing individuals who vary not only in country but also in demographics, such as occupation, income (relative to society), and status. Even within the same occupation, differences in other variables, such as pay, can masquerade as cultural differences (Bonache, Sanchez, & Zarraga-Oberty, 2009). Note, for instance, the differences in how people across the world perform the occupation of physician, ranging from high incomes, long hours, and huge patient loads in the United States to modest incomes, personalized attention, and 40-hour weeks in countries where medicine is socialized. Such differences challenge the assumption that simply because the samples in both countries involve physicians they are automatically "matched," thereby ruling out third factors and confounds. Indeed, often samples across countries cannot be matched on many extraneous variables, as perfect matches are nearly impossible because of wide variations in economic and social factors across countries.

For example, unlike the United States, there are countries such as China where state-owned rather than large private corporations dominate economic activity (Tsui, Schoonhoven, Meyer, Lau, & Milkovich, 2004). When researchers draw comparisons with countries where state-owned enterprises dominate the economic landscape, even matching for industry sector will not rid comparisons of selection bias, because organizations in the same sector (e.g., oil production and distribution) will still differ in meaningful ways, such as whether they are private or state-owned enterprises. Even samples of university students differ markedly across countries. In the United States a far greater proportion of the general population attends college than in countries where college attendance tends to be limited to the upper echelons of society or to a small proportion of students who excel in the public school system.

Matching should therefore proceed cautiously and only on variables likely to cause confounded results. Researchers should look carefully at economic (e.g., relative standard of living, economic system, and tax structure), political, and social factors, and to the greatest extent possible, samples should be matched. In addition, comparisons of multiple samples per country would be helpful. In regard to the physician example, one could have samples of American physicians from different settings, such as private practice versus public health facilities, or rural versus urban settings. If all Americans, regardless of setting, score higher on the measures, one gains confidence that results might be due to culture. As one compares more and more occupations and continues to replicate the same pattern of results, a reliable pattern of cultural differences may emerge.

Given that matching is probably bound to be imperfect because countries have some unique characteristics that cannot be equated, and also because some countries are likely to be more homogeneous than others on the measures and/or relationships of interest, statistically controlling for third variable effects may be a suitable alternative to matching. However, decisions concerning whether to use a third variable as a control should be made cautiously because some of these controls may turn out to be effects rather than causes of results, and therefore controlling for them would yield erroneous conclusions (Meehl, 1971). Moreover, using large numbers of statistical controls requires gathering as much information as possible about the samples, being mindful of the practical limitations in survey length that might adversely affect response rates.

In exploring the possible influence of confounding variables, researchers should not assume that matching samples on measures that call for subjective appraisals necessarily equates the two samples in the objective factors underlying such appraisals. Consider, for example, the case of social support, whose effects on the stressor-strain relationship have been widely studied (e.g., Viswesvaran, Sanchez, & Fisher, 1999). A majority of measures of social support rely on subjective appraisals of received support. Reports of social support are influenced by the extent to which societies are collectivistic versus individualistic and, therefore, interpretations of what constitutes an adequate level of support may vary considerably across countries (Triandis, 1994a). Thus, matching samples on the extent to which individuals feel that they had support from supervisors, co-workers, or even family members may be misleading, given the variations on what various cultures would consider an adequate level of support. Similarly, subjective appraisals of working conditions are likely to differ as a function of what constitute normal working conditions in the country. For example, the deplorable conditions of a sweatshop may not look so bad to rural workers who do not count on better ways to make a living.

## CONCLUSION

We advocate a series of administrative and methodological choices as potentially instrumental in (a) successfully completing and publishing large-scale CC/CN studies and in (b) assessing and minimizing the kind of language and selection threats that are often confounded with culture effects. First, we argued that a somewhat centralized approach including a small number of "central" researchers, which we have dubbed tongue-in-cheek as the "NATO" model, may expedite successful completion of refereed publications involving large-scale CC/CN studies. Clear and preestablished rules regulating researcher participation and authorship can be instrumental in preventing potential delays and conflicts among participating researchers. More decentralized and participatory models may allow more in-depth examinations of cross-cultural phenomena, but such models are also at higher risk of being stalled because of a myriad of interpersonal and administrative issues surrounding large-scale CC/CN studies. Our review of challenges in this sort of research focused on a series of confounds that may threaten the reliable identification of cultural effects, including language, sampling, and response biases. We reviewed methodological choices such as using within-participant designs and counterbalancing language order that undoubtedly minimize the many confounds that threaten large-scale CC/CN studies. However, we are suggesting that confounds, third-variable effects, and others issues of sample and measurement equivalence are an intrinsic part of CC/CN research, whose total eradication is nearly impossible. Therefore, researchers should always be ready to acknowledge and assess these threats rather than assume that they have successfully controlled them. Perhaps more important, we propose a theoretical approach to large-scale CC/CN research aimed at investigating construct rather than merely measurement equivalence.

---

### Best Practices Recommendations

Administrative Issues

- Assemble a central team of international researchers with enough experience in the peer-reviewed publication process. Try to recruit central team members who have a history of prior collaboration and mutual trust. Formulate a prestudy contract laying out the rules, rights, and benefits of participation, and have members endorse it.
- Rely on the central team for the formulation of study goals and design. Consider incorporating various research agendas into the design, so that the study does not become a one-person event but a true team project.
- Use team members as internal reviewers for manuscript drafts in a simulated peer-review process. Create an internal culture of delivering fast, honest feedback on manuscript drafts. This is easier to do when there is a central team as opposed to an absolute project leader whom others do not dare to criticize.
- Assemble a noncentral team of international collaborators. Provide these collaborators with detailed sampling criteria and sampling guidelines, and delegate local data collection to them because they know best how to reach a suitable sample and ensure an adequate response rate.

Measurement and Sampling Issues

- Have researchers and translators work together, such that psychometric criteria are used to decide when a back-translated scale is sufficiently close to the original version. Appraise translators of the statistical consequences of their specific translation choices and have them modify translations accordingly.

*(continues)*

---

---

**Best Practices Recommendations (*Continued*)**

- Use translators who are both bilingual and bicultural to ensure the meaning equivalence of translations, especially those of scale anchors.
- Assess English proficiency before assuming that respondents from non-English speaking countries can answer questionnaires in English.
- Consider counterbalancing the administration of a linguistically different version of the same questionnaire and assessing potential order effects.
- To gauge the manner in which the construct is expressed across cultures, consider using the MCSD, in which international researchers produce items depicting how the same construct is differentially expressed and gauged in various cultures.
- Do not assume that matching always rules out potential confounds, because countries have unique characteristics that cannot be fully equated. Consider statistically controlling for third-variable effects as an alternative to matching, but proceed cautiously because controls may turn out to be substantive effects rather than confounds, and they may unnecessarily increase survey length and adversely impact response rates.

---

## REFERENCES

Bandura, A. (1986). *Social foundations of thought and action: A social cognitive theory.* Englewood Cliffs, NJ: Prentice-Hall.

Berry, J. (1969). On cross-cultural comparability. *International Journal of Psychology, 4,* 119–128. doi:10.1080/00207596908247261

Bollen, K. A. (1989). *Structural equations with latent variables.* New York, NY: Wiley.

Bonache, J., Sanchez, J. I., & Zarraga-Oberty, C. (2009). The interaction of expatriate pay differential and expatriate inputs on host country nationals' pay unfairness. *The International Journal of Human Resource Management, 20,* 2135–2149. doi:10.1080/09585190903178062

Bond, M. H., & Yang, R. (1982). Ethnic affirmation versus cross-cultural accommodation. *Journal of Cross-Cultural Psychology, 13,* 169–185. doi:10.1177/0022002182013002003

Boyacigiller, N. A., & Adler, N. J. (1991). The parochial dinosaur: Organizational science in a global context. *Academy of Management Journal, 16,* 262–290.

Brislin, R. W. (1986). The wording and translation of research instruments. In W. J. Lonner & J. W. Berry (Eds.), *Field methods in cross-cultural research* (pp. 137–164). Newbury Park, CA: Sage.

Byrne, B. M. (1994). *Structural equation modeling with EQS and EQS Windows*. Thousand Oaks, CA: Sage.

Byrne, B. M., Shavelson, R. J., & Muthén, B. (1989). Testing for the equivalence of factor covariance and mean structures: The issue of partial measurement invariance. *Psychological Bulletin, 105*, 456–466. doi:10.1037/0033-2909.105.3.456

Candell, G. L., & Hulin, C. L. (1986). Cross-language and cross-cultural comparisons in scale translations. *Journal of Cross-Cultural Psychology, 17*, 417–440. doi:10.1177/0022002186017004003

Cheung, G. W., & Rensvold, R. B. (2000). Assessing extreme and acquiescence response sets in cross-cultural research using structural equations modeling. *Journal of Cross-Cultural Psychology, 31*, 187–212. doi:10.1177/0022022100031002003

Church, A. T., & Lonner, W. J. (1998). The cross-cultural perspective in the study of personality: Rationale and current research. *Journal of Cross-Cultural Psychology, 29*, 32–62. doi:10.1177/0022022198291003

Geisinger, K. F. (1994). Cross-cultural normative assessment: Translation and adaptation issues influencing the normative interpretation of assessment instruments. *Psychological Assessment, 6*, 304–312. doi:10.1037/1040-3590.6.4.304

Ghorpade, J., Hattrup, K., & Lackritz, J. R. (1999). The use of personality measures in cross-cultural research: A test of three personality scales across two countries. *Journal of Applied Psychology, 84*, 670–679. doi:10.1037/0021-9010.84.5.670

Hong, Y., Morris, M.W., Chiu, C., & Benet-Martinez, V. (2000). Multicultural minds; A dynamic constructivist approach to culture and cognition. *American Psychologist, 55*, 709–720. doi:10.1037/0003-066X.55.7.709

Hulin, C. L. (1987). A psychometric theory of evaluations of item and scale translations. *Journal of Cross-Cultural Psychology, 18*, 115–142. doi:10.1177/0022002187018002001

Hulin, C. L., Drasgow, F., & Komocar, J. (1982). Application of item-response theory to analysis of attitude scale translations. *Journal of Applied Psychology, 67*, 818–825. doi:10.1037/0021-9010.67.6.818

Hulin, C. L., & Mayer, L. J. (1986). Psychometric equivalence of a translation of the Job Descriptive Index into Hebrew. *Journal of Applied Psychology, 71*, 83–94. doi:10.1037/0021-9010.71.1.83

Iwata, N., Umesue, M., Egashira, K., Hiro, H., Mizoue, T., Mishima, N., & Nagata, S. (1998). Can positive affect items be used to assess depressive disorder in the Japanese populations? *Psychological Medicine, 28*, 153–158. doi:10.1017/S0033291797005898

Katerberg, R., Smith, F. J., & Hoy, S. (1977). Language, time, and person effects on attitude scale translations. *Journal of Applied Psychology, 62*, 385–391. doi:10.1037/0021-9010.62.4.385

Lazarus, R. S. (1966). *Psychological stress and the coping process*. New York, NY: McGraw-Hill.

Liu, C. (2003). *A comparison of job stressors and job strains among employees holding comparable jobs in Western and Eastern societies*. Unpublished doctoral dissertation, University of South Florida, Tampa.

Liu, C., Borg, I., & Spector, P. E. (2004). Measurement equivalence of a German job satisfaction survey used in a multinational organization: Implications of Schwartz's culture model. *Journal of Applied Psychology, 89*, 1070–1082. doi: 10.1037/0021-9010.89.6.1070

Lonner, W. J. (1990). An overview of cross-cultural testing and assessment. In R. W. Brislin (Ed.), *Applied cross-cultural psychology* (Vol. 14, pp. 56–76). Newbury Park, CA: Sage.

Lytle, A. L., Brett, J. M., Barsness, Z. I., Tinsley, C. H., & Janssens, M. (1995). A paradigm for confirmatory cross-cultural research in organizational behavior. *Research in Organizational Behavior, 17*, 167–214.

Marian, V., Spivey, M., & Hirsch, J. (2003). Shared and separate systems in bilingual language processing: Converging evidence from eyetracking and brain imaging. *Brain and Language, 86*, 70–82. doi:10.1016/S0093-934X(02)00535-7

Maruyama, M. (1984). Alternative concepts of management: Insights from Asia and Africa. *Asia Pacific Journal of Management, 1*, 100–111. doi:10.1007/BF01733683

Meehl, P. E. (1971). High school yearbooks: A reply to Schwarz. *Journal of Abnormal Psychology, 77*, 143–148. doi:10.1037/h0030750

Narayanan, L., Menon, S., & Spector, P. E. (1999). A cross-cultural comparison of job stressors and reactions among employees holding comparable jobs in two countries. *International Journal of Stress Management, 6*, 197–212. doi:10.1023/A:1021986709317

Raju, N. S., Laffitte, L. J., & Byrne, B. M. (2002). Measurement equivalence: A comparison of methods based on confirmatory factor analysis and item response theory. *Journal of Applied Psychology, 87*, 517–529. doi:10.1037/0021-9010.87.3.517

Ralston, D. A., Cunniff, M. K., & Gustafson, D. J. (1995). Cultural accommodation: The effect of language on the responses of bilingual Hong Kong Chinese managers. *Journal of Cross-Cultural Psychology, 26*, 714–727. doi:10.1177/002202219502600612

Riordan, C. M., & Vandenberg, R. J. (1994). A central question in cross-cultural research: Do employees of different cultures interpret work-related measures in an equivalent manner? *Journal of Management, 20*, 643–671.

Ross, N. (2004). *Culture and cognition: Implications for theory and method*. Thousand Oaks, CA: Sage.

Ryan, A. M., Chan, D., Ployhart, R. E., & Slade, L. A. (1999). Employee attitude surveys in a multinational organization: Considering language and culture in assessing measurement equivalence. *Personnel Psychology, 52*, 37–58. doi:10.1111/j.1744-6570.1999.tb01812.x

Rybowiak, V., Garst, H., Frese, M., & Batinic, B. (1999). Error orientation questionnaire (EOQ): Reliability, validity, and different language equivalence. *Journal of Organizational Behavior, 20,* 527–547. doi:10.1002/(SICI)1099-1379(199907)20:4<527::AID-JOB886>3.0.CO;2-G

Sanchez, J. I., Spector, P. E., & Cooper, C. L. (2000). Adapting to a boundaryless world: A developmental model of the expatriate executive. *The Academy of Management Executive, 14,* 96–106. doi:10.5465/AME.2000.3819309

Sanchez, J. I., Spector, P. E., & Cooper, C. L. (2006). Frequently ignored methodological issues in cross-cultural stress research. In P. T. P. Wong & L. C. J. Wong (Eds.), *Handbook of multicultural perspectives on stress and coping* (pp. 187–201). New York, NY: Springer. doi:10.1007/0-387-26238-5_9

Schaffer, B. S., & Riordan, C. M. (2003). A review of cross-cultural methodologies for organizational research: A best-practices approach. *Organizational Research Methods, 6,* 169–215. doi:10.1177/1094428103251542

Siu, O. L., & Cooper, C. L. (1998). A study of occupational stress, job satisfaction, and quitting intention in Hong Kong firms: The role of locus of control and organizational commitment. *Stress Medicine, 14,* 55–66. doi:10.1002/(SICI)1099-1700(199801)14:1<55::AID-SMI764>3.0.CO;2-X

Spector, P. E. (1988). Development of the Work Locus of Control Scale. *Journal of Occupational Psychology, 61,* 335–340. doi:10.1111/j.2044-8325.1988.tb00470.x

Spector, P. E., Cooper, C. L., Sanchez, J. I., O'Driscoll, M., Sparks, K., Bernin, P., . . . Yu, S. (2001). Do national levels of individualism and internal locus of control relate to well-being: An ecological-level international study. *Journal of Organizational Behavior, 22,* 815–832. doi:10.1002/job.118

Spector, P. E., Cooper, C. L., Sanchez, J. I., O'Driscoll, M., Sparks, K., Bernin, P., . . . Yu, S. (2002). Locus of control and well-being at work: How generalizable are Western work findings? *Academy of Management Journal, 45,* 453–466. doi:10.2307/3069359

Spector, P. E., Cooper, C. L., Sanchez, J. I., Sparks, K., Büssing, A., Dewe, P., . . . Wong, P. (2002). The pitfalls of poor psychometric properties: A reply to Hofstede's reply to us. *Applied Psychology, 51,* 174–178. doi:10.1111/1464-0597.00085

Spector, P. E., Sanchez, J. I., Siu, O. L., Salgado, J., & Ma, J. (2004). Secondary control, socioinstrumental control, and work locus of control in China and the U.S. *Applied Psychology, 53,* 38–60. doi:10.1111/j.1464-0597.2004.00160.x

Spector, P. E., Van Katwyk, P. T., Brannick, M. T., & Chen, P. Y. (1997). When two factors don't reflect two constructs: How item characteristics can produce artifactual factors. *Journal of Management, 23,* 659–677. doi:10.1177/014920639702300503

Spirrison, C. L., & Choi, S. (1998). Psychometric properties of a Korean version of the revised NEO-Personality Inventory. *Psychological Reports, 83,* 263–274.

Triandis, H. C. (1994a). Cross-cultural industrial and organizational psychology. In H. C. Triandis, M. D. Dunnette, & Leatta M. Hough (Eds.), *Handbook of industrial and organizational psychology* (pp. 103–172). Palo Alto, CA: Consulting Psychologists Press.

Triandis, H. C. (1994b). *Culture and social behavior*. New York, NY: McGraw-Hill.

Tsui, A. S., Schoonhoven, C. B., Meyer, M., Lau, C. M., & Milkovich, G. (2004). Organization and management in the midst of societal transformation: The People's Republic of China. *Organization Science, 15*, 133–144. doi:10.1287/orsc.1040.0063

van de Vijver, F., & Leung, K. (1997). *Methods and data analysis for cross-cultural research*. Thousand Oaks, CA: Sage.

Vandenberg, R. J., & Lance, C. E. (2000). A review and synthesis of the measurement invariance literature: Suggestions, practices, and recommendations for organizational research. *Organizational Research Methods, 3*, 4–70. doi:10.1177/109442810031002

Viswesvaran, C., Sanchez, J. I., & Fisher, J. (1999). The role of social support in the process of work stress: A meta-analysis. *Journal of Vocational Behavior, 54*, 314–334. doi:10.1006/jvbe.1998.1661

Weisz, J. R., Rothbaum, F. M., & Blackburn, T. C. (1984). Standing out and standing in: The psychology of control in America and Japan. *American Psychologist, 39*, 955–969. doi:10.1037/0003-066X.39.9.955

Werner, O., & Campbell, D. (1970). Translating, working through interpreters, and the problem of decentering. In R. Carroll & R. Cohen (Eds.), *A handbook of method in cultural anthropology* (pp. 398–420). New York, NY: Natural History Press.

# 6

# ETHICAL CHALLENGES TO CONDUCTING MULTINATIONAL ORGANIZATIONAL RESEARCH

BRENT J. LYONS, FREDERICK T. L. LEONG, AND ANN MARIE RYAN

In recent years, organizational psychologists have shown increasing interest in researching multinational organizations (Erez, 2010; Gelfand, Erez, & Aycan, 2007; Gelfand, Leslie, & Fehr, 2008). This increase has largely reflected how the context of work has changed in light of rapid globalization of research from local to cross-cultural and global (Erez, 1994). As a wave of cross-cultural research has spread across all fields of organizational research, understanding the impact of culture on organizations and their practices is thought to be imperative to ensure the well-being of the workforce within and across countries (Aycan & Kanungo, 2001). Many organizations have changed their structures to reflect the fact they no longer have distinct physical entities (i.e., a single or central office) because multinational organizations and multicultural teams operate across national and geographic boundaries. Members of multinational organizations that operate across cultural boundaries are required to have a shared understanding of organizational interests, goals, and practices (Erez, 1994). This change in the context of work has inspired the development of conceptual frameworks that emphasize the importance of examining similarities and differences among cultures, as well as how organizations, teams, and individuals operate in a global and multinational context. Along with the development of these conceptual frameworks, research on multinational and cross-cultural organizational research has also investigated new taxonomies of cultural beliefs and values relevant to multinational organizational functioning, as well as detailed the benefits of taking a multinational and cross-cultural approach for multinational organizations (for reviews, see Gelfand et al., 2007; Gelfand, Raver, & Ehrhart, 2002).

The recent surge in multinational research has been followed by recommendations for such research to adopt multidisciplinary and integrationist perspectives in theory development and practice that take into consideration the extent to which sociocultural context (i.e., environmental factors internal and external to the organization) influences behavior (Aycan, 2000; Aycan & Kanungo, 2001). Organizational scholarship has a history of using the imposed-etic approach by applying Western-based frameworks to non-Western cultural contexts (Aycan, 2000; Tsui, 2004; Tsui, Nifadkar, & Ou, 2007), and as a result, little is known about best practices for research in cultures outside America and Europe. Thus, some fundamental issues and challenges facing multinational organizational research remain unaddressed.

One specific challenge is the emergence of ethical dilemmas associated with conducting organizational research in a multinational context. No guidelines exist to help organizational psychologists assess and monitor potential cross-cultural ethical dilemmas, and little is known as to the extent and impact of those dilemmas. In this chapter, our intent is to highlight how U.S.-based ethical guidelines regulating research by American organizational psychologists do not account for many ethical dilemmas potentially facing organizational psychologists conducting cross-cultural multinational research. We make recommendations for how organizational psychologists can move toward ensuring their ethical research practices are sensitive to the potential for ethical dilemmas.

## MULTINATIONAL ORGANIZATIONAL RESEARCH AND ETHICS

Considering the impact that culture has on values and beliefs about appropriate ethical practices (Lefkowitz, 2011), it is imperative for organizational psychologists conducting multinational research to carefully consider the cultural context of their research to avoid potential ethical dilemmas and to appropriately address those that do occur. Aycan and Kanungo (2001) suggested that uncritical adaptation of Western-evolved practices and techniques to other sociocultural environments may not be effective in fully capturing the phenomena of interest because doing so does not consider the sociocultural context in which that phenomenon manifests (Tsui et al., 2007). As psychologists are becoming more involved globally, psychology worldwide is benefiting from enhancements in global thinking and dialogue (Pettifor, 2007). With more and more organizational psychologists doing research in social contexts with diverging values and expectations, the scope of problems related to cross-cultural research, including those related to ethics, is expected to increase.

Because ethical standards inform researchers of appropriate research conduct, it is crucially important that ethical guidelines appropriate for multinational organizational research be established. Ethical dilemmas created by value or belief conflicts between organizational psychologists from one country and those in other countries in which they are conducting their cross-cultural research are core ethical concerns for multinational researchers. With no guidelines in place, organizational psychologists have limited awareness as to how their practices can lead to ethical dilemmas in other cultures. For example, obtaining written consent may be problematic in societies that possess no written language or in societies with a strong relationship between the legal system and ethical codes (for a review of informed consent issues faced by multinational pharmaceutical companies, see Lee, 2010). Furthermore, as another example, evidence suggests that financial inducements considered high in rural India are miniscule relative to levels considered appropriate or incentivizing in the United States (Ariely, Gneezy, Loewenstein, & Mazar, 2009). Therefore, appropriate levels of participant pay are likely to differ widely across countries. Indeed, the lack of ethical standards for multinational research reflects an emerging ethical challenge.

Generally speaking, psychologists adhere to ethical guidelines established by their organizing associations. For example, analytical psychologists—primarily in Europe but also worldwide—adhere to the code of ethics established by the International Association for Analytical Psychology (2010), and organizational psychologists in the United States adhere to the ethical standards laid out by the American Psychological Association's (APA's) "Ethical Principles of Psychologists and Code of Conduct" (hereinafter referred to as the APA Ethics Code; APA, 2010; see also http://www.apa.org/ethics). The APA Ethics Code notes that the implementation of its ethical standards may vary depending on the context (e.g., international location) and that the researcher must consider cultural context when adopting the standards. Indeed, APA Ethics Code Principle E: Respect for People's Rights and Dignity requires that

> Psychologists are aware of and respect cultural, individual, and role differences, including those based on age, gender, gender identity, race, ethnicity, culture, national origin, religion, sexual orientation, disability, language, and socioeconomic status and consider these factors when working with members of such groups. Psychologists try to eliminate the effect on their work of biases based on those factors, and they do not knowingly participate in or condone activities of others based upon such prejudices.

Even though the APA Ethics Code requires that researchers consider the standards in an international context, it does not highlight the specific issues for researchers, nor does it provide specific guidance about how to uphold the ethical standards in a culturally sensitive manner, leaving major gaps when applied to multinational organizational research. Therefore, the APA Ethics Code is generally insufficient for ethical dilemmas that may emerge when research is conducted in countries for which the standards do not resonate or in multinational organizations that span several countries or cultures.

The current APA Ethics Code (2010) has detailed standards pertaining to sensitivity of group differences and nondiscrimination but primarily in the domestic context. For example, Standard 2.01 requires that psychologists only serve within their boundaries of competence by obtaining appropriate training, supervision, experience, and consultation where an understanding of factors associated with age, gender, race/ethnicity, religion and culture, and so forth, is essential for implementing their research or practice. Further, Standard 3.01 prohibits "unfair discrimination" based on characteristics such as gender, race, ethnicity, religion, sexual orientation, or any basis proscribed by law. Standard 3.02 describes a specific set of behaviors in which psychologists should not engage (e.g., "Psychologists do not engage in sexual harassment"). As the introduction to the APA Ethics Code indicates, "The ethical standards set forth enforceable rules for conduct as psychologists" (p. 2). Although such enforceable standards are important in setting minimum thresholds of acceptable behavior and making it possible to legally enforce the standards if any psychologists violate them, such specific statements leave unaddressed certain problems created in multinational research contexts. By urging psychologists to "eliminate the effect of biases in their work," the code provides a framework for culturally sensitive practices and incites an awareness of cultural considerations (see Principle E of the APA Ethics Code). However, the behavioral specificity of the APA Ethics Code does not address an entire range of ethical challenges faced by organizational psychologists when conducting cross-cultural research in other countries, on multicultural teams, and in multinational organizations. Recent advancements in the field of ethics have led to the development of the "Universal Declaration of Ethical Principles for Psychologists" (hereinafter referred to as the Universal Declaration; Gauthier, 2008), which has a primary goal of articulating moral principles that can aid in the development of more specific ethical guidelines for cross-cultural research. We discuss this effort in more detail below.

Ethical guidelines regulating cross-cultural research require a degree of contextualization that captures values and beliefs relevant to the country (or countries) where the research is being conducted. More generally, Tsui et al. (2007) highlighted the necessity of contextualizing organizational research by deriving theories about phenomena and adapting methods of inquiry to specific cultural contexts. However, Tsui et al. recognized that this is difficult because oftentimes the relevant sociocultural context is not obvious to outside researchers, which can result in cultural bias by which researchers impose their own frameworks on phenomena to which they may not necessarily apply (Erez, 2010). How researchers respond to potential ethical dilemmas is influenced by their "lens" that they bring to the research process. That is, by using their own lens, researchers may not be using the right methodology or asking the right questions, resulting in not only biased outcomes but also potential ethical dilemmas that could result in undue harm to participants or the sacrificing of research opportunities (e.g., reduced access to samples).

Ethical guidelines regulating the ethical practices of multicultural biomedical researchers have far surpassed those of organizational psychologists. In the next section, we highlight advancements in biomedical research ethics that can provide insight into the issues that organizational psychologists may face and how some of those issues have been tackled by the medical field.

## INTERNATIONAL ETHICS FOR MEDICAL RESEARCH

Organizational psychologists are not the first to encounter ethical challenges in conducting international and multinational research. Medicine has a longer history in facing these challenges, and a brief review of these developments should enlighten our current discussion. In light of collaborative research about the HIV/AIDS epidemic, biomedical ethicists have taken a progressive approach in developing ethical guidelines that regulate the research of physicians who work with international samples. As a result, medical research has taken the lead in confronting ethical challenges for cross-cultural research, and we believe that it is valuable for organizational researchers to become aware of, and learn from, this movement.

The Declaration of Helsinki, issued by the World Medical Association in 1964 (later revised in 2008), and the subsequent guidelines constructed by the Council for International Organizations of Medical Science (CIOMS; 2002) in collaboration with the World Health Organization (WHO) represent the first international movement toward developing ethical regulations for research with human subjects in a cross-cultural context.

The basic premise underlying the Declaration of Helsinki is that research should weigh concerns about participant well-being most heavily in that protecting vulnerable (e.g., economically and medically disadvantaged) populations is expected to take precedence over interests in benefitting science and society. The Declaration of Helsinki (reprinted in Exhibit 6.1) outlines a series of principles intended to guide the regulation of international medical research. For example, Principle 15 describes how research designs

EXHIBIT 6.1
Declaration of Helsinki (World Medical Association, 2008)

Ethical Principles for Medical Research Involving Human Subjects Adopted by the 18th WMA General Assembly, Helsinki, Finland, June 1964, and amended by the:

29th WMA General Assembly, Tokyo, Japan, October 1975
35th WMA General Assembly, Venice, Italy, October 1983
41st WMA General Assembly, Hong Kong, September 1989
48th WMA General Assembly, Somerset West, South Africa, October 1996
52nd WMA General Assembly, Edinburgh, Scotland, October 2000
53rd WMA General Assembly, Washington, DC, October 2002
(Note of Clarification on paragraph 29 added)
55th WMA General Assembly, Tokyo, Japan, October 2004
(Note of Clarification on Paragraph 30 added)
59th WMA General Assembly, Seoul, Korea, October 2008

## A. INTRODUCTION

1. The World Medical Association (WMA) has developed the Declaration of Helsinki as a statement of ethical principles for medical research involving human subjects, including research on identifiable human material and data.

    The Declaration is intended to be read as a whole and each of its constituent paragraphs should not be applied without consideration of all other relevant paragraphs.
2. Although the Declaration is addressed primarily to physicians, the WMA encourages other participants in medical research involving human subjects to adopt these principles.
3. It is the duty of the physician to promote and safeguard the health of patients, including those who are involved in medical research. The physician's knowledge and conscience are dedicated to the fulfillment of this duty.
4. The Declaration of Geneva of the WMA binds the physician with the words, "The health of my patient will be my first consideration," and the International Code of Medical Ethics declares that, "A physician shall act in the patient's best interest when providing medical care."
5. Medical progress is based on research that ultimately must include studies involving human subjects. Populations that are underrepresented in medical research should be provided appropriate access to participation in research.
6. In medical research involving human subjects, the well-being of the individual research subject must take precedence over all other interests.
7. The primary purpose of medical research involving human subjects is to understand the causes, development, and effects of diseases and improve preventive, diagnostic, and therapeutic interventions (methods, procedures, and treatments). Even the best current interventions must be evaluated continually through research for their safety, effectiveness, efficiency, accessibility, and quality.
8. In medical practice and in medical research, most interventions involve risks and burdens.
9. Medical research is subject to ethical standards that promote respect for all human subjects and protect their health and rights. Some research populations are particularly vulnerable and need special protection. These include those who cannot give or refuse consent for themselves and those who may be vulnerable to coercion or undue influence.
10. Physicians should consider the ethical, legal, and regulatory norms and standards for research involving human subjects in their own countries as well as applicable international norms and standards. No national or international ethical, legal, or regulatory requirement should reduce or eliminate any of the protections for research subjects set forth in this Declaration.

EXHIBIT 6.1  *(Continued)*

## B. PRINCIPLES FOR ALL MEDICAL RESEARCH

11. It is the duty of physicians who participate in medical research to protect the life, health, dignity, integrity, right to self-determination, privacy, and confidentiality of personal information of research subjects.
12. Medical research involving human subjects must conform to generally accepted scientific principles, be based on a thorough knowledge of the scientific literature, other relevant sources of information, and adequate laboratory and, as appropriate, animal experimentation. The welfare of animals used for research must be respected.
13. Appropriate caution must be exercised in the conduct of medical research that may harm the environment.
14. The design and performance of each research study involving human subjects must be clearly described in a research protocol. The protocol should contain a statement of the ethical considerations involved and should indicate how the principles in this Declaration have been addressed. The protocol should include information regarding funding, sponsors, institutional affiliations, other potential conflicts of interest, incentives for subjects, and provisions for treating and/or compensating subjects who are harmed as a consequence of participation in the research study. The protocol should describe arrangements for poststudy access by study subjects to interventions identified as beneficial in the study or access to other appropriate care or benefits.
15. The research protocol must be submitted for consideration, comment, guidance, and approval to a research ethics committee before the study begins. This committee must be independent of the researcher, the sponsor, and any other undue influence. It must take into consideration the laws and regulations of the country or countries in which the research is to be performed as well as applicable international norms and standards but these must not be allowed to reduce or eliminate any of the protections for research subjects set forth in this Declaration. The committee must have the right to monitor ongoing studies. The researcher must provide monitoring information to the committee, especially information about any serious adverse events. No change to the protocol may be made without consideration and approval by the committee.
16. Medical research involving human subjects must be conducted only by individuals with the appropriate scientific training and qualifications. Research on patients or healthy volunteers requires the supervision of a competent and appropriately qualified physician or other health care professional. The responsibility for the protection of research subjects must always rest with the physician or other health care professional and never the research subjects, even though they have given consent.
17. Medical research involving a disadvantaged or vulnerable population or community is only justified if the research is responsive to the health needs and priorities of this population or community and if there is a reasonable likelihood that this population or community stands to benefit from the results of the research.
18. Every medical research study involving human subjects must be preceded by careful assessment of predictable risks and burdens to the individuals and communities involved in the research in comparison with foreseeable benefits to them and to other individuals or communities affected by the condition under investigation.
19. Every clinical trial must be registered in a publicly accessible database before recruitment of the first subject.
20. Physicians may not participate in a research study involving human subjects unless they are confident that the risks involved have been adequately assessed and can be satisfactorily managed. Physicians must immediately stop a study when the risks are found to outweigh the potential benefits or when there is conclusive proof of positive and beneficial results.

*(continues)*

EXHIBIT 6.1 *(Continued)*

21. Medical research involving human subjects may only be conducted if the importance of the objective outweighs the inherent risks and burdens to the research subjects.
22. Participation by competent individuals as subjects in medical research must be voluntary. Although it may be appropriate to consult family members or community leaders, no competent individual may be enrolled in a research study unless he or she freely agrees.
23. Every precaution must be taken to protect the privacy of research subjects and the confidentiality of their personal information and to minimize the impact of the study on their physical, mental, and social integrity.
24. In medical research involving competent human subjects, each potential subject must be adequately informed of the aims, methods, sources of funding, any possible conflicts of interest, institutional affiliations of the researcher, the anticipated benefits and potential risks of the study and the discomfort it may entail, and any other relevant aspects of the study. The potential subject must be informed of the right to refuse to participate in the study or to withdraw consent to participate at any time without reprisal. Special attention should be given to the specific information needs of individual potential subjects as well as to the methods used to deliver the information. After ensuring that the potential subject has understood the information, the physician or another appropriately qualified individual must then seek the potential subject's freely given informed consent, preferably in writing. If the consent cannot be expressed in writing, the nonwritten consent must be formally documented and witnessed.
25. For medical research using identifiable human material or data, physicians must normally seek consent for the collection, analysis, storage, and/or reuse. There may be situations where consent would be impossible or impractical to obtain for such research or would pose a threat to the validity of the research. In such situations the research may be done only after consideration and approval of a research ethics committee.
26. When seeking informed consent for participation in a research study, the physician should be particularly cautious if the potential subject is in a dependent relationship with the physician or may consent under duress. In such situations the informed consent should be sought by an appropriately qualified individual who is completely independent of this relationship.
27. For a potential research subject who is incompetent, the physician must seek informed consent from the legally authorized representative. These individuals must not be included in a research study that has no likelihood of benefit for them unless it is intended to promote the health of the population represented by the potential subject, the research cannot instead be performed with competent persons, and the research entails only minimal risk and minimal burden.
28. When a potential research subject who is deemed incompetent is able to give assent to decisions about participation in research, the physician must seek that assent in addition to the consent of the legally authorized representative. The potential subject's dissent should be respected.
29. Research involving subjects who are physically or mentally incapable of giving consent, for example, unconscious patients, may be done only if the physical or mental condition that prevents giving informed consent is a necessary characteristic of the research population. In such circumstances the physician should seek informed consent from the legally authorized representative. If no such representative is available and if the research cannot be delayed, the study may proceed without informed consent provided that the specific reasons for involving subjects with a condition that renders them unable to give informed consent have been stated in the research protocol and the study has been

EXHIBIT 6.1   *(Continued)*

approved by a research ethics committee. Consent to remain in the research should be obtained as soon as possible from the subject or a legally authorized representative.

30. Authors, editors, and publishers all have ethical obligations with regard to the publication of the results of research. Authors have a duty to make publicly available the results of their research on human subjects and are accountable for the completeness and accuracy of their reports. They should adhere to accepted guidelines for ethical reporting. Negative and inconclusive as well as positive results should be published or otherwise made publicly available. Sources of funding, institutional affiliations and conflicts of interest should be declared in the publication. Reports of research not in accordance with the principles of this Declaration should not be accepted for publication.

## C. ADDITIONAL PRINCIPLES FOR MEDICAL RESEARCH COMBINED WITH MEDICAL CARE

31. The physician may combine medical research with medical care only to the extent that the research is justified by its potential preventive, diagnostic, or therapeutic value and if the physician has good reason to believe that participation in the research study will not adversely affect the health of the patients who serve as research subjects.

32. The benefits, risks, burdens, and effectiveness of a new intervention must be tested against those of the best current proven intervention, except in the following circumstances:

    ■ The use of placebo, or no treatment, is acceptable in studies where no current proven intervention exists, or
    ■ Where for compelling and scientifically sound methodological reasons the use of placebo is necessary to determine the efficacy or safety of an intervention and the patients who receive placebo or no treatment will not be subject to any risk of serious or irreversible harm. Extreme care must be taken to avoid abuse of this option.

33. At the conclusion of the study, patients entered into the study are entitled to be informed about the outcome of the study and to share any benefits that result from it, for example, access to interventions identified as beneficial in the study or to other appropriate care or benefits.

34. The physician must fully inform the patient which aspects of the care are related to the research. The refusal of a patient to participate in a study or the patient's decision to withdraw from the study must never interfere with the patient–physician relationship.

35. In the treatment of a patient, where proven interventions do not exist or have been ineffective, the physician, after seeking expert advice, with informed consent from the patient or a legally authorized representative, may use an unproven intervention if in the physician's judgment it offers hope of saving life, re-establishing health, or alleviating suffering. Where possible, this intervention should be made the object of research, designed to evaluate its safety and efficacy. In all cases, new information should be recorded and, where appropriate, made publicly available.

*Note.* From *WMA Declaration of Helsinki—Ethical Principles for Medical Research Involving Human Subjects,* by the World Medical Association, 2008, Ferney-Voltaire, France: World Medical Association. Copyright 2012 by World Medical Association. All rights reserved. Reprinted with permission.

need to be approved by an ethics committee containing individuals who are well-versed in the laws and regulations of the region in which the research is being conducted. The Declaration of Helsinki has influenced the formulation of international, regional, and national legislation and codes of ethical conduct, including the CIOMS (2002) "International Ethical Guidelines for Biomedical Research Involving Human Subjects" (hereinafter referred to as the Guidelines).

In response to the outbreak of the HIV/AIDS pandemic and advancements in research practices of medicine and biotechnology, in 1993 CIOMS in cooperation with WHO established the Guidelines (later revised in 2002). The CIOMS Guidelines consist of 21 guidelines intending to apply the principles of the Declaration of Helsinki to the regulation of international research, and particularly biomedical research being conducted in disadvantaged countries. The CIOMS Guidelines emphasize how the application of ethical principles needs to account for ethical values, emphasizing the application of ethical regulation in local circumstances and the establishment of adequate mechanisms for ethical review.

According to the CIOMS Guidelines, all research involving human subjects should be conducted in accordance with three basic ethical principles: respect for persons (i.e., individuals should be treated as autonomous independents), beneficence (i.e., the research design should maximize benefits and minimize harm to participants), and justice (i.e., distributive justice; equitable distribution of both burdens and benefits of participation across participants). Of particular interest to this chapter, several concerns proposed by CIOMS have relevance to issues faced by organizational psychologists. For example, Guideline 4 emphasizes that the language used in informed consent procedures (oral or written) needs to meet the participants' level of understanding and that researchers must ask questions to ensure that participants understand the information. Researchers also need to consider that the process of obtaining informed consent differs across cultures: In some regions, researchers need to obtain approval from community leaders before acquiring consent, although individual participant informed consent is required for all research projects. Likewise, in line with Guideline 4, organizational psychologists would need to develop culturally appropriate ways of communicating information that is necessary for the adherence to this informed consent process when researching organizations that spread across non–U.S. contexts.

Another example from the CIOMS Guidelines relevant to organizational psychologists is Guideline 8, which is concerned with risks to groups of persons. According to this guideline, research about certain topics may present risks to social groups (e.g., race, ethnicity, gender) that may have different meaning or effects across cultural contexts. For example, depending on a culture's values and beliefs, information might be published that could stigmatize a group or expose its members to discrimination. Such information, for example, could indicate that a certain group has higher susceptibility to a mental illness or holds beliefs not valued by an institution or organization. Guideline 8 requires that research be sensitive to such considerations and that researchers report and publicize (e.g., publish) the research in a manner respectful to all those involved. According to this guideline, organizational researchers would need to ensure that their practices are being monitored by the culturally relevant ethics review committees or independent monitoring board to ensure that such considerations are met.

Since the publication of the CIOMS 1993 Guidelines, several international organizations have issued ethical guidelines regulating medical research and clinical trials. Two examples include the *Report of the Equivalent Protections*, published by the U.S. Department of Health and Human Services (DHHS; 2003) and the *Guideline on Good Clinical Practice*, published by the International Conference on Harmonization (ICH; 1996). The *Report of Equivalent Protections* was developed to provide assurance to U.S. agencies that biomedical and behavioral research being conducted on their behalf in foreign countries was adopting protective procedures that are at least equivalent to those regulated by U.S. Title 45 of the Code of Federal Regulations. This approach makes it the principal responsibility of the research institutions that receive federal research funding to ensure that adequate protection is occurring when conducting research in non–U.S. contexts. For example, the *Report of Equivalent Protections* guidelines make it the responsibility of the researchers to ensure that an appropriate ethical approval committee is established that consists of qualified reviewers who would be similar to those on institutional review boards in the United States (IRB; DHHS, 2003).

*Good Clinical Practice*, published by ICH (1996), is a set of international ethical standards for designing, implementing, and reporting clinical trials that involve the participation of human subjects. The standards are designed to be consistent with the Declaration of Helsinki in that the primary purpose is to protect participants' well-being. The objective is to provide standards that are applicable to the European Union, Japan, and the United Arab Emirates regulating how clinical data are accepted as ethical by authorities in these various countries.

Established guidelines of ICH and the U.S. Office for Human Research Protections that ultimately stemmed from CIOMS and the Declaration of Helsinki have a strong regulatory and legal influence on physicians researching abroad. These principles and guidelines all share a common theme in stressing that the well-being of participants is of utmost importance and ensuring that well-being in the context of international research involves taking into considering culture-specific values and practices. Without such guidelines, serious ethical dilemmas may emerge. Without similar guidelines established for organizational psychologists, the risk of ethical dilemmas impacting the respect, beneficence, and justice (CIOMS, 2002) of participants in multinational organizational research is a concern that is more difficult to resolve.

## RECOMMENDATIONS

In offering our recommendations for addressing the ethical challenges in conducting multinational organizational research, we use a tripartite theoretical framework that consists of universal, group, and individual dimensions. Leong (1996) presented a multidimensional and integrative model of cross-cultural counseling and psychotherapy based on Kluckhohn and Murray's (1950) tripartite framework. He proposed that cross-cultural therapists need to attend to all three major dimensions of human personality and identity, namely, the universal, the group, and the individual. The *universal* dimension is based on the knowledge base generated by mainstream psychology and the universal laws of human behavior that have been supported by substantial bodies of research. The *group* dimension has been the domain of both cross-cultural psychology as well as ethnic minority psychology and the study of gender differences. The third and final dimension, the *individual*, concerns unique individual characteristics and is more often covered by behavioral and existential theories in which individual learning histories and personal phenomenology are proposed as critical elements in the understanding of human behavior. Leong's integrative model proposes that all three dimensions are equally important in understanding human experiences and should be attended to by the counselor in an integrative fashion. We propose that this tripartite framework is also useful in examining the ethical challenges in conducting multinational organizational research.

In introducing his multidimensional integrative model, Leong (1996) used a famous quote from Kluckhohn and Murray's (1950) influential chapter "The Determinants of Personality Formation" that was published in their book *Personality in Nature, Society, and Culture*: "Every man [sic] is in certain respects: a) like all other men, b) like some other men, and c) like no other man" (p. 35). Kluckhohn and Murray's contention was that some of the determinants of personality are common features found in the makeup of all people. This could be interpreted as addressing the biological aspect of the biopsychosocial model (Engel, 1977) generally used in today's medical sciences. For certain other features of personality, however, Kluckhohn and Murray stated that most individuals are like some other individuals, suggesting the importance of social grouping, whether that grouping is based on culture, race, ethnicity, gender, or social class. Last, they wrote that "each individual's modes of perceiving, feeling, needing, and behaving have characteristic patterns which are not precisely duplicated by those of any other individual" (p. 37). Each person's individuality, often the focus of social learning theories and models, is thus implied. This suggests that all persons have distinct social learning experiences that can influence their values, beliefs, and cognitive schemas.

Extending that tripartite framework to our current discussion of ethical challenges, we believe that these ethical issues can be addressed at those three levels, namely, the universal, group, and individual. At the universal level, our research practices should be guided by ethical principles that are relevant across countries, professional associations, organizations, and universities. On the group level, researchers are members of countries and professional organizations that also provide structure and guidance for research projects. In the final analysis, those universal principles and group standards and guidelines will be enacted at the individual level, where a particular researcher is involved in a particular research project and has to make individual decisions regarding the ethical challenges.

## Universal Dimension

In 2002, the General Assembly of the International Union of Psychological Science assembled an ad hoc joint committee, consisting of members from five countries, to develop the Universal Declaration. Their primary goal was to articulate principles and values that provide a common moral framework for psychologists around the world, and a framework that can also aid in the development of more specific standards as appropriate for particular cultural contexts. The Universal Declaration aspires to inspire world psychological organizations to develop and evaluate the ethical and moral relevance of their codes of ethics:

> This Universal Declaration describes ethical principles and related values for the international psychology community. It provides a shared moral framework that will help members of the psychology community to recognize that they carry out their activities within a larger social context, and that they need to act with integrity in the development and application of psychological knowledge and skills and in a manner that benefits humanity and does not harm or oppress persons or peoples. (Gauthier, 2008, p. 1)

The focus of the Universal Declaration is aspirational rather than specific and prescriptive. In other words, the principles outlined therein are universal; however, the specific application of its principles is intended to vary across cultures and to occur at a local level, ensuring that principles are relevant to local beliefs and values (Gauthier, 2008). The Universal Declaration proposed four general principles to help aid international organizations in their evaluation and development of ethical codes: (a) Principle I: Respect for the Dignity of Persons and Peoples, (b) Principle II: Competent Caring for the Well-Being of Persons and Peoples, (c) Principle III: Integrity, and (d) Principle IV: Professional and Scientific Responsibilities to Society.

Respect for the Dignity of Persons and Peoples asserts that all individuals, regardless of social status, demographics, or other capacities, are entitled to equal moral consideration and respect for the dignities of people. Examples of related values include fair and just treatment of others, privacy for individuals, free and informed consent, and respect for customs and beliefs of cultures. As respect for the dignity of persons and peoples is expressed differently in different cultures, psychologists are encouraged to acknowledge and respect such differences.

Competent Caring for the Well-Being of Persons and Peoples calls for psychologists to work for the benefit of others and do no harm, including maximizing benefits, minimizing harm, and correcting undue harm. Psychologists are encouraged to apply their knowledge and skills that are appropriate for social and cultural context.

Integrity calls for psychologists to be honest and engage in truthful, open, and accurate communication. It also includes managing and correcting for potential biases and other conflicts that could result in harm to others.

Professional and Scientific Responsibilities to Society states that psychologists will contribute to knowledge of human behavior and use this knowledge to improve the well-being of individuals, communities, and society. Responsibilities differ across cultures, and knowledge, therefore, needs to be interpreted in a way that is culturally appropriate.

The principles espoused in the Universal Declaration can provide a general framework for analyzing and resolving ethical issues in international and multinational research projects. However, it is necessary but not sufficient for the development of culturally sensitive ethical guidelines for specific cultural contexts, because they do not specify standards for behaviors of American organizational psychologists researching abroad. Indeed, as recommended by the Universal Declaration and implemented by the European Federation of Professional Psychologists Association's (1995) "Meta-Code of Ethics," ethical standards and regulations need to be contextualized within the culture of interest and are expected to vary across cultural contexts (Ritchie, 2008). However, the Universal Declaration was not designed to offer behaviorally specific recommendations and offers no practical guidance for researchers. The Universal Declaration instead introduces a framework by which more behaviorally specific guidelines can be developed for American organizational psychologists conducting multinational research. This is why there is a need to address ethical challenges across all three dimensions.

In many ways, the Universal Declaration is quite similar to the Declaration of Helsinki in that both seek to identify universal ethical principles with which to guide research. Whereas the Declaration of Helsinki is primarily concerned with medical research balancing participant well-being with the interests of science and society to protect the vulnerable, the Universal Declaration seeks to do the same for psychologists around the world. Just as the Declaration of Helsinki (with its 18 principles) has gone on to influence the formulation of international, regional, and national legislation and codes of conduct for medical research, we anticipate that the Universal Declaration will do the same for psychological science. However, as we discussed earlier, the universal dimension is only one of the three dimensions in which ethical challenges play out.

## Group Dimension

As mentioned above, the Universal Declaration is necessary but not sufficient in providing guidance to U.S. psychologists conducting international and multicultural research projects. Each organizational psychologist who conducts international or cross-cultural research belongs to multiple groups. They are citizens in a country with its own unique set of laws and regulations. They are also often members of professional organizations, such as the APA or the Association for Psychological Science, with their own set of ethical standards and guidelines. In addition, many of them are members of universities and research organizations that provide further oversight to their research activities through such regulating bodies such as IRBs. In addition to the Universal Declaration outlined above, individuals conducting multinational organizational research also need to attend to these multiple groups and their pronouncements and regulations.

For American organizational psychologists, some relevant standards can be found in the APA Ethics Code (e.g., Principle E). However, as White (2007) observed, in cultures with different values, political and economic systems, it may be imposing to insert U.S.-centric ethics in a research setting. There is no doubt that American psychologists conducting cross-cultural research will face similar issues in obtaining informed consent. Such concerns are voiced by the Universal Declaration's principle of Respect for the Dignity of Persons and Peoples, in which psychologists are asked to attend to social context when obtaining informed consent. However, the APA Ethics Code does not provide specific guidance on how researchers working within the context of the U.S.-based IRB can account for such culturally variant and contextually specific provisions (Leong & Lyons, 2010).

In addition, as Leong and Lyons (2010) observed, the APA Ethics Code largely reflects a U.S. concept of human rights, emphasizing beneficence and nonmaleficence, fidelity and responsibility, integrity, and justice as its core ethical principles. If U.S. IRBs evaluate research proposals of psychologists conducting research in other countries, it is possible that the values and beliefs of those research participants will not be recognized in the research process. IRBs in the United States greatly emphasize how it is participants' right to have autonomy in informed consent (i.e., individual agency in choice to participate in research or not), as opposed to a value, particularly when related to groups identified as vulnerable or in need of protection. Constructions of autonomy differ across cultures, and this should have implications on how informed consent is operationalized (London, 2002). In general, in many countries, U.S. IRBs are at a disadvantage for having little familiarity with some key contextual issues necessary for assessing the ethical standards of a research protocol (London, 2002). No ethics code is currently in place that provides guidance for researchers working within the context of IRBs, so they are able to account for contextually relevant factors in evaluating a research protocol without including ethnocentric assumptions and biases in the decision making process (Leong & Lyons, 2010). These complexities and limitations of the APA Ethics Code in providing guidance to U.S. psychologists highlight the need to consult other guidelines (Leong & Lyons, 2010).

In response to the pressing need for specific standards for psychologists conducting cross-cultural and international research, Leong and Lyons (2010) recommended referring to APA's "Resolution on Culture and Gender Awareness in International Psychology" (hereinafter referred to as the APA Resolution), which was formulated by the Council of Representatives on July 28, 2004 (see Exhibit 6.2). We propose that this APA Resolution serve as another group-level framework to guide the study and understanding of the ethical challenges inherent in conducting multinational organizational research. The passing of this resolution was largely influenced by the realization of a set of issues facing the world of psychology. Although the majority of psychologists live outside the United States (Hogan, 1995), U.S. leadership in world of psychology and organizational research (Tsui et al., 2007) is perceived as disproportionately influential, partly because of access to research funds, an abundance of U.S. publication outlets, and the wide acceptance of the English language. As a result, U.S.-grounded, -normed, and -structured measures dominate U.S. empirical research practices, and U.S. assessment procedures, tests, and normative standards have been used extensively in other countries, sometimes without consideration of cultural differences that affect reliability and validity. Ultimately, materials need to be developed and disseminated that will facilitate the training of organizational psychologists to conduct culturally appropriate multinational research.

## EXHIBIT 6.2
### American Psychological Association (APA) Resolution on Culture and Gender Awareness in International Psychology

Let it be resolved that the American Psychological Association will:

1. Advocate for more research on the role that cultural ideologies have in the experience of women and men across and within countries on the basis of sex, gender identity, gender expression, ethnicity, social class, age, disabilities, and religion.
2. Advocate for more collaborative research partnerships with colleagues from diverse cultures and countries leading to mutually beneficial dialogues and learning opportunities.
3. Advocate for critical research that analyzes how cultural, economic, and geopolitical perspectives may be embedded within U.S. psychological research and practice.
4. Encourage more attention to a critical examination of international cultural, gender, gender identity, age, and disability perspectives in psychological theory, practice, and research at all levels of psychological education and training curricula.
5. Encourage psychologists to gain an understanding of the experiences of individuals in diverse cultures, and their points of view and to value pluralistic world views, ways of knowing, organizing, functioning, and standpoints.
6. Encourage psychologists to become aware of and understand how systems of power hierarchies may influence the privileges, advantages, and rewards that usually accrue by virtue of placement and power.
7. Encourage psychologists to understand how power hierarchies may influence the production and dissemination of knowledge in psychology internationally and to alter their practices according to the ethical insights that emerge from this understanding.
8. Encourage psychologists to appreciate the multiple dilemmas and contradictions inherent in valuing culture and actual cultural practices when they are oppressive to women, but congruent with the practices of diverse ethnic groups.
9. Advocate for cross-national research that analyzes and supports the elimination of cultural, gender, gender identity, age, and disability discrimination in all arenas—economic, social, educational, and political.
10. Support public policy that supports global change toward egalitarian relationships and the elimination of practices and conditions oppressive to women.

*Note.* From *Resolution on Culture and Gender Awareness in International Psychology,* by the American Psychological Association, 2004, Washington, DC: American Psychological Association. Copyright 2004 by the American Psychological Association. Available at http://www.apa.org/about/governance/council/policy/gender.aspx

With the passing of the APA Resolution, the APA drew attention to 10 critical areas of consideration (listed in Exhibit 6.2). Specifically, Resolutions 2, 3, and 5 advocate that psychologists be critical of applying U.S. psychological research and practices to other cultures and adopt a highly collaborative and pluralistic approach to research such that organizational research practices are largely influenced by input from organizational members in the cultures under investigation. On the basis of this resolution, a call to action to critically consider the cross-cultural challenges in conducting ethical multinational research would be both timely and useful.

In essence, the APA Resolution goes above and beyond the narrow set of "dos and don'ts" inherent in the APA Ethics Code and makes recommendations on how American organizational psychologists can promote more research that is collaborative, respects other cultures, seeks to improve the well-being of persons in other countries, recognizes power hierarchies, and seeks to eliminate or reduce discrimination in organizations. At the same time, as a resolution of the APA, it is a set of nonbinding areas of consideration that still leaves considerable room for interpretation and variation in implementation. Indeed, there are no consequences for any American organizational psychologist who chooses not to follow the resolution.

**Individual Dimension**

Although we recommend that individuals who are conducting multinational organizational research seek guidance for ethical challenges from the Universal Declaration, the APA Ethics Code, and the APA Resolution, ultimately it is the individual researcher who has to make those ethical decisions. The universal and group dimensions are important levels of analysis, but the actual ethical decision making occurs at the individual level.

What we offer here are several recommendations to provide more information and guidance to individual organizational psychologists who are conducting multinational organizational research. Much in the same way that the International School Psychology Association has evolved their own code of ethics to deal with the ethical challenges created by international and cross-cultural research, Leong and Lyons (2010) argued that the same process has to occur within APA as it deals with the challenges of globalization. They concluded their review of the problem by a call to action for APA, particularly their Committee on International Relations in Psychology and the Division of International Psychology, to begin to assess and evaluate the nature and extent of ethical problems in conducting cross-cultural research among its members.

Specifically, Leong and Lyons (2010) argued that APA needs to provide much more systematic attention to the ethical challenges created by the increasing international and cross-cultural research being conducted by its members. Potential efforts suggested by Leong and Lyons include compiling a casebook of ethical challenges in conducting international research as a baseline activity. This in turn can be followed by a task force to create a position paper that would comprehensively address the issues raised in the Leong and Lyons article, with a series of recommendations.

An extension of that recommendation from Leong and Lyons (2010) that is specific to multinational organizational research being conducted by U.S. psychologists would be to have the Society for Industrial and Organizational Psychology (SIOP; APA Division 14) assemble a parallel task force. The mission of this SIOP task force would be to assess the extent of the problem (e.g., how many members are currently conducting cross-cultural research), review the literature, assemble case studies, and provide guidance to its members on how to address the ethical challenges of conducting multinational organizational research. As the recommendations from this new task force generate more attention, research, and scientific inquiry and study into these matters, the knowledge acquired needs to be fed back into the training arena so that current and future organizational psychologists can be educated about the proper conduct of international and cross-cultural research much in the same way that they have been educated about the ethical conduct of research in the domestic realm. Next, we discuss specific ethical dilemmas that American organizational psychologists may face when conducting multinational organizational research.

## POTENTIAL ETHICAL CHALLENGES

In this section, we highlight examples of specific ethical dilemmas that organizational psychologists may face when conducting research on multinational organizations, multicultural teams, and cross-cultural comparisons among individuals. Each is an example of a dilemma regarding the research practices of psychologists outlined in Section 8 of the APA Ethics Code. For example, challenges regarding voluntary informed consent (Standard 8.02), incentives (8.06), deception (8.07), and debriefing (8.08) are discussed as specific ethical standards in the APA Ethics Code that do not provide specific guidance to American organizational psychologists and may lead to dilemmas in multinational research. For each example, we describe how considering the universal, group, and individual dimensions of Kluckhohn and Murray's (1950) tripartite framework can help American organizational psychologists who are conducting multinational research make their research practices sensitive to such ethical dilemmas.

### Voluntary Informed Consent

*Scenario:* Professor Jones is delighted that he has been able to secure permission from an organization with manufacturing plants in 11 countries to collect data to test the influence of culture on a set of theoretical propositions. He is particularly pleased that although in the United States it would often take 2 weeks to secure enough interviewees for his pilot work, and his primary study survey response rate was only 40%, in Vietnam and Ecuador he had his interview schedule filled up in minutes and had close to a 100% response rate to his surveys. He attributes the difference to cultural norms regarding cooperativeness.

A basic ethical mandate in conducting research is to ensure that participants are voluntarily participating in the research and are fully aware of what they are consenting to be part of (APA Ethics Code Standard 8.02).[1] When conducting research in organizations globally, the concept of voluntary participation necessitates particular attention. In countries with strong government protection of workers' rights, individuals may feel assured that refusing to take part in a research study has no repercussions. However, in locations with less legal protection for workers, refusal to participate may be seen as too risky by workers, particularly if economically a loss of a job is devastating. Similarly, in high power distance locations, individuals defer to those at higher levels in the social hierarchy (Hofstede, 1980). Refusal to meet a request from an authoritative figure such as a distinguished researcher or senior level manager may be considered as grounds for sanction by coworkers, supervisors, and others in some cultural contexts. Thus, a researcher working on a multinational research project needs to pay particular attention to the nature of the consent process in locations where "voluntary" may not be viewed as voluntary by workers or where refusal to take part in research might be viewed negatively by organizational higher-ups. In the scenario, Professor Jones's high level of cooperation could indeed be due to cultural norms leading individuals to be more inclined to accede to requests for assistance, but it could also be because of concerns about negative consequences being associated with noncooperation in the workplace.

Throughout this volume, mention has been made of ensuring not just literal translation correctness but also construct equivalency. Similarly, researchers need to attend to how their consent form or request to participate is understood within a particular cultural context. Bhutta (2004) reviewed medical research on the use of informed consent procedures in developing countries and concluded that little attention is given to understanding what constitutes "informed" for different cultures. The same care that is applied to translation processes and equivalence in surveys and tests should be provided to the written and oral procedures for obtaining consent to

---

[1]APA Ethics Code Standard 8.05 also applies to this discussion. Standard 8.05 specifies under which conditions psychologists may dispense with informed consent, such as when research would not reasonably be assumed to create distress or harm (e.g., study of normal educational practices studied in educational settings). Indeed, what creates harm or distress (including legal, financial, or employment distress) varies across cultures; therefore, organizational psychologists conducting multinational research would need to attend to country-specific factors that could create harm or distress before choosing to dispense with informed consent.

participate, as well as to any recruitment materials. Fitzgerald, Marotte, Verdier, Johnson, and Pape (2002) noted that ''research participants in a less-developed country can comprehend a complex consent form if sufficient care is taken to provide them with information'' (p. 1301). However, Adams et al. (2007) also noted that Western researchers may regularly include information in informed consent procedures that some cultural groups would see as unnecessary and inappropriate; a flexible approach to what informed consent might look like across cultures is required rather than a one-size-fits-all consent protocol.

Research investigations regarding culture and consent are rare, but hypotheses regarding likely connections can be derived from knowledge of cultural differences in values. For example, those who are high in uncertainty avoidance seek to reduce the unpredictability of the future (Hofstede, 1980). In cultural contexts with higher levels of uncertainty avoidance (e.g., Latin American countries; House, Hanges, Javidan, Dorfman, & Gupta, 2004), more information about the research process and what will occur may be desired. Research on how collectivism relates to acquiescence to research requests in the workplace, and how power distance relates to refusal rates may also be informative.

According to the Universal Declaration, it is a universal principle across cultures and countries that all research participants are entitled to a truly informed consent (Respect for the Dignity of Persons and Peoples), and it is important for psychologists to attend to the cultural context that makes their participation voluntary (i.e., free of coercion) and informed (i.e., truly understood). At the group level, the APA Resolution is particularly useful in advocating that researchers study how cultural power hierarchies influence participant behaviors (Resolution 6) and how socio-cultural context influences participants' understanding and acceptance of the consent procedures (Resolution 5; for an example, see House et al., 2004). Case examples could be assembled by the APA and SIOP task forces to provide guidance for individual organizational psychologists as they make decisions about informed consent procedures in a given cultural context.

In our scenario, Professor Jones should start by engaging local cultural experts from Vietnam and Ecuador in reviewing his consent procedures. Such a review might reveal ways in which to word consent so that participants understand it is voluntary and not related to their employment status. Survey data collection procedures might require different approaches in different locations, where a face-to-face informed consent might be needed rather than just reading a written consent document. Although such changes might lower Professor Jones's response rate, he can be more assured that the consent obtained was indeed voluntary and informed.

## Incentives

*Scenario:* Professor Kim has been very successful in securing grant funding for her research, which then allows her to offer incentives, such as $50 gift cards for retailers, to participants. She is now expanding her data collection from the U.S. to employees in Tijiuana, Mexico, and plans to offer similar incentives for participation. A colleague points out to her that she should make her research dollars stretch further as a comparable incentive in Mexico would be a lot less than $50. Another colleague also questions whether her incentive is almost coercive, noting that it would be difficult to refuse to participate in a study when it involves turning down the equivalent of many hours of wages in a high-poverty area. Professor Kim wonders whether it is fairer to treat everyone identically in terms of exact amount given or in terms of value of the incentive and also whether differential valuing of an incentive might introduce a confound into her research study.

In the United States, incentives for participating in research, such as payments, are considered appropriate as long as they are not so large as to be considered coercive (Standard 8.06; APA Ethics Code). When conducting multinational research in organizations, one must consider carefully whether similar incentives can and should be used. In the scenario, Professor Kim recognized that the meaning of an incentive can vary on the basis of economic differences across countries; one can also argue that the meaning of receiving any incentive can differ across cultures that are economically comparable. In our own research, we have recognized that providing small tokens of appreciation for completing a survey (e.g., a pencil) would be considered polite and appropriate in some Asian cultures, whereas a pencil as a token of appreciation would have considerably less meaning in many Western societies. In collecting data in some South American countries, we found that a coupon for a free lunch was viewed as a more meaningful and attractive incentive than money, whereas in other countries this was not as valued as much as an equivalent amount of cash.

According to the Universal Declaration, researchers should aspire to treat all research participants with respect and dignity (Principle I: Respect for the Dignity of Persons and Peoples); as the meaning of respect associated with compensation values varies across cultural contexts, organizational psychologists need to attend to these differences. In line with the APA Resolution, at the group level, researchers considering incentives need to do their homework regarding what is culturally appropriate and what is incentivizing in that context. However, they must also guard against the inducement being difficult to refuse. Corporations have long dealt with how economic contexts might influence the fairness of equivalent compensation packages and often struggle with how to set compensation, particularly for expatriates (Bonache,

Sanchez, & Zárraga-Oberty, 2009; Sims & Schraeder, 2005). So too must researchers keep economic context in mind to be fair in their multinational research. Accumulating case examples of compensation strategies to help guide practices of other researchers could provide the foundation for training individual organizational psychologists to navigate the social and economic systems that impact the meaning of incentives in a given cultural context.

Professor Kim would do well to consult local cultural experts regarding the use of incentives and the appropriateness of incentives within the local Mexican context. She might consider conducting some pilot work to uncover what incentives are viewed in comparable ways to those she is offering in the United States, so as to create a parallel inducement to participate.

## Deception

*Scenario:* Professor Smith has obtained approval from his university's IRB to conduct a study involving mild deception. To see how individuals react to team members with various characteristics, he has created a simulation with one team member who is a confederate, or actor, unknown to the other participants who believe all are taking part in a job-related training program. In accordance with his approved protocol, participants are thoroughly debriefed at the end of the simulation. As he collects data at training sites across countries, he is surprised with the level of outrage expressed in some locations at the mild deception involved. However, while those in the United States are sometimes surprised that the confederate was not acting genuinely, they generally appreciate the need for the deception to evaluate how individuals interact.

APA holds the use of deception to be ethically sound only when it is justified by the study's significant prospective scientific, educational, or applied value; when it is not reasonably expected to cause physical pain or severe emotional distress; and when alternative procedures with no deception are not feasible (APA Ethics Code Standard 8.07). However, cultural differences in how deception is viewed may make the ethical soundness of the same procedure different across contexts. For example, Seiter, Bruschke, and Bai (2002) found that culture interacted with type of deception and perceived motive for deception to affect how acceptable a deception was considered across American and Chinese students.

The Universal Declaration considers the well-being (Competent Caring for the Well-Being of Persons and Peoples) and honest (Integrity) treatment of participants to be universal principles of ethical guidelines. When conducting research that involves deception, even of a mild form such as not fully disclosing the exact purpose of a study, it is important that the cross-cultural researcher investigate the acceptability of such deception within each cultural context studied. It is important for organizational psychologists to understand how cultural ideologies shape views about deception. Procedures may have to be altered or explanations and debriefings enhanced in certain locations to ensure that individuals fully understand what has occurred and that there are no harmful effects from the deception. Individual organizational psychologists could make their decisions about deception on the basis of case examples and training.

Professor Smith might take several steps to ensure that his use of deception is culturally acceptable. First, in consulting with local ethics review boards and local experts, he may have been forewarned regarding the reactions to his procedure. This information might have been used to alter the level and nature of deception to one more culturally acceptable, to create clearer consent procedures that inform of the possible deception, or to create enhanced debriefing procedures to justify the deception and to ensure no harmful effects occur.

## Debriefing

*Scenario:* Professor Alvarez has been conducting research on personality's influence on behavior in team contexts for quite some time and has recently begun collecting data with a large multinational firm. She collects personality inventory data from team members, as well as ratings of team functioning and performance. Her typical procedure for debriefing participants is to provide them with some useful information regarding her research so that they might gain an appreciation for how personality affects behavior at work. In conducting a debriefing session in Amsterdam, she finds participants demanding that she show them their personality assessment scores, something that she has never done.

APA Ethics Code Standard 8.08 outlines appropriate debriefing and feedback procedures, but Ryan and Tippins (2009) noted that in some countries, the norms regarding feedback on assessment are to provide scores and interpretative information, whereas in other contexts, little individualized information is given so as to protect material security. In the Universal Declaration, researchers should aspire to ensure their participants are treated with respect, dignity (Respect for the Dignity of Persons and Peoples), and honesty (Integrity). But researchers need to be aware of cultural differences in expectations of feedback and ensure that their process provides what is expected or clarifies why it will not be provided. Organizational psychologists can achieve this by building collaborative relationships with researchers in diverse cultures and by investigating cultural norms regarding debriefing procedures. Here again, procedures may need to be vetted by experts in the cultural contexts because an implicit assumption in one context (e.g., that specific feedback is not given unless stated) may be very different from implicit assumptions in another (e.g., that feedback is always given unless stated otherwise). The accumulation of case examples can help guide and train organizational psychologists as they implement debriefing procedures in a variety of cultural contexts.

Professor Alvarez should consult with local cultural experts and local review boards prior to beginning her research to determine whether her procedures might be normative or exceptional. In this case, knowing that her lack of feedback provision would be a surprise to participants, she could develop a more detailed informed consent that highlights this point as well as provides some clear justification as to why that feedback is not provided. Alternatively, Professor Alvarez might consider whether the provision of feedback, while more demanding on her time and resources, might be essential to gaining participation in this cultural context.

## CONCLUSION

One overarching theme of the dilemmas presented in this chapter is that when operating across cultures, differences in meaning and interpretation of what is superficially similar occur, and those different inferences can mean that something that is ethically quite appropriate in one context may not be so in another. The importance of establishing ethical practices means that considerably more time and effort must go into the research process when working multinationally. We encourage organizational researchers to not only use local experts to review research materials but also to review consent procedures and processes from an ethical perspective within that culture's norms. Finally, we also propose that the ethical challenges arising from multinational organizational research can be analyzed in light of the multi-level tripartite framework of the universal, group and individual dimensions of human identity and behaviors.

---

**Best Practice Recommendations**

- Consider how cultural differences can lead to ethical dilemmas in multinational organizational research.
- Address potential ethical challenges in multinational organizational research by considering ethical guidelines that emphasize common moral frameworks around the world.
- Consider how standards for ethical practice are highly contextualized to the culture or country under investigation and adapt procedures accordingly.

*(continues)*

---

**Best Practices Recommendations (*Continued*)**

- Encourage professional organizations to develop guidelines and case examples for dealing with cross-cultural ethical dilemmas in multi-national organizational research.
- Pay attention to the nature of the consent process in locations where "voluntary" may not be viewed as voluntary by workers or where refusal to take part in research might be viewed negatively by organizational higher-ups.
- Attend to how a consent form or request to participate is understood within a particular cultural context.
- Consider what is a culturally appropriate incentive that is not coercive, when incentives are offered for participation.
- Alter procedures or enhance explanations and debriefings to ensure that individuals fully understand any deception used.
- Be aware of cultural differences in expectations of feedback and ensure that the process provides what is expected or clarifies why it will not be provided.
- Use local experts to review research materials.

## REFERENCES

Adams, V., Miller, S., Craig, S., Niyima, S., Droyoung, L., & Varner, M. (2007). Informed consent in cross-cultural perspective: Clinical research in the Tibetan autonomous region, PRC. *Culture, Medicine and Psychiatry, 31*, 445–472. doi:10.1007/s11013-007-9070-2

American Psychological Association. (2004). *Resolution on culture and gender awareness in international psychology*. Retrieved from http://www.apa.org/about/governance/council/policy/gender.aspx

American Psychological Association. (2010). *Ethical principles of psychologists and code of conduct*. Retrieved from http://www.apa.org/ethics/code/index.aspx

Ariely, D., Gneezy, U., Loewenstein, G., & Mazar, N. (2009). Large stakes and big mistakes. *The Review of Economic Studies, 76*, 451–469. doi:10.1111/j.1467-937X.2009.00534.x

Aycan, Z. (2000). Cross-cultural industrial and organizational psychology: Contributions, past developments, and future directions. *Journal of Cross-Cultural Psychology, 31*, 110–128. doi:10.1177/0022022100031001009

Aycan, Z., & Kanungo, R. N. (2001). Cross-cultural industrial and organizational psychology: A critical appraisal of the field and future directions. In N. Anderson, D. S. Ones, H. Kepir-Sinangil, & C. Viswesvaran (Eds.), *International handbook of work and organizational psychology* (Vol. 1, pp. 285–409). London, England: Sage.

Bhutta, Z. A. (2004). Beyond informed consent. *Bulletin of the World Health Organization, 81,* 771–782.

Bonache, J., Sanchez, J. I., & Zárraga-Oberty, C. (2009). The interaction of expatriate pay differential and expatriate inputs on host country nationals' pay unfairness. *International Journal of Human Resource Management, 20,* 2135–2149. doi:10.1080/09585190903178062

Council for International Organizations of Medical Science. (2002). *International ethical guidelines for biomedical research involving human subjects.* Retrieved from http://www.cioms.ch/ frame_ guidelinesnov_2002.htm

Engel, G. L. (1977, April 8). The need for a new medical model: A challenge for biomedicine. *Science, 8,* 129–136. doi:10.1126/science.847460

Erez, M. (1994). Toward a model of cross-cultural industrial and organizational psychology. In H. C. Triandis, M. D. Dunnette & L. Hough (Eds.), *Handbook of industrial and organizational psychology* (2nd. ed., Vol. 4, pp. 559–608). Palo Alto, CA : Consulting Psychologists Press.

Erez, M. (2010). Cross-cultural and global issues in organizational psychology. In S. Zedeck (Ed.), *Handbook of industrial and organizational psychology* (pp. 807–854). Washington, DC: American Psychological Association.

European Federation of Professional Psychologists Association. (2005). *Meta-code of ethics.* Retrieved from http://www.rewi.uni-jena.de/rewimedia/Downloads/LS_Ruffert/Et hical_Codes/EFPA_Meta_Code+of+Ethics.pdf

Fitzgerald, D. W., Marotte, D., Verdier, R. I., Johnson, W. D., & Pape, J. W. (2002). Comprehension during informed consent in a less-developed country. *The Lancet, 360,* 1301–1302. doi:10.1016/S0140-6736(02)11338-9

Gauthier, J. (2008). Universal declaration of ethical principles for psychologists. In J. E. Hall & E. M. Altmaier (Eds.), *Global promise: Quality assurance and accountability in professional psychology* (98–105). New York, NY: Oxford University Press.

Gelfand, M. J., Erez, M., & Aycan, Z. (2007). Cross-cultural organizational behavior. *Annual Review of Psychology, 58,* 479–514. doi:10.1146/annurev.psych.58.110405.085559

Gelfand, M. J., Leslie, L., & Fehr, R. (2008). In order to prosper, organizational psychology should . . . adopt a global perspective. *Journal of Organizational Behavior, 29,* 493–517. doi:10.1002/job.530

Gelfand, M. J., Raver, J. L., & Ehrhart, K. (2002). Methodological issues in cross-cultural organizational research. In S. Rogelberg (Ed.), *Handbook of industrial and organizational psychology research methods* (pp. 216–246). New York, NY: Blackwell.

Hofstede, G. H. (1980). *Culture's consequences: International differences in work-related values.* London, England: Sage.

Hogan, J. D. (1995) International psychology in the next century: Comment and speculation from a U.S. perspective. *World Psychology, 1,* 9–25.

House, R., Hanges, P., Javidan, M., Dorfman, P., & Gupta, V. (Eds.) (2004). *Culture, leadership, and organizations: The GLOBE study of 62 societies*. Thousand Oaks, CA: Sage.

International Association for Analytical Psychology. (2010). *IAAP code of ethics*. Retrieved from http://iaap.org/iaap-overview/iaap-ethics/code-of-ethics-responsibilities-procedures.html

International Conference on Harmonization. (1996). *ICH harmonized tripartite guideline for good clinical practice EG(R1)*. Retrieved from http://www.hhs.gov/ohrp/international/

Kluckhohn, C., & Murray, H. A. (1950). Personality formation: The determinants. In C. Kluckhohn & H. A. Murray (Eds.), *Personality in nature, society, and culture* (pp. 35–48). New York, NY: Knopf.

Lee, S. B. (2010). Informed consent: Enforcing pharmaceutical companies' obligations abroad. *Health and Human Rights, 12*, 15–28.

Leong, F. T. L. (1996). Toward an integrative model for cross-cultural counseling and psychotherapy. *Applied and Preventive Psychology, 5*, 189–209. doi:10.1016/S0962-1849(96)80012-6

Leong, F. T. L., & Lyons, B. (2010). Ethical challenges for cross-cultural research conducted by psychologists from the United States. *Ethics & Behavior, 20*, 250–264. doi:10.1080/10508421003798984

London, L. (2002). Ethical oversight of public health research: Can rules and IRBs make a difference in developing countries? *American Journal of Public Health, 92*, 1079–1084.

Pettifor, J. L. (2007). Toward a global professionalization of psychology. In M. J. Stevens & U. P. Gielin (Eds.), *Toward a global psychology: Theory, research, intervention, and pedagogy* (pp. 73–97). Mahwah, NJ: Erlbaum.

Ritchie, P. L. J. (2008). Codes of ethics, conduct, and standards as vehicles of accountability. In J. E. Hall & E. M. Altmaier (Eds.), *Global promise: Quality assurance and accountability in professional psychology* (pp. 73–97). New York, NY: Oxford University Press.

Ryan, A. M., & Tippins, N. (2009). *Designing and implementing global selection systems*. New York, NY: Wiley-Blackwell. doi:10.1002/9781444310924

Seiter, J. S., Bruschke, J., & Bai, C. (2002). The acceptability of deception as a function of perceivers' culture, deceiver's intention, and deceiver–deceived relationship. *Western Journal of Communication, 66*, 158–180. doi:10.1080/10570310209374731

Sims, R. H., & Schraeder, M. (2005). Expatriate compensation: An exploratory review of salient contextual factors and common practices. *Career Development International, 10*, 98–108. doi:10.1108/13620430510588301

Title 45. Public Welfare. 45 C.F.R. § 46 (2009).

Tsui, A. S. (2004). Contributing to global management knowledge: A case for high-quality indigenous research. *Asia Pacific Journal of Management, 21*, 491–513. doi:10.1023/B:APJM.0000048715.35108.a7

Tsui, A. S., Nifadkar, S., & Ou, Y. (2007). Cross-national cross-cultural organizational behavior research: Advances, gaps, and recommendations. *Journal of Management, 33*, 426–478.

U.S. Department of Health and Human Services. (2003). *Report of the equivalence protection working group*. Retrieved from http://www.hhs.gov/ohrp/international/

White, M. T. (2007). Guidelines for IRB review of international collaborative medical research: A proposal. *The Journal of Law, Medicine, and Ethics, 27*, 87–94. doi: 10.1111/j.1748-720X.1999.tb01440.x

World Medical Association. (2008). *Declaration of Helsinki*. Retrieved from http://www.wma.net/en/30public ations/10policies/b3/

# 7

# THE TRIALS AND TRIBULATIONS OF CROSS-CULTURAL RESEARCH

MICHELE J. GELFAND

We shall not cease from exploration
And the end of all our exploring
Will be to arrive where we started
And know the place for the first time.

—T. S. Eliot

Those of us who do cross-cultural research usually have a story of precisely when we began our journey into that global territory. For some, the interest might have developed at a very young age; for others, it might have been happenstance, having stumbled into the field after doing work within one culture for many years. The litany of reasons why we venture into the world of cross-cultural research is also very diverse—for some, it might be to discover general universal principles; for others, it is to uncover the "thick description" of a particular culture (Geertz, 1973); and for still others, it might be to simply understand the complex elephant of what culture is, addressing fundamental issues of human nature.

Although the beginnings of and passions for doing cross-cultural research are varied, researchers ultimately share many common experiences along the bumpy road of cross-cultural research—experiencing many of the joys and delights, on the one hand, and many of the trials, frustrations, and disappointments, on the other. Unfortunately, the restrictions of journal

This research is based on work supported in part by the U.S. Army Research Laboratory and the U.S. Army Research Office under Grant W911NF-08-1-0144.

179

space and norms that focus researchers on reporting hypotheses, procedures, and results make it difficult to collectively realize that many of the issues that they encounter along the way are, in fact, common. The conference "Conducting Multinational Research Projects in Organizational Psychology: Challenges and Opportunities," which took place at Michigan State University in October 2009 was a great success in helping researchers to share their research stories and to collectively make explicit what is often not discussed or implicit across many individuals. Whether you call the occasion an academic conference detailing complex research programs or a collective therapy session, sharing these stories is critical for building institutional knowledge in cultural science, for giving a realistic preview to newcomers entering the field, and for empowering all of us with information that can help facilitate high-quality cross-cultural research.

In this chapter, I detail some of my own experiences conducting cross-cultural research, including, among others, a quantitative study of tightness–looseness across 33 nations (Gelfand, Raver, et al., 2011) and a qualitative study of subjective culture in the Middle East (ME) that I embarked upon across eight nations (Gelfand, 2008). I begin with my own serendipitous entry into the field and place it in a historical context, discussing the intellectual heroes who have had a great influence on my own thinking. I then discuss some lessons learned, accumulated across many studies and from a lot of time spent in the cultural trenches. Because there are many good academic treatments of the issues that arise in the cross-cultural research process (see the volume on methodology in the seminal *Handbook of Cross-Cultural Psychology* [Triandis & Berry, 1980]; see also Cohen, 2007; Gelfand, Raver, & Holcombe Ehrhart, 2002; Matsumoto & van de Vijver, 2011), in this chapter I discuss specific examples of my own work, some published and some unpublished, to more vividly illustrate the issues that one invariably encounters when venturing into cross-cultural research territory.

## STUMBLING INTO CROSS-CULTURAL PSYCHOLOGY

My own personal journey into cross-cultural research began, to echo T. S. Eliot (1943), when I was forced to step out of my cultural comfort zone and had the acute realization of just how much had been fundamentally shaped by American culture. I was a junior in college, a sheltered kid from Long Island, when I ventured off to London for a semester. I remember the strange sounds, sights, and smells of the United Kingdom, and being completely overwhelmed—dazed and confused—from experiencing the culture shock that comes with being away from one's own familiar territory. I vividly remember a phone conversation with my father that was arguably the beginning of my journey of becoming a cross-cultural psychologist. I was telling him about how strange it was that people in my study abroad group would go to Paris, Amsterdam, Scotland, and the like, for just a few days. My father responded, in his Brooklyn accent, "Well, imagine it's like going from New York to Pennsylvania!" That metaphor gave me so much comfort that the very next day I booked a low-budget tour to Egypt. It was just like going from New York to California, I reasoned (much to my father's dismay!). Those travels, and later living on an Israeli Kibbutz, sparked a lifelong passion for understanding the dynamics of culture. I was fascinated with basic questions, such as: How is it that culture shapes the self so profoundly, yet culture is so invisible and taken for granted? How does culture develop, how is it sustained, and how does it change over time? How does culture contribute to misunderstandings and conflict at the individual, organizational, and national levels?

When I was back at Colgate University for my senior year, I was fortunate to find that Carolyn Keating, a cross-cultural psychologist, was teaching a cross-cultural human development class. Keating was a student of Marshall Segall, and it was in that course that I became exposed to their great work from the 1960s in Africa that showed that even basic psychological processes—such as visual perception—are not necessarily universal. At the time, the notion that humans do not vary in fundamental ways of perceiving the physical world—space, size, distance, or color—went largely unquestioned in psychology. Segall, Campbell, and Herskovits (1966) turned this assumption on its head. Taking a largely empiricist and Brunswikian perspective, they argued that people use whatever cues they have learned through their past experience to perceive objects, a process they referred to as *ecological cue validity*. Their research, done across 15 countries, indeed showed that Europeans were much more susceptible to classic illusions, such as the Müller–Lyer illusion and the Sander parallelogram illusion. Aside from these fascinating differences in deep psychological processes, I was intrigued by their explanation of the findings: In explaining such differences, Segall et al. advanced the *carpentered world hypothesis*, which suggests that individuals who experience a lot of rectangular angles in their environment (which is more the case in Western cultures as compared with non-Western cultures) would be more likely to interpret nonrectangular figures as representations of rectangles, thereby exacerbating these types of visual illusions. I found this work—namely, that *culture* is a prime source of experience that causes different habits of inference to arise—to be completely fascinating, and it was my first entrée into the wide world of cross-cultural research.

It was in that course that I also became inspired by work that had been done in the "culture and personality school" in the 1950s and 1960s, and in particular, on how socialization processes and personality factors vary within a particular society (i.e., Benedict, 1946; Mead, 1928) and how culture shapes, and is shaped by, personality across different societies (B. B. Whiting & Whiting, 1975; J. W. M. Whiting & Child, 1953). I was intrigued by the ecological approach in B. B. Whiting and Whiting's (1975) classic work *The Children of Six Cultures*. Their theory highlighted the role of the physical environment (e.g., climate, terrain), history (e.g., migrations), and maintenance systems (e.g., subsistence patterns, social structure), as important factors that shape children's learning environment, which in turn were thought to affect the development of adult personality (including learned and innate components) and projective expressive systems. Although the theory had a largely deterministic flavor and drew heavily on psychoanalysis, which was of less interest to me, the broad view of culture—and the idea that one could use the scientific method to understand it—was incredibly inspiring to that sheltered kid from Long Island!

After I graduated from college, I was determined to go to graduate school to study culture and psychology, yet it was clear that there were no PhD degrees in this field. In a fateful conversation, Keating recommended that I talk to Richard Brislin, then head of the East–West Center at the University of Hawaii and expert in cross-cultural training, about graduate programs in the field. After listening to my interests, Brislin declared that I should work with Harry Triandis at Illinois. The rest was history.

Triandis was an incredible mentor who influenced my thinking and my approach to science. The sheer breadth and depth of his study of culture—both basic cultural processes and culture's applications to personality, social, and organizational psychology—is forever inspiring to me. His classic early work on the *Analysis of Subjective Culture* (1972) has influenced my thinking to this day. Triandis was highly influenced by the work of Herskovits (1955), who defined *culture* as the human-made part of the environment, consisting of both *physical* elements (e.g., tools, bridges, educational systems, religious institutions) and *subjective* elements (e.g., beliefs, attitudes, norms, values). Triandis set out to further explore subjective culture and was the first to develop methods to systematically identify social psychological constructs, such as categorizations, associations, attitudes, beliefs, expectations, roles, and norms across cultural groups. His work showed that coherent themes cut across these different elements of subjective culture—for example, individualism and collectivism, which we later examined in terms of its vertical and horizontal elements (Triandis & Gelfand, 1998). Another major contribution of the *Analysis of Subjective Culture* was that, similar to the work of B. B. Whiting and J. W. M. Whiting (and later Berry, 1979), it placed the thematic elements of subjective culture into a larger ecological and historical framework. The theoretical framework that was developed included *distal antecedents* (e.g., climate) and *historical events* (e.g., wars), *proximal antecedents* (e.g., occupations, language used, religion), and *immediate antecedents of action* (which included all the elements listed above), which result in patterns of action. The *Analysis of Subjective Culture* set the stage for large-scale studies on dimensions of culture that took hold in the 1980s and had a strong influence on my later interest in tightness–looseness and the structure of everyday situations. Triandis's work on the dynamics of culture (Trafimow, Triandis, & Goto, 1991) inspired my later interest in culture by situation interactions in the domain of negotiation and conflict (Gelfand & Realo, 1999; Morris & Gelfand, 2004).

Aside from the breadth of his theoretical training, Triandis gave me a big dose of the methodological realities that one confronts in doing cross-cultural research. His admiration for both *emics* (culture-specific elements) and *etics* (culture-general elements), and his insistence on using multiple methods, inspired me to use qualitative interviews, surveys, experiments, and archival methods, among others. He grounded me in the rich history and debates in the field, which I believe are critical to convey to new scholars (Kashima & Gelfand, 2011). Above all, Triandis's optimism, modesty, and good humor helped to bring the human element into science. His philosophy—that it is important to be passionate about one's work, to not take yourself too seriously, and to not be afraid to be controversial—has served as an important reminder to me throughout my career on the bumpy road of cross-cultural research.

## VIEWS FROM THE TRENCHES: TRIALS AND TRIBULATIONS OF CROSS-CULTURAL RESEARCH

As a graduate student in the early 1990s, I read many papers about the issues that one confronts when doing cross-cultural research, but these challenges, which seem like distal abstractions as a student, come to life when you begin doing the work. The cross-cultural research process, as I described it (Gelfand, Higgins, et al., 2002), involves a road map wherein one has to make numerous judgment calls, or crucial decisions that need to be made without a hard or fast rule (McGrath, 1982). The research process is also cultural in that the very issues that researchers often seek to study—values, norms, beliefs, assumptions—also infiltrate every stage of the process, from deciding what is a worthy question (which itself is value laden; Gelfand, Leslie, & Fehr, 2008); to creating a multicultural research team (in which cultural intelligence is critical for managing cultural diversity); to designing and implementing a particular research method (which involves unique cultural reactions, differential motivations, and ethical issues); to analyzing, interpreting, and publishing the data. In this respect, methods are infused with culture; they are difficult to separate. As Shweder (1990) once aptly remarked, "You can't take the stuff out of the psyche and you can't take the psyche out of the stuff" (p. 22). So too is the case with conducting cross-cultural research.

## Theory as the Starting Point

Probably the best advice I got when starting to do cross-cultural research was on the importance of having a strong theory. Because of the sheer number of "rival hypotheses" that can explain one's findings (other than culture), having a strong theory provides one with much greater confidence that the results are not due to extraneous factors. *Theory* here refers to both the constructs of interest (What is the construct space? How is it operationalized?) and the relationships between constructs. Cross-cultural research is complex because the theory of the construct itself requires serious consideration, particularly given the risk of "imposing" etic constructs on other cultures (Berry, 1980). Many, including myself, deal with this issue statistically—can one demonstrate that the scales being used have similar factor structures, similar loadings, and are in essence "equivalent" (Berry, Poortinga, Segall, & Dasen, 1992). One of my first research projects on sexual harassment did just this. I used simultaneous factor analysis in multiple samples to demonstrate that the Sexual Experiences Questionnaire (SEQ), which had been developed in the United States, had the same structure in Brazil (Gelfand, Fitzgerald, & Drasgow, 1995). Over time, however, I became skeptical with using this statistical approach to justify the theory of the construct because it assumes that the construct space itself—which has almost always been derived from Western theory and Western samples in the vast majority of cases—has been "mapped" appropriately. From a psychometric perspective, although factor analysis can illustrate whether certain items or dimensions are relevant (are similar) or are contaminated (are not working well in other cultures), or both, it cannot reveal whether important dimensions of a construct have been neglected or omitted (e.g., whether certain dimensions of harassment are novel in Brazil). This is a theoretical issue and requires a deep understanding of the cultural context. I often find myself asking, why would a construct developed in the United States necessarily have the full range of variation that is needed to capture realities of the phenomenon in another context? For example, Ramesh and Gelfand (2010) showed that although job embeddedness was a universal predictor of turnover, family embeddedness was an important (but heretofore neglected) predictor of turnover in India (and even in the United States). Farh and Earley (1997) showed that if one wants to understand organizational citizenship behavior in China, new dimensions (unearthed in interviews about what constitutes the construct) and new measures need to be added to the construct for it to be relevant in China. To be clear, it is not necessarily the case that new dimensions and items need to be added to a construct or measure, but assuming that the construct space "travels" perfectly is problematic.

Theory also guides the choice of samples. For example, in early work that I did on culture and procedural justice, I theorized that voice was much more important in high power distance than low power distance cultures. I selected Turkey (which is high on power distance) and Costa Rica (which is low on power distance) because they are both collectivistic societies; thus, I was trying to, generally speaking, isolate the cultural variable of interest. Our sampling of cultures for a multination study on cultural tightness–looseness was likewise guided by theory of the predictors of the construct. I theorized that population density, history of territorial conflict, resource scarcity, human disease, and natural disasters are predictive of tightness–looseness, and consulted extant archival databases (see the discussion below of the promise and pitfalls of archival databases) to choose nations that reflected substantial variation on these variables (Gelfand, Raver, et al., 2011). In other work (Kashima et al., 1995), we sampled nations so as to have variability on the individual, collective, and relational self to examine culture and gender influences on these constructs. Compared with representative sampling, this approach reflects *theoretical* sampling (Boehnke, Lietz, Schreier, & Wilhelm, 2011) that aims to maximize the variability of nations according to the theory being tested.

Theory also guides measures, whether they are mediators, moderators, or control variables. The importance of unpacking cultural differences has long been discussed in cross-cultural psychology (B. B. Whiting & Whiting, 1975). Merely showing country or other group differences does not elucidate the reasons for the effects, making it critical to try to illuminate the cultural phenomenon explaining the differences found. Although much work has used survey measures of personal values (e.g., of individualism–collectivism) as potential mediators, cultural mediators need not be based on value measures on surveys—they can be based on descriptive norms (Shteynberg, Gelfand, & Kim, 2008; Zou et al., 2009); the structure of situations, roles, and networks (Gelfand, Raver, et al., 2011; Kitayama, Markus, Matsumoto, & Norasakkunkit, 1997; Morris, Podolny, & Ariel, 2000); implicit measures (Kitayama & Karasawa, 1997); and artifacts or cultural products (Morling & Lamoreaux, 2008), among other variables. Unpacking cultural differences is a tricky business, but ultimately theory is critical for identifying potential mechanisms and alternative explanations for country or group differences.

## Cultural Legwork

In my experience, compared with doing research on one sample, cross-cultural research takes much longer and requires considerably more legwork before one even launches a study. For example, gaining access to samples and developing a highly functioning cross-cultural research team are critical for a successful cross-cultural project and require time, resources, cultural skills, a lot of patience, and some degree of pure luck. Building networks of people who are interested in the same questions, committed to the same publication goals, are willing and able to do all that is required to complete the process (translations, piloting, implementing, and interpreting data), and are on the same time frame with the necessary resources is a daunting task. Managing expectations—which can be very different depending on one's cultural background—is critical from the very start of a research project. A number of basic questions need to be addressed before launching a project. Will all collaborators be authors on the study? (I personally believe this is important, having been influenced on this issue with Triandis.) Is the research question and method appropriate in the local context? How will translations be handled? Who "owns the data?" Are funding agencies involved, and does this have implications for local collaborators? Are there ethical issues that need to be discussed involving the participants, the researchers, or both? For example, in a project in which I have been examining culture and negotiation in the ME, the funding agency (Department of Defense; DoD) clearly wants to be acknowledged on publications that result. Yet for some projects, it became clear that acknowledging the DoD would place collaborators in some countries at a huge reputational risk. Knowing this, I was able to negotiate with the DoD that in some cases we cannot acknowledge the funding agency. Having honest discussions about the goals of the research, where one wants to publish it, authorship, funding, and time frames for the work is critical for the success of a multicultural research team. Of course, "honest discussions" themselves are culturally constructed, and considerable trust and cultural skills are critical for dealing with controversial issues and the invariable relationship, task, and process conflict that can occur in multicultural collaborations. There is the added temptation, in my experience, of dealing with these issues using e-mail discussions, but e-mail is too "lean of a medium" (Daft & Lengel, 1984) to accommodate the complexity of these tasks. In my own work, I try to meet face to face often, talk on Skype (at least you can gauge nonverbals), and communicate frequently to ensure that everyone is fully comfortable with the many issues involved in the research.

Having agreed on the nature of the collaboration, one is then in a position to get the research started. This itself also takes considerable time, energy, and patience. Whereas in my own unicultural work in the lab or field, I can typically get my surveys or experiments ready for testing relatively quickly, implementing cross-cultural research involves many other steps. When using an experiment or survey across cultures, it is critical to discuss and modify the questions, methods, and designs with local collaborators, and critically, to expect this cultural input to change one's plans.

For example, in a recent collaboration, I created a multicultural team involving collaborators from Egypt, Iraq, Jordan, Lebanon, Pakistan, Turkey, and the United Arab Emirates to understand important subjective culture—values, focal concerns, beliefs, and norms—in the ME region. Because there is very little research on the psychology of culture in the ME, I thought it was critical to use qualitative methods to gain a "thick description" (Geertz, 1973) before developing surveys, experiments, or other methods. I settled on conducting interviews in all of these countries using the methodology pioneered in the *Analysis of Subjective Culture* (Triandis, 1972) as the platform, which involves word associations, antecedents and consequences of relevant constructs, and methods to illuminate situational variation in the constructs. Before developing the interview protocols, I read through numerous books and articles about the region, and then drafted a list of potential constructs to discuss with the ME team. These constructs were then the subject of many discussions within the team, and various questions were dropped as other questions were added. Based on this input, I drafted the next version of the interview protocols, which included interview probes on the psychology of connections (*wasta*), fate, honor (*sharaf, irdh*), face and public image (*wujah*), respect, modesty, dignity, values, trust, negotiation, conflict, revenge, forgiveness and apologies, and collaboration. This next draft was then the subject again of numerous discussions and iterations. After several months, we settled on a final set of protocols to pilot with local focus groups. Although the process was very time consuming, with this extensive cultural legwork I could be much more confident that the interview protocols reflected important focal concerns and would yield valuable "cultural fruit."

Before even piloting the protocols (which is critical to do before launching the interviews), we had a lot more work to do to get ready to launch the study. First, there was the anguishing process of translation. All protocols were originally written in English and had to be translated into Arabic, Farsi, Turkish, and Urdu. Once translated into the local language, we had different translators back-translate them into English so we could compare the original English version and the back-translated version. Invariably there were many discrepancies, so we then needed to figure out where the differences in translation occurred (was it a problem in the original translation? or was the back-translation the culprit?). In my experience, translations often reveal problems that have a basis in poor English, for example, double-barreled statements, colloquial language, metaphors, and idioms that don't even make sense to English speakers! As a rule of thumb, I have always assumed that the English version will need to be modified in addition to the translated version. Another rule of thumb is that one should estimate the time needed to do translations and then double or even triple this time to have a realistic estimate. Coordinating numerous translations (wherein there might need to be different changes that are standardized across all materials) takes considerable time. For example, in our study of tightness–looseness across 33 nations (Gelfand, Raver, et al., 2011), our study materials were in 21 languages, and the translation process took a full year to complete.

When one has confidence in the final translated materials, it is time to pilot the methods. Piloting is critical for the quality of cross-cultural research projects (Gelfand, Higgins, et al., 2002). All methods—experiments, interviews, surveys—need to be carefully examined for numerous criteria before implementing the research: Are participants familiar with the tasks, comfortable with them, motivated by them? Do they understand the instructions in the intended way? How do they react to the experimenter, interviewer, or other "epistemic authority" running the study? Are they perceived as ethically acceptable? Is there a problem with using deception if applicable? Is there ample time for the study? Are the incentives appropriate in all cultural groups? Piloting the study before data collection, in my experience, always results in important changes. For example, our pilots of the interview study discussed previously revealed a lot of perceived overlap in the questions that made participants less motivated. As a result of this feedback, we had to further condense and reorganize the protocols. Our pilots also revealed that we needed to spend more time building rapport, particularly in rural areas, to make people more comfortable answering the questions, some of which were highly sensitive.

Many of the pilots that I have conducted illustrate how the methodological choices we make are often laden with Western assumptions that, ironically, can relate to the very questions we are asking. Put differently, the very "stuff" that we're interested in looking at cross-culturally is found in cultural issues that one encounters in the method. For example, in Gelfand and Realo (1999), we were interested in examining how accountability produces very different effects in negotiation depending on the cultural context. Much research on accountability in the United States in the 1970s and 1980s showed that accountability produces competition in negotiation: In fact, negotiators assume that their constituencies want them to be competitive (Benton & Druckman, 1973; Gruder, 1971). It is not surprising that accountability activated competitive construals and behaviors, and resulted in lower negotiation outcomes for individualistic samples. We reasoned that accountability need not produce competition in all cultures as it does in the individualistic United States; rather, we hypothesized that accountability acts as a norms enforcement mechanism, producing whatever is normative in the cultural environment. To test this, we first conducted research in the United States among Asian Americans and Caucasians and showed that, in fact, among collectivists (Asian participants), accountability activated cooperative construals and behaviors, and resulted in higher negotiation outcomes. These effects were reversed in unaccountable negotiations, when, in effect, negotiators were released from normative pressures to do what is expected. Interestingly, when we tried to pilot the material in Japan for a follow-up study, we had a very difficult time getting our manipulations of accountability to work. In fact, low accountability situations were seen as having very high accountability, even after numerous pilots, making it difficult for us to run the study in Japan (at least as a scenario study). In retrospect, it is not particularly surprising that getting the manipulations of accountability to be equivalent in the United States and Japan is challenging, given that Japan is a very tight culture with much higher monitoring (Gelfand, Raver, et al., 2011) and thus has higher naturally occurring accountability as compared with the United States. Thus, what is perceived to be a low-accountability situation in one culture may be seen as a high-accountability situation in a culture with a higher base rate, in general, of monitoring. This one example aside, it is critical to ensure that one's manipulations are understood in the same way and have equal strength before data collection, even if the manipulation has worked time and time again in one's own cultural context.

In addition to having equal cognitive comprehension of the task instructions, it is important to ensure that participants in all cultures have equal motivation to perform the task. In other words, comprehension of the task is not enough; it also must be equally engaging across groups. Again, ironically enough, the very nature of the research question that is being addressed can reveal cultural issues in motivation in the method. For example, in Gelfand, Higgins, et al. (2002) we were interested in cross-cultural differences in egocentric biases in negotiation. Much research in the field of negotiation has illustrated that negotiators tend to view their own behaviors as more fair than others (Thompson & Loewenstein, 1992), which leads to more aggressive behavior, less concession making, and ultimately lower outcomes (Babcock & Loewenstein, 1997). In Gelfand, Higgins, et al. (2002), we theorized that serving biases of fairness in negotiation would be consistent with ideals within individualistic cultures, in which the self is served by focusing on one's positive attributes to stand out and be better than others but would be disruptive to ideals in collectivistic cultures, in which the self is served by focusing on one's negative characteristics to blend in and maintain interdependence with others (Heine, Lehman, Markus, & Kitayama, 1999). We first did a number of survey and scenario studies to examine cultural differences in egocentric biases of fairness in conflict in the United States and Japan, and then in our last study, we set out to examine how differences in egocentric biases affect hard negotiation outcomes. We created a simulation that required students to assume rules and to negotiate over four issues. The context for the negotiation, we thought, was very interesting and engaging—namely, a negotiation between two distinguished honor student clubs over space, time, and other issues on which they needed to coordinate. We piloted the task in the

United States, and it was a smashing success. Students reported that it was very motivating and enjoyable. When piloting in Japan, however, we found that the task completely flopped—the students reported being uncomfortable and unmotivated with the issues that in their cultural eyes seemed very atypical. It became clear from discussions that this was a vertical individualistic task and produced negative reactions in Japan. Unbelievably, the very same question that we were interested in (cultural differences in how much people like to stand out and their implications for negotiation in different cultures) became embedded in our research tasks! We went back to the drawing board and developed a new buyer and seller task that proved to be much more motivating and relevant in both contexts (Gelfand, Higgins, et al., 2002). Without this extensive piloting, we would have missed the fact that even though it would have been possible to translate the original honor's club task, and have it be equally comprehensible in both cultures, participants would not have been equally motivated to engage in the simulation in Japan, and our results would be very difficult to interpret.

In other work we (Gelfand, Brett, et al., 2011) have done, pilots and focus groups have often revealed that the methods that we export abroad are far too decontextualized to be understandable and motivating in other cultures. In our interview questions, for example, we initially asked questions such as "Is compromise good or bad?" and later adapted the questions to have tags to reflect the *circumstances* under which is it good or bad. In our interviews, respondents in general in the ME needed to know with whom, about what issues, and in what circumstances we were asking about compromise, negotiation, *wasta*, revenge, forgiveness, apologies, among other constructs. We rarely found that our American counterparts asked for this information. In experiments we have likewise found it important to include much more information in the case materials for the instructions and study materials to make any sense. For example, in our case *At Your Service* (Brett & Gelfand, 2008), we had individuals negotiate either as part of a team or as part of a dyad in the United States and Taiwan. The case involved a relationship between two individuals who were either trying to form a deal to own a restaurant together (i.e., a deal-making context) or were trying to dissolve a relationship that had been subject to many problems (i.e., a disputing context). When we first wrote the case, we included details only about the issues to be resolved. Yet pilot studies in Taiwan revealed that they could not negotiate the case without more information about the people, their histories, their relationship, and so on. Put simply, it was too low context for a high-context culture (Hall, 1976).

Other Western assumptions also sneak into researchers' methods. For example, in the time-as-money Western culture, researchers often assume that participants can read the materials, get into roles, answer questions, and negotiate a case in a remarkably short time. In the same Taiwan–U.S. study (Brett &

Gelfand, 2008) discussed above, we ran the study in 90 minutes, but we found that more than 50% of the Taiwanese participants failed to reach agreement in that time. We found some very interesting results, but to trust the findings, we had to rerun the entire study to ensure that our results were not a methodological artifact of not having enough time to negotiate. Ultimately, the results of our follow-up experiment were identical, giving us confidence in the theory. Nevertheless, in this case, it was clear to us that the same amount of time that is needed in one culture to complete a study might be highly problematic in another.

In summary, the above descriptions and examples make clear that it is important to choose a task collaboratively with all local researchers that will ensure equal familiarity, comprehension, motivation, and ethicality in the study and illuminate any potential problems in the implementation of the task. Either focus groups or pilot analyses should be held in each culture, and the results of these preliminary analyses should be used to make substantive changes in the protocols. In the pilot test or focus groups, I have found it useful to employ comprehension and motivation checks (Berry, 1980) or use judgmental methods with which experts evaluate the stimuli (Segall et al., 1992).

## Methodological Tradeoffs and the Importance of Triangulation

McGrath (1982) instilled in me the idea that all methods are flawed and each has strengths and weaknesses. In cross-cultural research, all methods have additional cultural baggage (Gelfand, Higgins, et al., 2002), and many rival hypotheses can threaten one's confidence in the interpretation of cultural differences that are found. Because of this, I have always found that to the greatest extent possible, it is important to see one's theory replicated with more than one method—that is, to see that the results triangulate.

For example, questionnaires or surveys have a number of advantages—they may be less intrusive than other methods (e.g., laboratory experiments, discussed below) and provide the ability to collect data on a wide range of questions at any one time. Cross-cultural challenges to surveys abound, however, including potential differences in motivation, understanding of instructions, validity, reliability, and response sets, making it important to replicate findings with another method. In our study of cultural tightness–looseness (Gelfand, Raver, et al., 2011), we measured the strength of norms and degree of sanctioning across 33 nations with Likert survey measures (e.g., "There are many social norms that people are supposed to abide by in this country"; "In this country, if someone acts in an inappropriate way, others will strongly disapprove"; "People in this country almost always comply with social norms"). Because survey measures can be subject to response sets and a lack of equivalence, it is important to perform proctrustes factor analysis in all cultures to examine the structure of the measure and also check to see whether standardization is required. In addition to these issues, differential motivation to respond (e.g., social desirability) and potential differences in the interpretation of the items also make it critical to gather additional data from other sources in order to provide convergent validity for one's survey measure. For example, we have more confidence in the Likert scale, given that tightness–looseness scores were strongly correlated with nonsurvey measures, including expert ratings on the construct, higher monitoring in society (more police per capita), and more severe punishments (e.g., the death penalty) for crime. The questionnaire measure was also correlated with unobtrusive measures, including the percentage of people who write with their left hand (a very visible indication of being "deviant" from norms) and with greater accuracy of public clocks in cities, indicating a greater concern with order and uniformity. By showing that our tightness–looseness scores were correlated with other indicators (Gelfand, Raver, et al., 2011), rival hypotheses due to response sets or differences in meaning of items, among many other issues, were reduced. In another study that relied on surveys of perceptions of conflict episodes in which we used multidimensional scaling to examine the dimensions on which people perceive conflicts in the United States and Japan (Gelfand et al., 2001), we coupled this method with analyses of newspaper accounts of conflicts in the *New York Times* and Japanese *Yamiuri*. Both analyses illustrated that although cooperation versus competition (or win–lose) frames were universal, U.S. conflicts were perceived to be much more competitive (win oriented) than those in Japan. In this case, cultural documents such as newspapers can help to provide additional confidence that one's theory generalizes beyond one method.

As another example, experiments offer numerous advantages in that they provide a controlled research environment and allow for greater inferences in causal relationships. Laboratory research is also beneficial in that it enables one to assess implicit attitudes in addition to explicit self-reported attitudes. Yet laboratory research, particularly in cross-cultural settings, can present many problems that can reduce confidence in the interpretability of the results. As noted earlier, it is critical that laboratory tasks and procedures are equally understood by and motivating to individuals across different cultures. The very artificiality of the laboratory environment (and the role-playing manipulations that I often use) can be unfamiliar to people outside of the West, making it critical to replicate one's theories with another method. In our research on accountability using laboratory experiments (Gelfand & Realo, 1999) or self-serving biases (Gelfand, Higgins, et al., 2002), for example, it was important to see that our effects were also replicated using scenario-based measures.

Interviews and other qualitative methods are another useful method in cross-cultural research in that they enable one to gain depth on a research question and often afford more of an understanding of emic perspectives that are especially useful in early stages of cross-cultural research. Interviews are also essential when dealing with illiterate populations. Many difficulties and judgment calls arise, however, when implementing this method. For example, characteristics of the interviewer need to be carefully chosen for their cultural appropriateness (e.g., in the ME, using female interviewers for female samples). The ways in which interviewers gain trust, develop rapport, and probe the participants to answer questions can be very different in different cultures, making it important to try to negotiate a standardized interview process with one's collaborators before data collection. For example, in some cultures, revealing information about oneself is critical for the development of trust, yet in other cultures this would be seen as inappropriate, and a practice is perceived as threatening the objectivity of the data collection. Before our interviews in the United States and ME, we searched the literature for best practices in interviewing (it was not surprising that much of this was derived from interviews with Western samples), and with input from our collaborators, we designed an interview manual, which was discussed, revised, and finalized on the basis of the entire team's input. Other aspects of the interview process, such as tape or video recording, can have very different implications depending on the culture. For example, recording interviews could be highly sensitive in some cultures—particularly in very tight cultures, in which there is a concern about authorities hearing one's responses (e.g., my experience in Iran), making additional safeguards and assurances necessary. For example, in recent work on community negotiations in the United States and Egypt, I was not able to videotape the negotiations, as Egyptians would have considered this too invasive.

Many issues arise in determining how to extract, code, and interpret interview data. For example, in my project, I needed to first transcribe all interviews (which were between 1 and 2 hours per participant) from their native language from audio files to actual text in Arabic, Turkish, Urdu, and English. Each interview produced an average of 15 to 20 pages of actual text. Because I wanted to code the data in a standardized way, I needed to develop a method to reliably extract the answers. It took approximately 6 months to develop a process in which I felt confidence. I first developed a standardized manual for all team members to discuss. For each interview question, the ME and U.S. teams first completed extractions (i.e., the answers to questions) on two to three designated transcripts for reliability purposes. I took the most difficult interviews (those with the most variance in terms of where the answers could be found, some being found right after the questions were asked and others found later in the interview as well). I computed reliability across U.S. and ME collaborators, and after several iterations and resolving several disagreements (and updating our manual), I was able to have trust in the reliability of the process.

This process was far from completed. After all the data were extracted (approximately 1 year later for all questions), I needed to figure out what to do with the extracted data. I again sought to develop a standardized code development process that all collaborators could agree on and that was reliable and valid. I was very concerned at this stage with not viewing the data through our Western glasses and allowing emic concepts and themes to be identified in each country. The process that I created ultimately involved three phases. In the first phase, ME and U.S. teams separately examined the extracted answers for a particular interview question and constructed a list of possible codes or themes for their respective countries. For the construct of honor, for example, 1,769 codes, or an average of 103 codes per question, were generated across the teams! The second phase involved sorting and organizing these codes at a conceptual level by the U.S. team with input from our ME collaborators, as well as with input from extant research. Finally, the third phase involved writing a coding manual that described the code categories in detail and set forth procedures and guidelines for coding. Coding then was done with bilingual individuals with reliability checks. This process was implemented for all questions in the interview protocols. It is not surprising that these steps take a lot of time and resources. And as with other methods, it is important to triangulate interview findings with other methods to gain confidence in the results. For example, much of the interview analyses illustrated that honor and face loss become much more contagious across individuals in the ME than the United States, generally speaking. I am currently in the process of replicating these results with free recall methods, laboratory experiments, and computational models.

Finally, archival databases also have notable strengths in cross-cultural research in that they provide another unobtrusive source of cross-cultural data. Examples include ethnographies, which provide in-depth information about a given culture, and cross-cultural databases on ecological, sociological, economic, or political variables. These sources, however, also have notable weaknesses. Preexisting databases may only be available for a limited number of countries or variables. In addition, databases may label or assess constructs differently across cultures, and as such, comparisons are problematic. In addition, without a developed theory, the use of such sources can result in dustbowl empiricism. I have found it important to try to find convergent evidence when possible to help bolster my confidence in my own research using archival methods. For example, in the study of tightness–looseness (Gelfand, Raver, et al., 2011), I wanted to test the notion that ecological threats (e.g., lack of natural resources) and man-made threats (e.g., population density, human disease) are related to tightness. To assess the extent to which nations are subject to resource scarcity, I collected data on arable land, food production, food supply, and food deprivation from the Food and Agriculture Organization of the United Nations, as well as the percentage of farmland and access to safe water in each country from

Kurian's (2001) world ranking. Data on population density were taken from the *Atlas of World Population History* in the year 1500 but also from the United Nations in 2000. To assess threats due to human disease, I located a number of different sources to triangulate the results. The index of historical prevalence of pathogens was taken from Murray and Schaller's (2010) research, in which they constructed the disease prevalence index based on early epidemiological atlases. The World Health Organization (WHO) provided data for years of life lost to communicable disease and prevalence of tuberculosis—a highly communicable disease. Mortality rates for children under 5 were also gathered from the United Nations. By finding the theoretically expected results with multiple sources, one can have more confidence in the results of archival analyses. In addition, as with other methods, it is comforting to replicate one's results with a completely different method. For example, in recent research, I have been priming ecological conditions (e.g., population density) in the laboratory to examine the theory of tightness–looseness.

In summary, all methods clearly have strengths and weaknesses, and all are very useful, particularly in combination, when doing cross-cultural research. Each method varies considerably in its capacity for gaining depth about the phenomenon (interviews), control and causal inferences (laboratory experiments), unobtrusive nonreactive measures (observations, content analyses), and the ability to have standardized, structured responses (surveys). Above all, each method presents problems for interpreting results across cultures, rendering it essential to replicate with a complementary method when possible.

## CONCLUSION

As this chapter has, I hope, illustrated, cross-cultural research is a passion for me and a lifelong journey that brings many joys. It also presents many challenges at all stages of the research process that require many difficult judgment calls that do not necessarily have one right or wrong solution. To cope with the long and bumpy road, I have always relied on the use of theory, much cultural legwork, the wisdom of my collaborators, the triangulation of methods, and patience. Textbooks and journal articles on methodological issues in cross-cultural research can also provide very useful technical advice. It is also instructive, however, to share the stories, dilemmas, and serendipity that are behind the scenes of research lives to more vividly illustrate the issues that are invariably encountered when venturing into cross-cultural research territory. This is both empowering, as many researchers experienced at the Michigan State conference, "Conducting Multinational Research Projects in Organizational Psychology: Challenges and Opportunities," and critical for building institutional knowledge in an ever growing field.

**Best Practices Recommendations**

- Always have strong theory guiding cross-cultural research. Theory is needed for the construct itself, its relationships, sampling, design, and measures.
- Involve local collaborators in every step of the research process. They know much more than you do!
- Assume there will be considerable cultural legwork in building a multicultural team before data collection.
- Conduct multiple pilots before doing your research, and expect that this cultural input will change your plans. Culture is in the method too!
- Identify rival hypotheses for results before conducting research. Measure them, control for them, or both.
- Use multiple methods to triangulate your findings.
- Attend to equivalence in measurement and response biases when examining your results.
- Be passionate, but don't take yourself too seriously! (Advice from Harry Triandis.)

## REFERENCES

Babcock, L., & Loewenstein, G. (1997). Explaining bargaining impasse: The role of self-serving biases. The Journal of Economic Perspectives, *11*, 109–126. doi:10.1257/jep.11.1.109

Benedict, R. (1946). *The chrysanthemum and the sword: Patterns of Japanese culture*. Boston, MA: Houghton Mifflin.

Benton, A. A., & Druckman, D. (1973). Salient solutions and the bargaining behavior of representatives and nonrepresentatives. *International Journal of Group Tensions, 3*, 28–39.

Berry, J. W. (1979). A cultural ecology of social behaviour. In L. Berkowitz (Ed.), *Advances in experimental social psychology* (Vol. 12, pp. 177–206). New York, NY: Academic Press.

Berry, J. W. (1980). Introduction to methodology. In H. C. Triandis & J. W. Berry (Eds.), *Handbook of cross-cultural psychology* (Vol. 2, pp. 1–28). Boston, MA: Allyn & Bacon.

Berry, J. W., Poortinga, Y. H., Segall, M. H., & Dasen, P. R. (1992). *Cross-cultural psychology: Research and applications*. New York, NY: Cambridge University Press.

Boehnke, L., Lietz, P., Schreier, M. & Wilhelm, A. (2011). Sampling: The selection of cases for culturally comparative psychological research. In D. Matsumoto &

F. van de Vijver (Eds.) *Cross-cultural research methods in psychology* (pp. 101–129). Cambridge, England: Cambridge University Press.

Brett, J. M., & Gelfand, M. J. (2008). *At your service.* In J. M. Brett (Ed.), *Negotiation, teamwork, and decision-making exercises.* Northwestern University, Kellogg School of Management, Dispute Resolution Research Center, Chicago, IL.

Cohen, D. (2007). Methods in cultural psychology. In S. Kitayama & D. Cohen (Eds.), *Handbook of cultural psychology* (pp. 196–236). New York, NY: Guilford Press.

Daft, R. L., & Lengel, R. H. (1984). Information richness: A new approach to managerial behavior and organizational design. *Research in Organizational Behavior, 6,* 191–233.

Eliot, T. S. (1943/1971). *Four quartets.* New York: Harcourt. Farh, J.-L., & Earley, P. C. (1997). Impetus for action: A cultural analysis of justice and organizational citizenship behavior in Chinese society. *Administrative Science Quarterly, 42,* 421–444. doi:10.2307/2393733

Geertz, C. (1973). *The interpretation of cultures.* New York, NY: Basic Books.

Gelfand, M. J. (2008). *Dynamical models of culture and collaboration in the Middle East.* Principal Investigator on Grant W911NF-08-1-0144 from the U. S. Army Research Laboratory and the U. S. Army Research Office.

Gelfand, M. J., Brett, J. M., Imai, L., Gunia, B., Tsai, H. H., & Huang, D. (2011). *Team negotiation across cultures: When and where are two heads better than one?* Manuscript submitted for publication.

Gelfand, M. J., Fitzgerald, L., & Drasgow, F. (1995). The structure of sexual harassment: A confirmatory analysis across cultures and settings. *Journal of Vocational Behavior, 47,* 164–177. doi:10.1006/jvbe.1995.1033

Gelfand, M. J., Higgins, M., Nishii, L., Raver, J., Dominguez, A., Yamaguchi, S., . . . Toyama, M. (2002). Culture and egocentric biases of fairness in conflict and negotiation. *Journal of Applied Psychology, 87,* 833–845. doi:10.1037/0021-9010.87.5.833

Gelfand, M. J., Leslie, L., & Fehr, R. (2008). In order to prosper, organizational psychology . . . should adopt a global perspective. *Journal of Organizational Behavior, 29,* 493–517. doi:10.1002/job.530

Gelfand, M. J., Nishii, L. H., Holcombe, K., Dyer, N., Ohbuchi, K., & Fukumo, M. (2001). Cultural influences on cognitive representations of conflict: Interpretations of conflict episodes in the United States and Japan. *Journal of Applied Psychology, 86,* 1059–1074. doi:10.1037/0021-9010.86.6.1059

Gelfand, M. J., Raver, J. L., & Holcombe Ehrhart, K. (2002). Methodological issues in cross cultural organizational research. In S. Rogelberg (Ed.), *Handbook of industrial and organizational psychology research methods* (pp. 216–246). New York, NY: Blackwell.

Gelfand, M. J., Raver, J. L., Nishii, L., Leslie, L. M., Lun, J., Lim, B. C., . . . Yamaguchi, S. (2011, May 27). Differences between tight and loose societies: A 33-nation study. *Science, 332,* 1100–1104. doi:10.1126/science.1197754

Gelfand, M. J., & Realo, A. (1999). Individualism–collectivism and accountability in intergroup negotiations. *Journal of Applied Psychology, 84,* 721–736. doi:10.1037/0021-9010.84.5.721

Gruder, C. L. (1971). Relationship with opponent and partner in mixed-motive bargaining. *Journal of Conflict Resolution, 15,* 403–416. doi:10.1177/002200277101500311

Hall, E. T. (1976). *Beyond culture.* New York, NY: Anchor Books.

Heine, S. J., Lehman, D, R., Markus, H. R., & Kitayama, S. (1999). Is there a universal need for positive self-regard? *Psychological Review, 106,* 766–794. doi:10.1037/0033-295X.106.4.766

Herskovits, M. J. (1955). *Cultural anthropology.* New York, NY: Knopf.

Kashima, Y., & Gelfand, M. J. (2011). Culture: A brief history of meaning in psychology. In W. Stroebe & A. Kruglanski (Eds.), *Handbook of the history of social psychology* (pp. . New York, NY: Psychology Press.

Kashima, Y., Yamaguchi, S., Kim, U., Choi, S., Gelfand, M. J., & Yuki, M. (1995). Culture, gender, and self: A perspective from individualism–collectivism research. *Journal of Personality and Social Psychology, 69,* 925–937. doi:10.1037/0022-3514.69.5.925

Kitayama, S., & Karasawa, M. (1997). Implicit self-esteem in Japan: Name letters and birthday numbers. *Personality and Social Psychology Bulletin, 23,* 736–742.

Kitayama, S., Markus, H., Matsumoto, H., & Norasakkunkit, V. (1997). Individual and collective processes in the construction of the self: Self-enhancement in the United States and self-criticism in Japan. *Journal of Personality and Social Psychology, 72,* 1245–1267. doi:10.1037/0022-3514.72.6.1245

Kurian, G. T. (2001). *The illustrated book of world rankings.* New York, NY: Sharpe Reference.

Matsumoto, D., & van de Vijver, F. J. R. (2011). *Cross-cultural research methods in psychology.* Cambridge, England: Cambridge University Press.

McGrath, J. E. (1982). Dilemmatics: The study of research choices and dilemmas. In J. E. McGrath, J. Martin, & R. A. Kulka (Eds.), *Judgment calls in research* (pp. 69–102). Beverly Hills, CA: Sage.

Mead, M. (1928). *Coming of age in Samoa.* New York, NY: Morrow.

Morling, B., & Lamoreaux, M. (2008). Measuring culture outside the head: A meta-analysis of individualism–collectivism in cultural products. *Personality and Social Psychology Review, 12,* 199–221. doi:10.1177/1088868308318260

Morris, M. W., & Gelfand, M. J. (2004). Cultural differences and cognitive dynamics: Expanding the cognitive tradition in negotiation. In M. J. Gelfand & J. M. Brett (Eds.), *The handbook of negotiation and culture* (pp. 45–70). Palo Alto, CA: Stanford University Press.

Morris, M., Podolny, J., & Ariel, S. (2000). Missing relations: Incorporating relational constructs into models of culture. In Earley, P. C., & Singh, H. (Eds.), *Innovations in international and cross-cultural management, 52–90.* Thousand Oaks, CA.: Sage.

Murray, D. R., & Schaller, M. (2010). Historical prevalence of infectious diseases within 230 geopolitical regions: A tool for investigating origins of culture. *Journal of Cross-Cultural Psychology, 41*, 99–108. doi:10.1177/0022022109349510

Ramesh, A., & Gelfand, M. J. (2010). Should they stay or should they go: Job embeddedness in predicting turnover in individualistic and collectivistic cultures. *Journal of Applied Psychology, 95*, 807–823. doi:10.1037/a0019464

Segall, M. H., Campbell, D. T., & Herskovits, M. J. (1966). *The influence of culture on visual perceptions.* Indianapolis, IN: Bobbs-Merrill.

Shteynberg, G., Gelfand, M. J., & Kim, (2009). Peering into the "magnum mysterium" of culture: The explanatory power of descriptive norms. *Journal of Cross-Cultural Psychology, 40*, 46–69.doi: 10.1177/0022022108326196.

Shweder, R. A. (1990). Cultural psychology: What is it? In J. W. Stilger, R. A. Shweder, & G. Herdt (Eds.), *Cultural psychology: Essays on comparative human development* (pp. 1–43). New York, NY: Cambridge University Press.

Thompson, L., & Loewenstein, G. (1992). Egocentric interpretations of fairness and interpersonal conflict. *Organizational Behavior and Human Decision Processes, 51*, 176–197. doi:10.1016/0749-5978(92)90010-5

Trafimow, D., Triandis, H. C., & Goto, S. G. (1991). Some tests of the distinction between the private and the collective self. *Journal of Personality and Social Psychology, 60*, 649–655. doi:10.1037/0022-3514.60.5.649

Triandis, H. C. (1972). *The analysis of subjective culture.* New York, NY: Wiley.

Triandis, H. C., & Berry, J. W. (1980). *Handbook of cross-cultural psychology: Vol. 2. Methodology.* Boston, MA: Allyn & Bacon

Triandis, H. C., & Gelfand, M. J. (1998). Converging measurement of horizontal and vertical individualism and collectivism. *Journal of Personality and Social Psychology, 74*, 118–128. doi:10.1037/0022-3514.74.1.118

Whiting, B. B., & Whiting, J. W. M. (1975). *Children of six cultures: A psycho-cultural analysis.* Cambridge, MA: Harvard University Press.

Whiting, J. W. M., & Child, I. L. (1953). *Child training and personality: A cross-cultural study.* New Haven, CT: Yale University Press.

Zou, X., Tam, K.-P., Morris, M. W., Lee, S.-L., Lau, Y.-M., & Chiu, C.-Y. (2009). Culture as *common* sense: Perceived consensus vs. personal beliefs as mechanisms of cultural influence. *Journal of Personality and Social Psychology, 97*, 579–597. doi:10.1037/a0016399

# AFTERWORD: MULTINATIONAL RESEARCH PROJECTS IN ORGANIZATIONAL PSYCHOLOGY— THE FUTURE IS BRIGHT

ANN MARIE RYAN, FREDERICK T. L. LEONG,
AND FREDERICK L. OSWALD

To conclude this volume, we offer some observations that span the chapters and relate to conducting any multinational research project in organizational psychology. We also discuss what we see as key directions for future research.

## OBSERVATIONS

*Conceptualizing a research question to incorporate cultural considerations is not a simple task.*

Early on, organizational research and practice that incorporated a consideration of culture did so from a comparative viewpoint rather than from a developed theoretical one. Studies would compare a practice or examine an empirical relationship in two different nations with the hypothesis premised on the idea that if Hofstede (1980) showed that these nations have differences in cultural values, then there will be differences in study findings regarding the practice or relationship across the countries. Because of the admonishments of many regarding the deficiencies of this approach (for a thorough discussion, see Gelfand, Raver, & Holcombe Ehrhart, 2002), we have begun to see a much more well developed approach to incorporating culture into research questions in organizational psychology.

Specifically, in more recent research, we see (and hope to see more often) that culture is approached with a multilevel understanding, where nation is not equated with culture and nationality is not assumed to indicate an individual's values and beliefs (i.e., avoiding ecological fallacies). It is more commonplace to see meaningful discussion of how culture operates at and across multiple levels, as well as using levels of analysis for measurement of values and cultural practices that are more closely aligned with the research question. Also, as Ones et al. (Chapter 4) explained, cultural specificity should not be assumed to be the only explanation for differences in relationships found across cultures. In the current volume, this more deliberative and multilevel approach to the role of culture is apparent.

Note that a more thoughtful and thorough approach to conceptualizing culture does not necessarily mean theory must always exist a priori. A central point provided by Gibson, Szkudlarek, and McDaniel (Chapter 1) is that insights on how the conceptualization of teams differs across cultures came from a proximal approach arising from the data themselves, not from a priori theorizing about culture and teams. As Gibson et al. noted, proximal and distal approaches both have value. Gelfand (Chapter 7) further reinforced this in her discussion of the importance of emic approaches to not only building measures but also building theory. In our view, there is a much more conscious focus among organizational researchers recently around clearly specifying culture's role and providing meaningful theoretical explanations for it, regardless of how that conceptualization emerges.

*Consideration of measure equivalence and the cultural appropriateness of methodological choices is essential.*

The challenges of quality measurement and appropriate choice of methods pervade many questions that organizational psychologists tackle, especially in the work of those attempting to study issues on a global basis. Although clear guidelines have been developed for assessing the cross-cultural equivalence of measures used across borders (or translated versions of a measure, or both; see Byrne et al., 2009; Leong et al., 2010; van de Vijver & Leung, 1997; Vandenberg & Lance, 2000), there are still many challenges in implementing these best practices. Some methods require more advanced analytic tools that are not readily accessible or require a type of knowledge and skill that many researchers and practitioners may not develop in their typical day-to-day work. Some methods require large samples that may not be available (even in large multinational organizations). Many times, the organizational psychologist is operating under tight timelines imposed by the needs of the organization that do not allow for the additional steps of assessing measurement equivalence or allowing for a more time-intensive approach to gathering data. Often, resources simply are not budgeted to do a high-quality measurement equivalence study, and therefore researchers and practitioners do the best they can with available resources. The greater concern, though, is that conclusions may be well off-base if derived from measures that were not conceptually and psychometrically equivalent across the sample or if the methods used did not fit the cultural context. Further, as Lyons, Leong, and Ryan (Chapter 6) noted, a lack of equivalence or culturally inappropriate methodological choices also has ethical implications.

This volume provides a number of examples of how to best consider these issues. Bartram (Chapter 3) provided a thorough description of how to tackle issues of measurement equivalence and norm development. Sanchez and Spector (Chapter 5) illustrated the psychometric challenges inherent in multinational, multilingual research and ways to mitigate problems. Ng, Van Dyne, and Ang (Chapter 2) detailed the extensive steps required to establish the construct validity of a measure to be used cross-culturally.

Beyond measure equivalence, the volume also illustrates the many methodological choices that cross-cultural researchers make (e.g., what type of sample; whether to use experimental designs, surveys, interviews). The chapters provide numerous examples of how there may be extra steps and extra care needed as one progresses. For example, Ng et al. (Chapter 2) discussed the number of studies and samples required to validate a new construct. Gelfand (Chapter 7) detailed the potential trade-offs when attempting to choose a culturally sensitive approach to data collection in a given context.

Chapter 4, by Ones et al., provided a comprehensive discussion of how one can use meta-analytic techniques to address the question of cross-cultural generalization of relationships. Their chapter provided illustrations of the types of data that are available, as well as the types that are needed to correctly evaluate hypotheses regarding cultural variability.

In sum, cross-cultural research in organizations has moved beyond the relatively simple translation and use of measures and the application of familiar traditional methods to a much keener awareness of the multiple practical and theoretical considerations that must be evaluated by the researcher as he or she makes use of modern methods and measurement choices in conducting research across countries.

*Operational challenges require organization and planning, attention to detail, and adaptability—although these are traits that every researcher should possess, cross-cultural work requires them in abundance.*

The scope of large-scale multicountry projects often scares off even the most seasoned researcher. More than anything, it is clear that multinational research requires much more resources devoted to planning and much greater risk assessment and mitigation before commencing a project. In part, this is simply because of the scale of these projects and the size of the research teams requires more coordination. Beyond that, culture does not just add another layer or another checklist before carrying out a study, it requires novel and numerous considerations every step of the way.

Examples of operational challenges are highlighted in most chapters in this volume. Gelfand (Chapter 7) provided a number of examples of the importance of what she labels "cultural legwork" that is required in ensuring that a cross-cultural research project be successful. Lyons et al. (Chapter 6) targeted the ethical challenges associated with conducting cross-cultural research. Sanchez and Spector (Chapter 5) described how administrative choices influence methodological capabilities and discuss different variants of how one might approach a multinational research project. Ones et al. (Chapter 4) described their approach to ensuring that measures, methods, and operational decisions were held constant across cultural contexts in the International Generalizability of Expatriate Success Factors (iGOES) project. Gibson et al. (Chapter 1) explicitly noted that the characteristics they believe are essential to quality multinational research include "openness to the unexpected, acceptance of uncertainty, and appreciation of multiplicity" (p. 9).

*Cross-cultural research is rewarding for those who pursue it.*

The authors of works in this volume clearly demonstrated their enthusiasm and commitment to the projects they pursued. Ng et al. (Chapter 2) noted, "Notwithstanding the challenges we faced, the journey has been extremely rewarding" (p. 50). Gelfand (Chapter 7) stated, "Cross-cultural research is a passion for me and a lifelong journey that brings many joys" (p. 195). Gibson et al. (Chapter 1) opined, "Even if it is not always glamorous, it is always and forever enlightening!" (p. 9).

## DIRECTIONS

Although our observations provide some sense of where organizational psychology may be at currently vis-à-vis cross-cultural focus on research and practice, this volume has also hinted at what else may be required to make large-scale, multinational research projects less of an unusual exception by a handful of dedicated researchers and more part and parcel of how practice and research questions are typically approached. To that end, we offer a few suggestions.

*Do all of the above more.*

Although we have noted that the field has definitely moved forward in terms of expectations regarding conceptual development of cross-cultural research questions and quality of measurement and methods, it is also clear that there are many gaps out there unaddressed. There are areas in which few cross-cultural studies have been published (e.g., work–family conflict; Cohen, 2009) or areas in which studies are quite dated or in which use of more sophisticated conceptualizations, operationalizations, and analytic tools did not occur (i.e., no multilevel theory, no in-depth analysis of measurement equivalence, no use of hierarchical linear modeling or similar techniques to account for both culture and individual level effects adequately). The movement toward increasing sophistication and rigor in our conceptualization and standards for research practices should be maintained.

*Provide better guidance to practice.*

In our interactions with organizational psychologists working in corporate and consulting settings, we have noted a general clamoring for good information about what to consider when implementing programs and tools on a global basis (e.g., selection instruments, 360-degree feedback systems, leadership development programs). Yet, what research exists has not been sufficiently integrated and translated to provide meaningful practical advice. For example, Oswald (2008) emphasized the critical need to implement research methodologies that help understand, select, and develop managerial talent in light of economic globalization. Ryan and Delany (2010) recently provided a long list of unanswered questions regarding the role of culture in recruitment and selection (e.g., when and how should recruitment materials be culturally adapted, do recruiter–applicant similarity effects exist on culture or nationality)—similar lists could be generated for almost any area of organizational psychology practice.

Ng et al. (Chapter 2) provided a number of cogent examples of how they have been able to apply their multicultural research program in the course of teaching and executive development work. Similarly, Gibson et al. (Chapter 1) noted that they were able to produce a set of practical guidelines for implementing teams in a manner that incorporates the cultural backgrounds of the members. Bartram's (Chapter 3) focus was on a tool widely used in selection practice globally. The chapters here illustrated that high-quality multinational research projects can provide the needed guidance for practice.

*Encourage the next generation of researchers.*

The large, multiyear, highly successful projects described in this volume might intimidate students. One might expect that hearing others describe successful accomplishment of a research project would enhance a sense of efficacy for those thinking of pursuing cross-cultural topics; however, it can also increase hesitancy.

We feel that there are two key ways to further encourage young researchers to better consider culture in their research, even (or especially) on a small scale. First, students must be made aware that a global mind-set (Hough, Fandre, & Oswald, 2008) will be a requirement for new hires to almost any field. Workers in large corporations who lack cross-cultural competence and sensitivity will often be much less likely to be successful than those with a similar lack in the past. Second, curricula must be revised and cocurricular experiences created that ensure the development of needed skills to work and research in a broad array of cultural contexts (Ryan & Gelfand, 2011).

## CONCLUSION

Gelfand (Chapter 7) stated, "It is also instructive, however, to share the stories, dilemmas, and serendipity that are behind the scenes of research lives to more vividly illustrate the issues that are invariably encountered when venturing into cross-cultural research territory" (p. 195). The chapters in this volume provided that instruction in ways that we think will excite and encourage many more to tackle the large-scale multinational research projects that are very much needed in organizations and in organizational psychology. The paradigm shift to globalization requires that researchers develop models and methods to study organizations across multiple nations and cultures while dealing with the many practical constraints that inevitably accompany the real-world opportunity of multinational research.

## REFERENCES

Byrne, B. M., Oakland, T., Leong, F. T. L., van de Vijver, F. J. R., Hambleton, R. K., Cheung, F. M., & Bartram, D. (2009). A critical analysis of cross-cultural research and testing practices: Implications for improved education and training in psychology. *Training and Education in Professional Psychology, 3*, 94–105. doi:10.1037/a0014516

Cohen, A. (2009). Individual values and the work/family interface: An examination of high-tech employees in Israel. *Journal of Managerial Psychology, 24*, 814–832. doi:10.1108/02683940910996815

Gelfand, M. J., Raver, J. L., & Holcombe Ehrhart, K. (2002). Methodological issues in cross-cultural organizational research. In S. Rogelberg (Ed.), *Handbook of industrial and organizational psychology research methods* (pp. 216–246). New York, NY: Blackwell.

Hofstede, G. (1980). *Culture's consequences: International differences in work-related values*. Beverly Hills, CA: Sage.

Hough, L., Fandre, J., & Oswald, F. (2008). *Understanding and measuring global mindset: Development of the Global Mindset Inventory*. Glendale, AZ: Thunderbird School of Global Management.

Leong, F. T. L., Leung, K., & Cheung, F. M. (2010). Integrating cross-cultural psychology research methods into ethnic minority psychology. *Cultural Diversity & Ethnic Minority Psychology, 16*, 590–597. doi:10.1037/a0020127

O'Meara, K. (2011). Inside the Panopticon: Studying academic reward systems. In J. C. Smart & M. B. Paulsen (Eds.). *Higher education: Handbook of theory and research* (Vol. 26, pp. 161–220). New York, NY: Springer.

Oswald, F. L. (2008). Global personality norms: Multinational, multicultural, and managerial. *International Journal of Testing, 8*, 400–408. doi:10.1080/15305050802435201

Ryan, A. M., & Delany, T. (2010). Attracting job candidates to organizations. In J. L. Farr & N. T. Tippins (Eds.), *Handbook of employee selection* (pp. 127–150). New York, NY: Routledge.

Ryan, A. M., & Gelfand, M. (2012). Internationalizing the I-O psychology curriculum. In F. T. L. Leong, W. Pickren, M. M. Leach, & A. J. Marsella (Eds.), *Internationalizing the psychology curriculum in the United States: Meeting the challenges of globalization*. New York, NY: Springer.

van de Vijver, F., & Leung, K. (1997). *Methods and data analysis for cross-cultural research*. Thousand Oaks, CA: Sage.

Vandenberg, R. J., & Lance, C. E. (2000). A review and synthesis of the measurement invariance literature: Suggestions, practices, and recommendations for organizational research. *Organizational Research Methods, 3*, 4–69. doi:10.1177/109442810031002

# INDEX

for culture and language, 130–135
and sample equivalence, 140
Coon, H. M., 65
Cooper, C., 13
Cooper, Cary L., 123–124, 126
Cooper, R., 16
Cooperativeness, 168
Corporate settings, 4–6
Costa, P. T., 77
Council for International Organizations
of Medical Science (CIOMS),
153, 158
Country, 93n1
Covariance structures, 136–138
CQ. *See* Cultural intelligence
CQS (cultural intelligence scale),
34–35, 47–48
Crawford-Mathis, K., 38–39
Cronbach, L. J., 85
Cross-cultural/cross-national research
(CC/CN), 123–143
administrative issues in, 124–127
construct equivalence in, 136–139
culture vs. language effects in,
130–135
measurement and sampling issues
with, 127
response bias in, 135–136
sample equivalence between cultures
in, 139–142
translation of instruments for,
127–130
Cross-cultural generalization, 91–118
best practices for, 117
with intercontextual studies,
111–115
with intercultural studies, 106–111
with intracultural studies, 99–106
levels of analysis for, 91–94
meta-analytic cumulation in,
115–116, 118
statistical artifacts in, 94–99,
106–111, 116, 118
Cross-cultural research, 179–196. *See
also* Cross-cultural/cross-national
research (CC/CN)
cultural legwork for, 185–191
methodological tradeoffs in,
191–195
scholarly interest in, 179–183

theoretical foundation for,
184–185
triangulation in, 191–195
Crowne, K., 38, 39
Cultural accommodation, 133–135
Cultural adjustment, 40
Cultural clusters, 113
Cultural context
for bilinguals, 133
consent in, 169
constructs in, 184–185
exposure to, 180–181
in sampling, 111–112
theory in, 123
Cultural equivalence, 11
Cultural influences
on behavior, 64–65
with globalization, 3–4
on rating scales, 135–136
on subjective appraisals, 141–142
Cultural intelligence (CQ), 29–50
conceptualization of, 32–34
future directions for research on,
47–49
history of research on, 30–32
measurement of, 34–35
nomological network of, 35–43
scholarly interest in, 44–47
*Cultural Intelligence* (P. C. Earley &
S. Ang), 30
*The Cultural Intelligence Difference*
(D. Livermore), 30
Cultural intelligence scale (CQS),
34–35, 47–48
Cultural judgment and decision making
(CJDM), 39–40
Cultural response bias, 67–68
Cultural specificity, 104–106
Cultural tightness–looseness. *See*
Tightness–looseness
Cultural values, 64–67, 150–151
Culture
controls for, 130–135
country vs., 93n1
definitions of, 46, 63
effects of, 130–135
familiarization with, 169, 185–191
in hypothesis conceptualization,
201–202
in methodology selection, 202–203

cultural context in, 111–112
equivalence of, 139–142
errors in, 95, 98
matching, 140–142
in meta-analysis, 106, 108, 110
representativeness of, 93–94
theoretical basis for, 185
Sanchez, J. I., 138
Sander parallelogram illusion, 181
Sapir–Whorf hypothesis, 127. *See also*
    Whorfian hypothesis
Scalar equivalence, 93, 107
Scalar invariance, 116n8
Scale anchors, 130
Scales. *See* Rating scales
Schaller, M., 195
Schmidt, F. L., 32, 106n5
Schwab, D. S., 11
Scores
    average scale, 75–82
    on Big Five dimensions, 78–81
    conversion of, 60
    country-level, 75–82
    differences in, 59–61
    gender differences on, 82
    mean, 67, 105n4
    raw, 59–61
    standard, 60
Second-order sampling error, 106
Segall, M. H., 181
Seiler, S., 36
Seiter, J. S., 171
Self-awareness, 17–18
Self-disclosure, 193
Self-report measures, 46–48
SEM (structural equation
    modeling), 132
Sexual Experiences Questionnaire
    (SEQ), 184
Shannon, L. M., 38
Shen, W., 92
Shokef, E., 38
Short-term orientation, 64
Shweder, R. A., 183–184
Simplified Chinese language, 73–74
SIOP (Society for Industrial and
    Organizational Psychology), 167
SmithKline Beecham, 11
Social intelligence, 29
Social networks, 43

Society for Industrial and Organiza-
    tional Psychology (SIOP), 167
Sociocultural context, 150, 153
South Africa, 71–73
Specificity, cultural, 104–106
Spector, P. E., 107–110, 123–124, 126,
    136–137, 139
Sports metaphors, 14–16
Standard deviation
    computation of, 67
    in meta-analyses, 100–104, 108–109
    second-order, 106
Standard scores, 60
Stark, S., 37
Statistical analysis
    artifacts of, 94–99, 106–111,
        116, 118
    in construct validity, 137–138
    equivalence in, 184
Steel, P., 65
Sternberg, R. J., 30–32
Stewart, A. C., 39
Structural equation modeling
    (SEM), 132
Subgroups, 12
Subjective appraisals, 141–142
Subjective culture, 182–183
Sulloway, F. J., 100
Surveys, 191–192
Systematic bias, 60
Szkudlarek, B., 16, 17, 22

Takeuchi, R., 37–38
Tan, M. L., 39, 43
Tangirala, S., 40
Taras, V., 65–66
Tarique, I., 38
Tay, C., 38, 40–41
Teaching, 44
Teams and teamwork
    analysis, 18
    conceptualization of, 14–16
    defined, 10
    effectiveness, 10–14
    in proximal research, 16–22
Templer, K. J., 40
Temporal factors, 23
Tesluk, P. E., 37–38
Theoretical framework
    in archival methods, 194–195

Whorfian hypothesis, 127, 133, 134
Williams, M. E., 40
Wilson, C. E., 39
Within-group design, 134
Within-participant design, 131, 132, 134
WLCS. *See* Work Locus of Control Scale
Work environment
    adjustment to, 40
    constructs for, 137
    context of, 149–150
    interpretation of, 129
Workers' rights, 168
Work experience, international,
    37–39, 49

Work–life balance, 5
Work Locus of Control Scale (WLCS),
    107, 108, 136–137
Work performance. *See* Job
    performance
Work Teams Project, 10
World Health Organization (WHO),
    153, 158, 195
World Medical Association, 153
Worthley, R., 39

Yun, S., 37–38

Zellmer-Bruhn, M., 11, 14–22

# ABOUT THE EDITORS

**Ann Marie Ryan, PhD,** is a professor of organizational psychology at Michigan State University (MSU). Her major research interests involve improving the quality and fairness of employee selection methods, and topics related to diversity and justice in the workplace. She also has recently conducted research on work–nonwork conflict. In addition to publishing extensively in these areas, she regularly consults with organizations on improving assessment processes. She is a past president of the American Psychological Association's (APA's) Division 14 (Society for Industrial and Organizational Psychology [SIOP]) and past editor of the journal *Personnel Psychology*. Dr. Ryan has a long record of professional service on SIOP committees and National Academy of Sciences panels, and she currently serves on the Defense Advisory Committee on Military Personnel Testing. She received her PhD in psychology from the University of Illinois at Chicago.

**Frederick T. L. Leong, PhD,** is a professor of psychology at Michigan State University (MSU) in the industrial/organizational and clinical psychology programs. He is also the director of the Consortium for Multicultural Psychology Research at MSU. He has authored or coauthored more than 200 journal articles and book chapters and has edited or coedited 12 books. He is editor-in-chief of the *Encyclopedia of Counseling* and the *APA Handbook of Multicultural Psychology*. He is also editor of APA's Division 45 (Society for the Psychological Study of Ethnic Minority Issues) book series *Cultural, Racial and Ethnic Psychology* and founding editor of the *Asian American Journal of Psychology*. Dr. Leong is a fellow of APA Divisions 1, 2, 5, 12, 17, 29, 45, and 52; the Association for Psychological Science; the Asian American Psychological Association; and the International Academy for Intercultural Research. His major research interests center on culture and mental health, cross-cultural psychotherapy (especially with Asians and Asian Americans), cultural and personality factors related to career choice, and work stress. He is the past president of APA Division 45, APA Division 12—Section VI (Clinical Psychology of Ethnic Minorities), the Asian American Psychological Association, and the International Association of Applied Psychology's Division 16 (Counseling Psychology Division). Dr. Leong received his PhD in counseling and industrial/organizational psychology from the University of Maryland, College Park.

**Frederick L. Oswald, PhD,** is an associate professor in the industrial/organizational psychology program at Rice University. His research deals with employment testing and personnel selection in organizational, educational, and military settings. Specifically, his work involves defining, modeling, and predicting performance outcomes from measures of cognitive and motivational constructs (e.g., cognitive abilities, personality traits, situational judgment, job knowledge and skill, biographical data). His statistical work deals with psychological measurement, adverse impact, meta-analysis, and structural equation modeling. Dr. Oswald publishes his research in close collaboration with the graduate students he mentors, and he has a history of large-scale, grant-funded projects (e.g., U.S. Navy, College Board). Currently, he is an associate editor of the *Journal of Management* and *Journal of Business and Psychology*; he also serves on the editorial boards of the *Journal of Applied Psychology*, *Personnel Psychology*, *Psychological Methods*, *Organizational Research Methods*, *International Journal of Selection and Assessment*, and the *Journal of Research in Personality*. Dr. Oswald received his PhD in psychology from the University of Minnesota, Twin Cities Campus.